Library of
Davidson College

ETHICS AND ANTHROPOLOGY
Dilemmas in Fieldwork

ETHICS AND ANTHROPOLOGY
Dilemmas in Fieldwork

Michael A. Rynkiewich and James P. Spradley

Macalester College

ROBERT E. KRIEGER PUBLISHING COMPANY, INC.
MALABAR, FLORDIA

Original Edition 1976
Reprint Edition 1981

Printed and Published by
ROBERT E. KRIEGER PUBLISHING COMPANY, INC.
KRIEGER DRIVE
MALABAR, FLORIDA 32950

Copyright © 1976 by
John Wiley & Sons, Inc.
Reprint by Arrangement

174.9
E842

All rights reserved. No part of this book may be reproduced in any form or by any electronic or mechanical means including information storage and retrieval systems without permission in writing from the publisher.

Printed in the United States of America

Library of Congress Cataloging in Publication Data

Main entry under title:
Ethics and Anthropology   86-1531

   Reprint Originally published: New York:
Wiley, © 1976.
   Bibliography: p.
   1. Anthropological ethics — Addresses, essays, lectures. 2. Anthropological — Field work — Addresses, essays, lectures. I. Rynkiewich, Michael A.
II. Spradley, James P.
GN33.6.E83 1981   174'.9309   81-3698
ISBN 0-89874-349-4   AACR2

PREFACE

This book is a collection of case studies in the ethics of doing anthropology. Like all scientists, anthropologists cannot escape the profound influence of their personal preferences and cultural values. This book explores this ethical dimension of anthropology at the grass roots level. Each chapter presents a first-person account in which an anthropologist writes about a dilemma or series of problems that involved personal values and beliefs. We learn about the context in which a particular ethical dilemma arose, the conflicting choices faced by the author, the people involved, the emotions and doubts that emerged, and the partially satisfactory results and resolutions.

The impetus for this book came from our colleagues. We heard them recount difficult field experiences and argue over the merits of past professional decisions. We listened with interest and talked of our own dilemmas, discussing at length the values we espoused. But we were struck by the fact that the stories, lessons, and values, so important to anthropologists when they met informally, seldom made their way into the professional journals or monographs. Our students had little access to this rich collective experience except through their own personal encounters or when they heard our colleagues speak to them. Perhaps most important, we began to realize that the ethical dilemmas and partial solutions that anthropologists were working out all over the world were important data for our developing professional standards. And so we asked several colleagues to recount a significant experience that involved a dilemma of professional ethics. We requested them to avoid discussions about *ethics* per se, for this was not to be a book about abstract ethical principles. Neither was our purpose to present a history of ethical conflicts within the discipline, although that is an important task that needs to be done. In short, we asked each author to write a first-person narrative about a particular problem, how it arose, the questions they asked and tried to answer, how they lived through the dilemma and, finally, how they assessed the outcome.

The history of ethical problems in anthropology goes back at least as far as the censure of Franz Boas, the "father of American Anthropology," for writing a letter to *The Nation* to protest the U. S. government's use of anthropology as a cover for spying (see Stocking, 1968:273; *The Nation,* 1919, Vol. 109). More recently the American Anthropological Association has been rocked by two events that involved many anthropologists. The aborted Project Camelot allegedly involved anthropologists in contracts for secret research useful to the U.S. military in reacting to radical revolutions in other countries (see Horowitz, 1965; 1967). Alleged involvement by other anthropologists in secret research in support of counterinsurgency in Thailand opened wider the debate over ethics within the Association (See AAA statement, 1969; Wolf and Jorgensen, 1970).

Although these two events captured the attention of anthropologists and led to important debates about ethics in the discipline, they are difficult to use in teaching. Years later the charges alleging misconduct, the facts in the cases, and the ethical issues are all still ambiguous. Discussion of these events among anthropologists frequently escalates into heated arguments. It will take historians of anthropology many years to unravel and clarify the issues. In the meantime, we believe there is a need for case studies that deal with more ordinary ethical issues faced by anthropologists in the field and at home. Such studies, although not always dramatic, provide the foundation for further development of professional standards.

The American Anthropological Association has long been concerned with developing such standards. In December, 1948, the Council of Fellows adopted the "Resolution on Freedom of Publication," which urged all research sponsors to give anthropologists complete freedom to publish findings without censorship. In March, 1967, the "Statement on Problems of Anthropological Research and Ethics," was adopted as a step toward providing guidelines for anthropologists doing research. The most comprehensive statement was adopted in May, 1971: "Principles of Professional Responsibility." This statement is reprinted in the appendix of this book by permission of the American Anthropological Association. It deserves careful study and review by professional and student alike. All the important ethical statements of the Association as well as information on the role and function of the Committee on Ethics are available on request in a booklet titled, "Professional Ethics" (write to the American Anthropological Association, 1703 New Hampshire Avenue N.W., Washington, D.C., 20009).

James P. Spradley

Michael A. Rynkiewich

REFERENCES

American Anthropological Association

    1969   "Statement of the Executive Board of the A.A.A.," Bulletin of the AAA, Annual Report.

Boas, Franz

    1919   "Correspondence: Scientists As Spies," *The Nation,* Vol. 109.

Horowitz, Irving Louis

    1965   "The Life and Death of Project Camelot," *Trans-Action,* December.

Horowitz, Irving Louis (ed.)

    1967   "The Rise and Fall of Project Camelot: Studies in the Relationship Between Social Science and Practical Politics." Cambridge, Mass.: The M.I.T. Press.

Stocking, George W. Jr.

    1968   *Race, Culture and Evolution.* New York: The Free Press.

Wolf, Eric R. and Joseph Jorgensen

    1970   "The Thailand Issue and the Ethics Committee: A Reply to the A.A.A. Executive Board," *Newsletter of the American Anthropological Association,* Vol. II, No. 9.

CONTENTS

Introduction		1
Chapter 1	The Medicine Man David W. McCurdy	4
Chapter 2	Trouble in the Tank James P. Spradley	17
Chapter 3	Rights, Responsibilities, and Reports: An Ethical Dilemma in Contract Research Carol J. Pierce-Colfer	32
Chapter 4	The Underdevelopment of Anthropological Ethics Michael A. Rynkiewich	47
Chapter 5	The People of Enewetak Atoll versus The U.S. Department of Defense Robert C. Kiste	61
Chapter 6	The American Indian Movement and the Anthropologist: Issues and Implications of Consent Fay G. Cohen	81

Chapter 7	The Ethics of Fieldwork in an Urban Bar Brenda J. Mann	95
Chapter 8	Studying Elites: Some Special Problems Barbara Harrell-Bond	110
Chapter 9	The Anthropologist in the Field: Scientist, Friend, and Voyeur Judith Friedman Hansen	123
Chapter 10	Secret Societies and the Ethics of Urban Fieldwork Noel J. Chrisman	135
Chapter 11	Ethnology in a Revolutionary Setting June Nash	148
Chapter 12	Professional Standards and What We Study Laura Nader	167
Appendix	Principles of Professional Responsibility Adopted by the Council of the American Anthropological Association, May, 1971	183

ETHICS AND ANTHROPOLOGY
Dilemmas in Fieldwork

INTRODUCTION

In organizing the following cases we have not classified them according to specific ethical concerns raised by the authors. Most involve several issues interwoven into a complex situation.

In "The Medicine Man" (Chapter 1), David McCurdy takes us to India. You are living in a village as an anthropologist doing research; people around you are sick, and you have some knowledge of medicine. Should you help? Few people would say "No!" but how much should you do? Where does the anthropologist draw the line between the time-consuming activity of caring for the sick and getting on with the work of anthropological research? And should you prescribe medicine when you aren't sure of the disease? The answers to these and other questions are elusive and very personal.

In 1967 James Spradley set out to study an alcoholism treatment center near Seattle, Washington. After gaining permission from the King County sheriff for the research, he discovered a more pressing topic for investigation while at the treatment center. Should he seek permission to gather data on this topic when it would probably be denied, or go ahead and do the study "quietly"? And when your research leads to the discovery of injustice within public institutions, what is your responsibility? These issues are discussed in "Trouble in the Tank" (Chapter 2).

The two biggest recent trouble cases in anthropology concerned *secret* contract research for the United States government. Many anthropologists continue to take government contracts when they do not involve "secrecy clauses." This means that reports on the people studied will not be given to the government while being withheld from informants. But what should you do if the government changes this understanding halfway through the research? You are under pressure to give information to the government but to withhold it from those studied and the alternatives may be to give in or lose the contract. In "Rights, Responsibilities, and Reports: An Ethical Dilemma in Contract Research," (Chapter 3) Carol Pierce-Colfer discusses these conflicting responsibilities and her search for a solution.

Some ethical questions are not obvious, particularly to the uninitiated. Michael Rynkiewich, as a graduate student doing research, paid too much attention to some minor problems and missed the major issue. Only after his fieldwork was completed and he had returned to the United States did he realize that his responsibility to the people should have involved him more, rather than less, in their political discussions. Micronesians were faced with a choice between independence and union with the United States. The former seemed economically unfeasible, the latter seemed dangerous for a small minority with very little land to lose. These issues are discussed in "The Underdevelopment of Anthropological Ethics" (Chapter 4).

A similar issue was not difficult for Robert Kiste to see, as he points out in "The People of Enewetak Atoll versus The U. S. Department of Defense" (Chapter 5). The United States wanted to delay the return of a dislocated community so they could blow up TNT on the island where they once exploded atomic and hydrogen bombs. Should you help the Air Force convince the people of the need for such tests or help the people defend themselves from the Air Force's demands? Put in those terms the course of action seems clear, but how do you proceed?

Cases where the people's needs ran a poor second to the anthropologist's wants have made many American Indians reluctant to permit anthropologists in their midst again. Fay Cohen wanted to study the American Indian Movement's police patrols in Minneapolis, Minnesota. "What good will it do us?" AIM's leaders asked. Modifying her research plans to include the people's needs was only one strategy Ms. Cohen had to use in the constantly changing struggle to gain and maintain permission to carry out her fieldwork as she relates in "The American Indian Movement and the Anthropologist: Issues and Implications of Consent" (Chapter 6).

On the other hand, the people in the bar studied by Brenda Mann did not seem to care what she was doing. Because she conducted her research from the vantage point of an employee, it was difficult to make clear the aims of research. And, in a public setting, from whom does one seek permission? In "The Ethics of Fieldwork in an Urban Bar" (Chapter 7), Ms. Mann traces the development of these problems.

Some social situations are more closed than that of a bar. Barbara Harrell-Bond faced the problem of studying elite families in Sierra Leone. The people, much like ourselves, were not anxious to have an outsider take up their time and pry into the details of their lives. If you were successful in being accepted into such a group, how would you then, a year or two later, break off relations and leave? What responsibility do you have to people with whom you have become friends? Can you break off abruptly, go home, and publish the details of their lives for everyone to read? In Chapter 8, "Studying Elites: Some Special Problems," Ms. Harrell-Bond recounts how she dealt with these problems.

What if people are very responsive to your desire to be an anthropologist and a friend, so responsive that they permit you to see things and hear things that Americans would not let outsiders see and hear? Would you be embarrassed? Would you warn them again and again that you are recording everything in your field notes? Would you publish what you learn? Judith Hansen, in "The Anthropologist in the Field: Scientist, Friend, and Voyeur" (Chapter 9), tells how she weighed the goals of anthropology against the integrity of her informants.

Let us go one step further and examine the responsibilities of an anthropologist when he becomes a member of the group he is studying and the group is a secret society. Noel Chrisman found himself in the dilemma of being responsible to the secrecy required by the society he was studying and responsible to the profession and his sponsors to publish the results of his study. In Chapter 10, "Secret Societies and the Ethics of Urban Fieldwork," Mr. Chrisman explores the tension that arises from being both anthropologist and member.

June Nash probably faced more personal danger than any of the other anthropologists in this book. During her research a revolution was raging all around her. The opportunity for taking sides is never greater than in such a situation, nor are the consequences for making a wrong choice more serious. As in all polarized situations, the anthropologist is rarely fully committed to one side or the other. Many anthropologists would prefer to remain uninvolved observers, but the people or the situation may demand that such a stance be abandoned. Ms. Nash relates her experiences and the choices she made in "Ethnology in a Revolutionary Setting" (Chapter 11).

When you have several fieldwork sessions behind you and your work is accepted by your colleagues, you may begin to wonder what influenced your choices. Laura Nader takes such a backward look and asks some compelling questions about the criteria anthropologists use to choose research projects. In a careful examination of the values and interests that led her to study cultures on three different continents, Ms. Nader not only reveals the ethical considerations of her own fieldwork, but the values that influence anthropological research in general. Her "Professional Standards and What We Study" (Chapter 12) goes to the heart of anthropology and raises perhaps the mose fundamental ethical question: why do we choose to study what we study?

Ethical dilemmas have no simple solutions. Anthropologists work in situations where the values from different cultures impinge on the most critical decisions. In this book the authors have presented only partial answers and limited solutions to the specific problems faced. We present this record of experiences and case studies for thought and discussion. In doing this, we hope that this collection leads to a widening awareness of ethical issues faced by anthropologists.

1
THE MEDICINE MAN

DAVID W. McCURDY

David W. McCurdy (1935—   ) was born in New York City and educated at Stanford and Cornell where he received his doctorate in 1964. He taught at Colorado State University and then moved to Macalester College where he is associate Professor of anthropology and chairperson of the department of Sociology and Anthropology. He conducted fieldwork in India from 1961—1963 as a Ford Foreign Area Training Fellow, is coeditor of *Conformity and Conflict* (1970 and 1974), and coauthor of *The Cultural Experience* (1972) and *Anthropology: The Cultural Perspective* (1975).

The morning of May 6, 1962 dawned bright and clear. The village was already awake, its householders moving quietly to finish their chores before 100° temperatures overtook the day. I rose at 7 A.M., sleepily pulled the mosquito net from the side of my cot, and stood stretching in the north room of my mud-and-dung-plastered bamboo house. Searching for a clean shirt in an old and battered green metal trunk, I could hear, for the first time, the low murmur of voices in the front yard. "It sounds like some people are out there," I thought to myself. "I wonder who it can be so early?"

It didn't take long to find out. I dressed quickly and pushed open the front door. To my astonishment I looked out on a crowd. People filled the compound, women with infants, men smoking and talking on the verandah, an assortment of children sitting or playing quietly in the warmth of the early morning sun. "Rām, Rām," I said to them automatically. "Rām, Rām, Sāb (sahib)," they answered pleasantly.

Just then Kānjī Pārgī entered the yard, straining under the heavy weight of the water pot he had just filled and carried up from the village well. I had hired Kānjī two months earlier to look after the house. His work freed my time for research, and he proved to be an invaluable informant. "Yē koi hai, Kānjī (What is this, Kānjī)?" I said, gesturing toward the crowd. "Are all these people sick?"

"Yes, Sāb," he replied. "They are troubled with sore eyes and yesterday many people in the village came down with diarrhea. That is why so many have come today."

"But why have they arrived so early?" I said, thinking of the late night I had just put in typing field notes.

"That is bad, Sāb," Kānjī replied apologetically. "People don't know you sleep late. I will warn them to come later tomorrow."

It wasn't really the early hour that bothered me but the large number of villagers who had come for treatment. There must have been 25 people in the compound at that moment, and 5 or 10 more were likely to show up before the rush was over. If Kānjī's estimate was correct, a majority of them suffered from conjunctivitis, an often severe inflamation of the eye, or from diarrhea. Neither condition took too long to treat provided there were no complications. On the other hand there were always hard cases—an infected axe cut, a mysterious chest pain, weight loss, a sore liver, "fever"—and these required more time to diagnose and treat if, indeed, they could be dealt with at all. How much of the morning would I have to devote to these people?

To make matters worse, I had scheduled an interview for about 8:00 A.M. that day. A household head named Vākājī Kātarā had agreed to tell me about his son's wedding, which was now taking place. Bhil weddings are long affairs; they involve a series of rites culminating in the "walk around the fire" at the bride's house. Today Vākājī's son would exchange clothing with his affinal kin, collect money from relatives and friends who lived in Ratakote, and set off for the bride's village with his wedding party. I wanted to learn more detail about the wedding and to understand its significance better. Vākājī warned me to come early, however, explaining that once the clothing exchange started that morning, he would be unable to talk again until after his son was married. He would be too busy. I thought of the time it would take to treat all the people in my compound and doubted that I could make it. "How in hell am I going to do research around here if this keeps up?" I muttered to myself.

Research was also on my mind in the fall of 1960. I was sitting with my feet propped up on a chair in the cluttered office that served as the lounge for graduate students in the Department of Sociology and Anthropology at Cornell University. The mahogany doors and woodwork spoke of the room's earlier elegance, part of a suite that once belonged to the president of Cornell University. Now, filled with odd pieces of cast-off furniture, littered with an assortment of old tests and papers, unwashed coffee cups, and overflowing ashtrays, graduate students came here to relax or study. On this day I sat talking with a friend whose graduate career was at the same stage as mine.

"Am I relieved," I said. "Smith and Opler approved my research proposal. I have been working on that thing for six weeks and I didn't think they would ever like it."

"Where are you going to send it?" he asked.

"To Ford, NIMH, and NSF, but I really wrote it for the Ford Foundation. I'm going to have to change it a little for NSF. They should be more interested in the design than in the usefulness of the results. I don't really know what to do for NIMH, I'll have to ask around about that. I hope one of these foundations takes it."

Such talk was common during the fall. We were putting in late nights in preparation for our comprehensive examinations, reading extensively about the region in which we hoped to do fieldwork, studying a language, and trying to generate an acceptable field research proposal. The final task was particularly important. Without an attractive proposal no foundation would provide funds, and without funds, there would be no field trip. Fieldwork was essential to us. Faculty members and senior graduate students frequently spoke about "the field." Students who returned from the field seemed changed; they were somehow more mature as though working in another society gave them more confidence about themselves and their relationship to anthropology.

But fieldwork meant much more than residence in a community with an alien culture. Once there, we all knew that one task held highest priority: gathering of large amounts of high quality data for a thesis and several publications. Those of us who prepared for fieldwork that fall felt some anxiety about our ability to meet this requirement. We knew of students who had returned with less than adequate field notes and we heard statements like, "They say that Jack didn't get much material in the field. They aren't sure he has enough for a thesis. He may have to go back." On the other hand there were also dramatic successes. One student had extended his fieldwork to almost three years, returning home with more than 30,000 note cards filled with data! Stored on their sides, the cards were reputed to line an entire wall of his apartment and to contain the finest information ever collected by an anthropology student at Cornell. The message in both cases seemed clear; the more good material we collected in the field, the better.

The quality of the research proposal and the ties with a foundation it established also underscored the importance of field research. All of us had worked hard on our proposals; they seemed like the distilled efforts of lecture courses, seminar papers, and countless conferences with a graduate committee. Everyone knew that the foundations were selective; they regularly turned down some of the research proposals submitted to them. "Did you hear?" someone would say. "Harry has just been turned down by NSF. He didn't even get as far as the interview. That makes three rejections." We all believed that for some reason foundations didn't have confidence in Harry and his research design, which meant that they *did* have faith in those of us who received support. When we accepted a grant, we accepted a responsibility to the foundation. And with the grant came stronger pressures to pursue fieldwork successfully.

This sense of urgency was uppermost in my mind as I surveyed the villagers who waited for me to treat them that morning in 1962. I had come to India for one purpose: to conduct a study of acculturation among the Bhils of southern Rajasthan. "I'm not here to become a doctor or start a medical practice," I had said to myself again and again during the first months of research. I chose to work in Ratakote, a Bhil village in the Aravalli Hills, because a road had recently opened it up to outside contact, not because its people were sickly or needed medical attention. But now I faced the dilemma more clearly than ever before. One man waited to be interviewed, a strategically important informant. Twenty-five others waited to be treated, people plagued by illness and disease. In the back of my mind a larger question kept surfacing: "What was I going to be for the next year, be an anthropologist or a paramedic?"

Kānji made a hot cup of Staines instant coffee laced with goat's milk and sugar as I asked my guests if I might "take food" before turning to their ailments. Local customs were on my side for a few minutes at least. As I sat on the verandah waiting for my coffee to cool, J. K. Doshi joined me. He was my Indian assistant whom I had asked to join the project almost immediately upon arrival in southern Rajasthan. "Davidji," he said quizzically, "Just see all these people. What has brought so many today?"

"Well, Doshiji, it's because we're very popular here in Ratakote," I answered him wryly, for he knew why the villagers had come as well as I did. But his question made me recall the events of the past few months, the decisions I had made to help people, and the increasing tempo of involvement that eventually led to a demand for my services so evident today. Had I done something to cause the dilemma? Surely this did not happen to every anthropologist.

Or did it? Anthropological field work is unique in at least one respect. It creates a close social relationship between anthropologist and informant. I think that for many of us this intimacy and involvement with people was an important drawing card into anthropology. I had not come to India to define people like so many laboratory specimens or subjects for observation. Furthermore, the relationships that had developed even during these early months had facilitated my research. They involved obligations, responsibilities, mutual respect, and a willingness to assist. And I gladly accepted the fact that it was not a one-way street. But now something was happening in the way people defined by role in the village. I had unwittingly acquired an obligation to treat illness in this community. I had become a local healer without knowing it!

Perhaps it had been Amarnāth's headache that started it all. I met Amarnāth for the first time on the evening of my second day in Ratakote. He came with some other people to absorb the heat given off by my kerosene pressure lamp as it burned in the school room where Doshi and I temporarily resided. We had come to our present lodging through the good offices of Nārājī, the village headman. "As long as you behave yourselves you can stay in this village," he had said to us. "Until your new house is finished you will sleep in the school." Amarnāth said little this first evening. He sat with the others and listened to the steady stream of questions and my halting, interpreted, answers. "Where are you from?" "How did you travel here?" "Why did you come to Ratakote?" On subsequent nights I came to know Amarnāth better for he began to talk more openly, and I learned much from him during my first few weeks in the village.

One morning Amarnāth arrived at my door. "I have had a terrible headache for three days, Sāb," he said. "The pain is very sharp here below my eye and here, right over it. It comes up and goes down with the sun. Do you have any medicine that might help?"

I hesitated and thought to myself, "That sounds like a sinus infection. Aspirin would help the pain although I doubt that it would attack the infection."

"Sāb is not a doctor you know," Doshi interjected. Like many high-status Indians, he had seen many requests from others who needed aid, and was on guard against long-term obligations. He tried to protect me now.

On the other hand Amarnāth was already a friend. He had been more willing than any other villager to spend his time answering my questions. He was also in real pain; sinus infections that "come up and go down with the sun" are famous for their ferocity in southern Rajasthan. I took out the bottle of Bayer's aspirin I had brought to India with me, unscrewed the cap, and shook out four tablets. "Here," I said, handing them to Amarnāth, "Take two of these with some water now and two more later this afternoon. You had better rest today, too."

Amarnāth thanked me, turned around, and walked painfully down the path toward his house. But the next morning he returned again. "Sāb, the medicine you gave me was very good," he said. "I would like some more."

"Well, Doshi was right," I thought to myself with some annoyance. "Once you start this kind of thing it is hard to stop." With resignation I gave Amarnāth six more aspirin tablets and wondered if he would be back again the next day. But that was the end of the incident. Later I learned that Amarnāth had divided each of the six tablets in half so that they would last longer, and that he claimed even this smaller dose worked well. In the future his strategy would be copied by other villagers who cut each aspirin tablet I gave them in four parts, hoarded the pieces, and even offered them as gifts to relatives in other Bhil communities.

No one asked me for anything during the next three weeks. Doshi and I continued to live in the school and as the time went by, we became better known to the people who lived near us. Research progressed nicely; I mapped the village, began a census, and participated in several events including a memorial feast for an important man who had died six months earlier. My house, which had been rising slowly during this period, was finally completed in the middle of January. The headman had chosen the location for me, a hill in a central part of one of the village wards, and arranged for three men to do the work. The structure, itself, consisted of two rooms approximately 10 feet square and a covered verandah. Although it could not compare in elegance to the stone houses of other villagers, it was perfect for my needs and we wasted no time in moving in. That evening I gave a party for the men who had worked on the project, and, along with some neighbors who heard what was going on and invited themselves, we drank, talked, and sang late into the night. Most of us got drunk, and we paid for it with a severe hangover the next morning.

One man, Haujī, paid more dearly than the rest, as I learned from his brother about 10 A.M. "Sāb," he shouted as he hurried up to my house. "Haujī is very sick."

"What is the trouble with him?" I asked.

"He can hardly breathe and he is very hot. He felt bad after the party last night and he has been getting worse and worse. He is really bad. Can you come and look at him?"

I had known Haujī almost as long as Amarnāth. He had directed the men who built my house and I often sat with him talking about such things as the size of the rooms, the pitch of the roof, and the possibility of windows. As I spoke with him from day to day I also learned something of the misfortune that could so easily strike Bhil families. Haujī was born 40 years earlier in a house that stood only 300 yards from my own. When he was 18 years old he was married and continued to live with his parents, a Bhil custom for the youngest son. Over the years his parents died and his wife bore him four children, a boy and three girls. Then, only a year earlier fever struck the family, first afflicting his oldest, a daughter who would have married the next year, and eventually all the children. Haujī tried everything he could to restore their health. He brought them to the village devrā or god's house where the deity, Bherōji, agreed, speaking through a shaman, to cure the children. But this and later shamanistic rituals failed and the children grew worse. Haujī sacrificed a goat to his house god and he held a special ceremony to the goddess Sikōtri, fearing that she might be to blame for the illness. In the end two daughters and his son died and, in despair, he abandoned his unlucky house for a new one he constructed in the hills. Now his brother's tone of voice seemed to imply that Haujī might be on the verge of death. I left immediately to see if I could help.

I found Haujī lying on the ground under a pile of dirty quilts. He moaned and shook and hardly recognized anybody. He was flushed and feverish and his lungs both sounded congested. "I bet it's pneumonia," I said to Doshi who stood next to me. "There is nothing we can do here. He is going to die unless we get him to the government hospital in Udaipur fast. See if that is O.K. with his brother."

Haujī suffered terribly during the long bumpy ride to the district capital. Once there, he was admitted to a medical ward and eventually given a shot of penicillin. Within two hours his temperature dropped from 106 to 99° and he felt well enough to smile. With things apparently in hand, I left him in the company of his wife and brother and drove back to Ratakote.

The next day Nārājī, the headman, paid me a visit. "The whole village is talking about what you did yesterday, Sāb," he told me. "They say you must be kind to do a thing like that. They say you saved Haujī's life and that you must truly be a man of pārēm (love) to give up your own comfort for Haujī." Indeed, people I had never met came to see me during the next few days and more than once I was asked to describe Haujī's condition and how I had made the doctors at the hospital admit him and give him an injection. Some asked directly why I had been so kind as to do a thing like that.

Five days after his trip to the hospital, a very sick Haujī appeared at my door. He had "escaped" from the hospital because "people were dying in there." He had walked back to Ratakote, a distance of over 20 miles, and felt very weak. He was lucky to have received a shot of penicillin that was intended to last for a long period of time. I judged that he would recover with rest and a diet strong in protein and vitamins. I suggested that he eat some eggs, drink whole milk, and kill and eat a chicken now and then. I also promised to get him a bottle of vitamin tonic the next time I made a trip to Udaipur.

Although he complained about weakness for several months, Haujī felt well enough to resume normal activities within two weeks. Much to my surprise, he attributed his cure to the eggs he had eaten. "He does not like eggs very well," his wife explained to me later. "When you said that he must eat them it was like medicine. He told me that you must know about some power in the eggs. After he ate them for a few days he felt so much better that he wanted even more. Our chickens did not lay enough and I had to look for more at other houses. Haujī says 'you surely know the power of medicines but you hesitate to tell because you are modest.'"

From then on people tried to tap this hidden power. One day shortly after Haujī's recovery, a woman stopped me as I was walking toward the shrine of Mangra Bābā (hill god) to watch a ceremony. "Sāb, my baby is sick with fever, would you look at her? She just lies there." I stopped by her house but knew that there was little I could do. Fever was a disease to the people of Ratakote. People got fever, suffered with fever, and died from fever. For me, it was a symptom of other diseases, and by itself, it usually told me very little. I looked at the child, asked if anything else were wrong with it, and puzzled, had to claim ignorance about the little girl's affliction. "The baby is certainly sick," I told her. "I don't know what she has and I have no medicine that would do her any good. You should show her to the malaria control worker when he visits the village this week and if she gets worse, you could take her to the hospital in Udaipur."

Other inquiries followed this one over the next few weeks. I saw my first cases of conjunctivitis and diarrhea. I was asked what to do about a painful boil, angina pains, a burning sensation during urination, fever, stomach pains, weakness, lack of appetite, sexual impotency, and a variety of other conditions people suffered from. I responded with courtesy and sympathy and with advice if I could think of any. But I felt frustrated by a lack of medicine; there was nothing concrete I could do to help them.

March was the turning point. Amarnāth, whose house was close to mine, paid me a visit one evening. He favored one leg as he approached and I asked why he limped.

"It's the sore on my shin, Sāb," he replied. "It hurts more than usual tonight."

"What do you mean, more than usual?" I asked. "How long have you had it?"

"Oh, about seven years," he said. "It nearly healed once but I knocked it open again."

The sore was large, over an inch and a half in diameter and so obvious that I wondered how I had missed it before. An area of rough scar tissue surrounded the lesion, indicating a larger area of involvement sometime in the past. It seemed inflamed, which probably explained Amarnāth's present distress. "I bet it won't heal because the circulation is gone," I said looking at the wound. "I wonder how you could get a thing like that to close up? Look Amarjī, why don't you soak a clean cloth in some hot water and put that on the sore? It might help a little. Beyond that I don't know what you could do about it. I don't have anything for it here."

"That's all right, Sāb," Amarnāth told me. "I am used to it. After all, I have had it for a long time now."

I thought about his wound a few days later as the jeep lurched and jounced toward Udaipur over a road that traversed an endless series of rock outcroppings. "What would it be like to have an open sore that would not heal for seven years?" The road smoothed out a bit on the outskirts of the city, then became rougher as the bumpy blacktop started. Soon I could see the house in which my wife, Carolyn, and baby daughter, who had accompanied me to India, lived. They stayed with me from time to time in the village, but found life there difficult. We had rented a room with a porch and kitchen shed soon after arriving. I drove in from the village once each week to see them, buy supplies, clean up, and catch up on typing notes and other work. As I pulled up to the front door, I could see Carolyn talking with a Westerner dressed in a high-necked Indian coat and loose fitting pants. I kissed her and turned to meet the stranger. "This is Arthur Banks, the mission doctor from Kherewara we heard about," she said. "Vickie and I found him in the bazaar today and asked him home for tea while he waits for his bus to Kherewara."

I had heard of Dr. Banks from other acquaintances in the city. He had been on home leave in England when we first arrived in India, but had returned and was hard at work now at what he liked best, public health projects and general clinic work. I liked him immediately. It was not long before my concern about Amarnāth surfaced. "Seven years," he asked. "That's a long time. Why don't you try soaking his foot in a tub of hot water to start with and add some epsom salts. Then try penicillin ointment on it and keep it covered. If there is any circulation left you should be able to get some tissue to form." Before I could ask, he took out his pen and wrote a prescription for penicillin skin ointment. "Do you need anything else?" he asked, looking up from his small prescription pad.

Without hesitation, I said, "Could you give me something that would help with conjunctivitis? I see so much of that in the village. And is there anything that I could use to treat dysentery? People complain to me about that all the time too. I ought to warn you though, I don't feel too secure about giving drugs. I did spend some time in the Army Medical Service Corps but except for one course, I don't know much about tropical diseases."

"I can give you some things you can use safely," he replied assuringly. "Aureomycin eye ointment would be good for conjunctivitis. No telling what is causing the trouble and the ointment should get almost any kind of bacteria. But make sure you continue treatment for a few days after the infection is gone. If you don't you may grow a strain of bacteria that is resistant to the drug. As for dysentery the safest thing you could use would be insoluble sulfa. Just give them enough to do the job and impress on them the need to take it regularly."

The doctor finished his tea and left to catch the Kherewara bus. I visited a drugstore I had shopped at once before and had the prescriptions filled. I also bought surgical guaze, some antiseptic, adhesive tape, aspirin, and epsom salts. Returning to Ratakote, I stopped by Amarnāth's house and asked him to come by and let me look at the sore on his leg again. That evening he soaked his shin for an hour and received his first application of penicillin ointment.

I was pleased and Amarnāth was dumfounded when his wound healed completely in two weeks. But it was just the first in a series of cures I could now affect. The day after I began work on Amarnāth's shin I treated my first case of conjunctivitis. The afflicted person could barely open his swollen eyes in daylight and complained of a constant painful ache at night. The next day after only one treatment I could see no sign of infection. He felt no pain and claimed to be cured. Diarrhea turned out to be a more difficult disease to treat, but sulfa seemed to help.

Word of these successes spread rapidly and patients multiplied. I ran out of medicine in five days and hurried to buy more on my next trip to Udaipur. I was surprised to discover that the druggist now treated me as a medical specialist and would sell me anything I asked for. In fact he seemed to have caught on to my high potential as a customer. "Take sulfa by the 5000-tablet box," he recommended. "It is much less costly that way. And you will be needing much eye ointment this time of year. Why not buy six tubes? Have you got enough penicillin ointment left? You should probably have five or ten more tubes of that as well." Later I would discover that the avaricious druggist was correct. The parade of patients grew longer throughout the spring, and my supply of medicine was often strained.

So was my knowledge of disease. The infections, fevers, pains, and other infirmities that confronted me each day almost always included a mystery or two. Visits to Dr. Banks for advice helped with the diagnosis of some, and the manual he gave me entitled *The Tropical Dispensary Handbook* helped with others. But there would always be a few baffling ailments and I could only advise those afflicted with them to make the long trip to the hospital in Udaipur for tests and, hopefully, better informed opinion.

Most people ignored these limitations and by May, 1962 my future in medicine seemed assured. If I had had any thoughts about extricating myself from paramedical practice, they were dashed by the success of aureomycin, penicillin, sulfa, and the wonderfully fragile local bacteria that had never encountered antibiotics before. These medicines worked too well; village resentment over their denial would have driven me from Ratakote. Instead I continued medical activities, to run what really amounted to a clinic. Villagers marveled at the power of "Sāb's medicine." They bragged about it to their friends and relatives in other communities, and made it and me a status symbol for Ratakote. I found myself sought out by more and more people, strangers, from neighboring villages. One man even walked all the way to Ratakote from Udaipur because someone had told him that, "Sāb cures better than the hospital." If escape from this medical identity was impossible, the preservation of the field research project, to say nothing of my personal commitment to anthropology, graduate committee members, and the Ford Foundation, would require heightened efficiency and a greater degree of control over daily activities. Was there a way to conduct successful fieldwork?

Time was a major part of the problem. Fieldwork takes time. It can easily require four or five hours to type up a day's field notes, even more if one takes particularly long and successful interviews or has observed especially complex events. To complicate matters, the control and scheduling of time is often out of the ethnographer's hands. Informants are busy people; one interviews them at their convenience. Local events schedule themselves.

Treating patients used up valuable time, and the more patients there were the more time treatment took. Even worse patients interrupted research activity. They arrived at their own convenience, at any time during the day or night that suited them. They would catch me as I hurried to meet an informant for an interview, interrupt as I tried to type field notes, or pull me away from the observation of an interesting religious event. Frustration over time was a constant research companion.

I developed four strategies to deal with this problem. All attempted to schedule time more effectively, to organize daily activity so that there was more time for research. First, I scheduled office hours. Villagers had a tendency to show up for treatment early in the morning, and I formalized their inclination by setting treatment hours in the morning after breakfast, and in the evening around dinner time. I announced this to the headman and village elders, pleading that although I wanted to continue medical assistance, I was a student and needed time for my own work.

Stating hours was easier than enforcing them. I found it difficult to turn people away when they arrived at the wrong time. They had often walked for several miles from some distant part of Ratakote and it seemed heartless to make them wait or ignore their troubles. A second strategy, hiding, seemed to help this difficulty. To hide, I scheduled interviews in distant parts of the village or arranged to observe an event or activity at a place that could not be seen from my house. Since I did research when I was hiding, this strategy directly contributed to fieldwork. When villagers came for treatment and discovered I was not home, they decided it was better to stop by during morning or evening office hours. Eventually hiding became less necessary as a result.

A third strategy, exporting informants, was closely related to hiding. I discovered this strategy by accident while I was recovering from a bout of dysentary at my residence in Udaipur. Worried about the loss of research time due to illness, I asked Kānji to pay me a visit for two days. Interviews on this occasion proved so useful, and the time for typing them up so plentiful, that I repeated the process again later.

The fourth strategy, developing a medical staff, was probably most useful of all and turned office hours into work periods on many occasions. Since my arrival in Ratakote, I had worked closely with my research assistant, J. K. Doshi, and my village assistant, Kānji Pārgi. They shared in research activity and participated in the daily routine of household maintenance. They also helped with the treatment of sick villagers and, before long, learned the questions I asked patients and the treatments I prescribed for common ailments. Gradually they were able to take over much of the outpatient care that I would normally have had to provide. Kānji inherited "eyes" and "cuts." He developed a gentle skill with patients and his bandages often looked neater, and stayed on longer, than mine. Doshi handled the more sensitive cases, such as diarrhea, colds, and respiratory infections. He became an accomplished diagnostician, treating most cases and sending me the few remaining problems that baffled him. While my associates conducted sick call, I attended to research. I found office hours were an ideal time to catch up on note typing and even managed to schedule interviews, fairly certain that they could be completed without interruption.

The medical training of Kānji had a side effect that I thought was beneficial. The people of Ratakote were becoming more and more dependent on the relief from suffering that aureomycin, penicillin, and sulfa could provide. Yet I would soon leave the village, depriving them of access to these drugs. Kānji, I reasoned, now knew enough to treat most common ailments and could continue in medical practice indefinitely. When I asked him about it he readily agreed to the idea, but pointed out one difficulty. He would have to be able to buy drugs in Udaipur and he would have to develop some way to raise the necessary funds in Ratakote. The first problem was easy to solve. The druggist agreed to sell Kānjī drugs and Dr. Banks lent his authority to the arrangement. The second would be more difficult, because Bhils help each other for nothing as a matter of hospitality. The best we could do while I remained in the village was to extract a promise from people to pay for the cost of Kānjī's medicines.

Time management helped to facilitate research, but it could not cure the basic dilemma. Dealing with patients still took part of my time, and villagers continued to evade the controls I attempted to place on them. There were emergencies that necessitated trips to Udaipur, such as the time a leopard bit a man named Kālāji through the left arm or the occasion when a little girl named Nānī was hemorrhaging from her mucus membranes as the result of a Russel's-viper bite. Some villagers, particularly those who felt themselves to be important, would send for me when someone in their family was ill. Others would try to interrupt me during the day despite efforts to avoid them.

But I came to find time spent treating people was not completely wasted in the context of fieldwork. Curing could generate field data as well. Through medical activity I learned folk classifications of disease and treatment. Since Bhils tied disease so closely to the supernatural, medicine proved to be a gateway to religion. And through the clinic I gained a clear and valued identity in Ratakote. My willingness to help increased their willingness to trust. Through trust emerged more detailed, accurate information. Curing led to the good rapport so necessary to successful fieldwork.

Anthropological fieldwork will always engender conflict between the ethnographer's personal relationships and his research goals. Informants will always make demands on time that are normal from their perspective, and anthropologists will respond to these demands as best they can. In the end fieldwork must involve a compromise, a willingness to recognize that informants are people, too, and that their needs are bound to impinge on research. Yet it may be the anthropologist's response to these needs that permits research to succeed. It is not clear to me whether curing informants *should* be part of the response. It is evident that medicine and research can mix, and that I would probably find myself in the same dilemma again were I to work in another Indian village.

2
TROUBLE IN THE TANK

JAMES P. SPRADLEY

James P. Spradley is Professor of Anthropology at Macalester College, St. Paul, Minnesota. He received the Ph.D. in 1967 from the University of Washington. His first fieldwork in British Columbia led to the book, *Guests Never Leave Hungry: The Autobiography of James Sewid, a Kwakiutl Indian.* His major interest lies in the ethnography of American culture. He is the author of *You Owe Yourself a Drunk: An Ethnography of Urban Nomads,* and coauthor of *The Cocktail Waitress: Woman's Work in a Man's World* (with Brenda Mann), and *The Cultural Experience: Ethnography in Complex Society* (with David W. McCurdy). In 1969 he received the Stirling Award in Culture and Personality for his paper on the cognitive analysis of tramp culture. He has been chairman of the Committee on Ethics, American Anthropological Association, and a member of the Panel of Scholars on Career Education, U. S. Office of Education.

I

The faculty meeting began promptly at eight o'clock. On that Thursday morning in early June of 1967, I was beginning to think around the edges of a decision that would eventually grow into a series of ethical dilemmas. The chairman took his customary place at the head of the long seminar table and started the meeting.

"Grand Rounds will meet in Health Sciences 405 this morning at ten. It's a classic case of schizophrenia. Dr. Johnson will present the case and I hope you can all come." A moment of silence followed while he sorted through some papers in front of him. Then, while the other faculty members discussed the Summer Research Training Program for medical students, my thoughts drifted away to my own research program.

I had been on the faculty of the Department of Psychiatry at the University of Washington for nearly a year, yet I still felt somewhat like an outsider. Everyone else seemed to know what was expected of them and I often wished for the security of well-defined responsibilities. My training had not prepared me to give psychological tests or engage in therapy; I had no desire to become a junior psychiatrist. I taught one course in the spring and offered lectures on culture and illness from time to time. Beyond that I was free to become involved in the training of future psychologists, psychiatrists, and physicians. I could participate in patient related activities such as group therapy. I could also carry out research that was related to mental illness, provided I gathered the data in the greater metropolitan area of Seattle. I felt most comfortable doing research and other faculty understood that role. I was eager to begin a new project since I had recently completed research on a Kwakiutl Indian chief in British Columbia. But, I discovered, the choice to do research only presented me with a new set of alternatives and the necessity to make other choices.

The faculty meeting ended and I edged my way to the door and walked quickly up the long hallway toward the elevator. The Psychiatry Department occupied one wing of the seventh floor of the University Hospital. The two elevators stood opposite the nurses station and beyond them lay the other wing with patients. The doors opened and a stream of people flowed out; I stepped in, pushed the button for the third floor—Department of Pediatrics—and leaned against the back of the elevator to wait. I knew that whatever I decided to study could easily continue for a number of years. I wanted a project that was interesting, challenging, and thoroughly anthropological. Perhaps a study of the Greek immigrant community in Seattle would meet these criteria; it could even lead someday to research in Greece. I thought of other alternatives like the spiritualist counselors and religious healers who attracted clients from all over the city. I wondered if I studied their methods could I compare them to curing rituals in Africa or Asia? I might study the social structure of a psychiatric ward in any one of a number of hospitals, a project similar to what William Caudill, another anthropologist, had done more than 10 years earlier.

As the elevator stopped at the fourth floor to pick up a nurse I thought about the most likely possibility, a study of urban Indians. Many Native Americans had moved to Seattle from rural reservations and I could investigate their strategies for adapting to city life. A government agency that helped to relocate Native Americans from Alaska had an office near the University of Washington and when I approached the director about a possible study he seemed receptive, even enthusiastic.

But each week brought new ideas, new opportunities. The latest was an alcoholism treatment center. I saw the third floor light come on and when the doors opened I stepped out, went past the waiting area and down the hallway to the Department of Pediatrics. I had decided to see if Jim Oakland, a psychologist who worked there, had time for a cup of coffee in the hospital cafeteria. I wanted to talk to him about the possibilities and problems of studying an alcoholism treatment center.

Jim Oakland and I had taught together at Seattle Pacific College a few years earlier while we both did graduate work in different departments at the University of Washington. We frequently talked about our respective jobs and research interests. He had administered some psychological tests to James Sewid, the Kwakiutl Chief whose life history I had recently completed. From time to time I had made suggestions on the social and cultural aspects of his work in developing norms for the Edwards Personality Inventory. His office door was ajar and I pushed it open. "Do you have time for coffee? I want to tell you my latest idea for research." Without a hesitation, he jumped to his feet, reached for his coat, and we were on our way to the first floor of the hospital.

As we sipped coffee in a quiet corner of the busy cafeteria I told him what I knew. "There's a new residential treatment center for skid road alcoholics opening sometime this summer. The King County Sheriff's Department will operate the center; they plan to take drunks arrested in Seattle and keep them at the center for treatment instead of giving them a jail sentence. I don't know much about the details but it would be a chance to get in on the ground floor, the start of the treatment center, and study it's culture as it develops."

Jim listened with interest and then asked, "How would you go about doing the research?"

"I would drive out to the treatment center; the buildings are under construction now a few miles outside the city. I'd go maybe three or four days a week, maybe more, to observe and talk with the patients and staff. It would be like studying a small society. The drunks will undergo several months of treatment and I'd want to participate in the various kinds of therapy, observe the work program, eat meals with them, and just hang around to gather data on the informal aspects of the center. I might develop some questionnaires later on and use some personality tests. I'd do an ethnography of the treatment center—my goal would be to describe its culture.

"But why do an ethnography of an alcoholism treatment institution?" he asked. "What kind of contribution will it make? Do you have any larger goals in such a study?" His question went to the heart of my own values and I paused before answering. "Well, in addition to the pure scientific goals, I may be able to learn some things that could improve the treatment milieu and lead to a more effective program. I don't know much about alcoholism but the skid road drunk is the hardest to cure and most approaches haven't worked very well. Maybe I can make some contribution there."

We continued talking for nearly an hour about possible problems, about the goals of such a study, the strategies for collecting data, the ways it might lead to improved treatment, and how I felt about this study in contrast to the others I had considered. We talked again during the next week and by the middle of June all signs pointed toward a study of the alcoholism treatment center.

II

The cool, damp days of June gave way to the bright sun of early summer. Before I made a final decision on the project I tried to find out more about the planned treatment center, reviewed some of the literature on studying institutions, and worked out ideas for gathering data. A colleague in the Department of Psychiatry told me that a Mr. Ron Fagan, newly appointed director of the center, was the kind of person I would find receptive to research. I called Mr. Fagan and made an appointment to meet him. A thin, soft-spoken man in his early fifties, he greeted me warmly; his informal manner put me at ease immediately. He began talking about alcoholics and his hopes for the new facility that he called "Cedar Hills Alcoholism Treatment Center." Although he did not fully understand what approach I would take as an anthropologist, he said that at one time he had collaborated on an alcoholism research project with a sociologist from the university. He believed in the importance of such research. He would welcome the kind of study I wanted to do.

Before we finished talking I knew I would learn a great deal from Mr. Fagan. I also sensed that his work involved far more than a job. He had a lifelong dream to help the alcoholic, especially the "low bottom drunk" from skid road. He recalled his own experiences as we talked, how he had been on skid road in Seattle and San Francisco and other cities around the country, the struggle with drinking, his attempts to stop the vicious cycle, finally hitting bottom and finding help through Alcoholics Anonymous. Since his recovery he had worked in a variety of settings to help alcoholics.

I learned that each year the Seattle police arrested more than 10,000 drunks sending a steady stream of men to the city jail. After a few weeks or months to dry out, most ended up back on the streets only to find themselves arrested again. It was a revolving door. Ron emphasized that this system did little more than dry out the drunk and keep him away from the bottle for a few weeks. It treated the symptom, not the cause. The men needed help, not punishment. Alcoholism was a disease that could be treated and Cedar Hills would use the best treatment approaches yet developed, everything from medical care and group therapy to Alcoholics Anonymous. Of course they would not have room for all the drunks arrested each year but would select those most likely to respond to treatment. Ron said he would start hiring staff and selecting patients in the next few weeks and I could start my research almost immediately. He offered to let me sit in on interviews with prospective patients and record the development of selection procedures. It would only require the permission of Sheriff Jack Porter, the person ultimately responsible for the center. Confident of the Sheriff's support, Ron said he would arrange for an appointment. I agreed to prepare a brief written proposal.

On July 18 I sent the proposal to Sheriff Jack Porter. It stated my purpose: "This research project will focus on how Cedar Hills functions as a treatment center for alcoholics. A study will be made of the development of the center, the formal and informal organization of staff and patients, the daily activities of each, various types of therapy utilized, and the meaning of the center to the patients, staff, and visitors."

Three days later I sat in a comfortable, overstuffed chair in Sheriff Porter's spacious office with Ron Fagan. He agreed with Ron that my study of Cedar Hills was a good idea and thought it could add to developing an effective treatment program. I pointed out that such a study could add to our understanding of new institutions, provide a basis for evaluating various therapeutic approaches, and that publications on the study could help to inform the community about the center. I then asked him what kind of institution he had in mind at Cedar Hills.

"I feel we must have a custodial type rehabilitation center. Successful treatment of alcoholics demands an institution," he said, leaning forward slightly in his chair. "What do you mean by *custodial* rehabilitation center?" I asked. "There are many other types of institutions but it is necessary to have one with a controlled environment. As long as you have alcoholics and as long as the police have to handle them—somebody has to do it. We have the alcoholics and because no one else is doing it we felt we should attempt some type of rehabilitation program."

As he talked I sensed his deep commitment to reshaping the lives of repeated offenders, to changing the archaic system that only dispensed punishment. My image of a tough cop who had risen to the top in Washington State's most populated county began to fade. He talked of the work release program he had developed for county jail prisoners so they could continue on regular jobs while serving time. He expanded on his ideas for the treatment center: "I think our treatment at Cedar Hills should be as sophisticated as possible. A work program is important in therapy. A work program is also important for returning money to the taxpayer. But work is secondary; cure is the most important. I feel there is value in Alcoholics Anonymous, various therapeutic approaches, and that vocational rehabilitation is very important. If Cedar Hills hasn't changed in six months," he said, emphasizing each word, "We will have to take another good look at it. It must keep changing. We must have some follow-up. If we can follow up on 50 percent of the men who go through Cedar Hills, that is better than others are doing."

I left that meeting deeply impressed with these men who were working to make the effective treatment of chronic alcoholics a reality. I felt exhilarated, filled with anticipation of the research about to begin. Confusion over too many alternatives had given way in a few short weeks to a firm decision to study Cedar Hills Alcoholism Treatment Center. I felt good because I had selected a unique cultural milieu for research. I knew it was a project that could have direct application to a social science problem of immense proportions. At the same time I did not plan to become an applied anthropologist; I would not try to change institutions or individuals. I had even told Ron Fagan that in order to keep from influencing the development of Cedar Hills I would have to withhold much of what I observed until after the study was completed. During the next two years I was to become more deeply involved with transients and drunks from skid road than I could ever have imagined on that warm summer afternoon as I left Sheriff Jack Porter's office.

III

Before July ended I was deep into fieldwork. The treatment center, now nearing completion, still had no patients. In the mornings I visited the criminal court in Seattle to watch the daily parade of drunks, to hear their pleas of "Guilty," and to record the sentences handed out by the judge. Ron Fagan and a newly hired counselor were there to watch and select patients. I interviewed them both to learn their reasons for selecting some men and rejecting others. I visited Cedar Hills and gathered information on the history of the new center. My field notes grew as I wrote down everything I could from my observations and interviews.

By the end of the first week in August a group of men had been selected; they waited in the city jail for their transfer to the county treatment center. Each would receive a six-month sentence; those who responded to treatment quickly could expect an early release. I sensed an air of anticipation among the staff because, at last, the waiting would end and they could get down to the hard task of rehabilitating these derelicts from skid road. But then, at the last minute, a bureaucratic snarl developed over the source of funds to purchase food for the men taken from the Seattle city jail to the King County treatment center. I talked with the staff and others, listened to their frustrations, and recorded their reactions to the news that these first patients would never arrive at Cedar Hills. Some felt the delay was due to the long-time rivalry between the city and county police departments. Another month passed before the problem was solved and a new group of patients selected.

On the morning of September 14, I left home earlier than usual. I drove to the Public Safety Building in downtown Seattle where I met Bill Adams, a police officer who had recently joined the treatment center staff; together we would transport the first six patients to Cedar Hills. At last I could talk to patients, find out the reasons they volunteered for treatment, listen to how they felt about the new center, and hopefully come to understand their lives as alcoholics. The elevator brought the men from the jail on the seventh floor to the basement where they were escorted into a paddy wagon. We drove out of the police garage and headed south. More than 30 minutes later we pulled into the grounds of Cedar Hills, the new buildings and landscaping seemed a sharp contrast to the adjacent county dump, the acres of surrounding woods, and the six transients from skid road.

I still vividly remember one small incident that happened about ten o'clock that morning, although at the time it seemed almost too insignificant to record. Standing around in the basement of the multipurpose building trying to appear unobtrusive, I talked with these patients as they checked in their meager belongings and received green uniforms to wear while at the center. Several talked about the city jail: "Sure is crowded in there, lotta men are sleeping on the floor," one said. "The food was really terrible," added an older man, "I haven't had coffee in two weeks because I haven't been able to drink the coffee in there." Then two of the others began complaining that the police officers who arrested them had stolen their money. For an instant I felt vaguely uncomfortable, aware that Bill Adams and Sergeant Ron Colvin were listening to these complaints. One patient recalled: "I had a $20 bill when I was arrested and when I asked for the money in my property there was none." The other man claimed he had $22 when picked up for drunk but it also had disappeared. As the discussion ended and the men began to leave for their dormitory, Sergeant Colvin assured me that the money probably hadn't been taken. "These men are drunk when arrested and don't really know what they have in the way of money. This kind of complaint is rather common."

The days that followed brought more patients and Cedar Hills came alive with activity. I interviewed informants and participated in staff meetings, patient orientations, meals, card games, informal bull sessions, and always I made long and detailed notes on what I learned. Late in September I joined a group of new patients for coffee in the dining room. They were discussing the laws in some states that protected alcoholics from repeated arrests for drunkenness; the topic shifted to conditions in drunk tanks in various jails around the country. One man said bitterly, "I don't see how any judge could ever go to bed at night without a guilty conscience after sentencing these men." Another spoke with deep resentment: "Throwing a man in jail over and over again just makes him that much more bitter each time." An hour later I overheard two of these same men talking about their own arrest a few days earlier. It had occurred at the same time and they had gone to jail together. The police officer had ordered them to turn their pockets inside out, ostensibly looking for knives and any items of personal property. One had $17, the other $23, but when they were released from jail to come to Cedar Hills they got nothing back. They noticed I had overheard their complaints and one said, "You'd better not tell on us!" I assured them that I did not work for Cedar Hills and would not tell anyone. Then he said, "In this jail they don't even give you a receipt for the money they take." Only later would I come to fully appreciate the significance of this statement.

During the next few weeks my role as neutral but interested observer became accepted; more and more patients sought me out to talk—and almost always their concern focused on conditions in the jail. If a staff member approached during such a conversation, the subject changed or became very general. But when I was alone with individuals or groups of men, they talked freely, expressing their deep resentment of the power of the police. They spoke from long years of experience; many had served "life sentences on the installment plan," as one man called it. They told me about thefts and beatings, about policemen who roamed around skid road waiting and looking for drunks to pick them up on the least prevarication. Out of deep and angry feelings older men decried the drunk tank that they found almost unbearable, often forced to sleep there for several nights at a time on the cold cement floor. Others had witnessed drunks being robbed and beaten by policemen on skid road and in the jail. They stressed the impossibility of ever "beating a drunk charge" so that nearly everyone entered guilty pleas even when innocent. One man recalled, "I was picked up one time for panhandling or begging; I asked a man for a cigarette and they arrested me and brought me in to be booked but the officer in charge just said, 'Well, you haven't been picked up in this jail before, we'll just put down you were drunk.'"

About this time I went to one of the counselors at Cedar Hills, a recovered alcoholic himself who, in years past, had spent many weeks in jail on drunk arrests. One morning in late September we drove together from Seattle to Cedar Hills. "When you were drinking and running and in jail," I asked, "Were you ever mistreated by the police? I'm wondering if we can believe the stories the men report." I knew he would willingly tell me of his own experience; he also knew personally hundreds of other men he had worked with in Alcoholics Anonymous. After a moment he replied: "Yes, one time I was in an elevator and I said something that wasn't nice and the policeman started to beat me up. And as to getting rolled, that is very true, drunks are rolled by the police all the time." We talked for some time about the difficult problems these men faced with the police in Seattle and in other cities. And as we continued to drive the last few miles to Cedar Hills I began to feel vaguely unsure about the direction of my research.

IV

October brought a warm Indian summer to Seattle; the trees turned from green to red to gold and the university came alive again with returning students. I continued to gather data on Cedar Hills but now I struggled almost daily with the question I had comfortably resolved during the previous summer: "What should I study?" Should I go on investigating this new institution for the treatment and rehabilitation of alcoholics? Or should I study the much older system for the arrest and incarceration of drunks? Would it be right to use Cedar Hills as a base for interviewing informants about life in jail? If I did change the focus of my research and study the experiences of drunks with the Seattle Police, would it be right to hide this fact from Sheriff Jack Porter? Ron Fagan might accept this shift in my research goals but the Sheriff could hardly allow it. If I began systematic interviews about the jail I would still have to continue some research on Cedar Hills so as not to arouse suspicion among the security officers who worked at the treatment center. On the other hand, maybe I should ignore the stories about the police and stick to my original research goals. After all, I couldn't study everything; sooner or later I had to draw the line and exclude some things that could be investigated.

Jim Oakland knew of what I had learned during those first months of research and one day over lunch I told him, "I'm wondering if I should focus on interviews with patients about the jail, concentrating on their experiences there rather than on the treatment center? Or should I ignore the jail? I don't think I can study both and do justice to my original proposal." I half expected the next question for it was one I had thought about often. "How do you know these stories about the police and the jail are true?" he asked. "Most people would see your informants as merely bums and derelicts who can't be taken seriously."

"I'm not sure they *are* true," I told him, "In fact, up to now I've only thought of them as complaints that would have to be investigated. But I feel sure that something is going on at the jail that few people in Seattle know about. The whole system of arresting drunks seems to breed injustice. They make nearly 12,000 arrests each year and some men spend as much as six months in jail simply for appearing drunk in public. They could bail out for $20 every time if they only had the money. If conditions are half as bad as some men say, then it's a hell of a place. Almost all the men who come for treatment have spent years in and out of jail and they seem far more concerned about the police and doing time in jail than about their drinking. Some of them aren't alcoholics; they volunteer for Cedar Hills just to escape doing hard time in jail. It can't help but have a profound influence on any treatment program. It may be true, as one informant told me, "After 30 days in jail, you owe yourself a drunk." I wonder if there's some way to change the laws or something; I don't know, but as long as they keep arresting these men, any kind of treatment program will fight a losing battle." Jim agreed and as we left he encouraged me to seriously consider more concentrated research on the collective experience of these men with the police and in jail.

An unexpected event occurred a few days later to help me decide. On Tuesday, October 31, I sat in court waiting for things to begin. The bailiff rapped his gavel loudly several times; everyone stood in silence. "The Municipal Court Number One of Seattle is now in session. The Honorable James Noe presiding." I knew the procedure by heart and sat down to begin taking notes as I had done on many other mornings. I heard the city attorney begin the process: "Delmar Luden, you have been charged with drunk in public, how do you plead?" "Guilty." After a quick review of his previous record the judge announced, "Thirty days committed." It took 10 seconds from start to finish for Mr. Luden to have his day in court. Stephen Brady followed with a two-day suspended sentence. I wrote rapidly as the tempo picked up—the same charge, the same plea, and always the sentences. Suddenly the fourteenth name caught my attention—Charles Roberts. I looked more closely and saw a former patient from Cedar Hills walk from the holding tank into the courtroom and stand before the judge. Only a few days earlier I had talked with this man about the jail, his past, the treatment program, and his hopes for the future. I avoided looking directly at him for fear he might recognize me sitting there in the audience as a spectator watching him. Judge Noe asked a clerk to notify Cedar Hills and then said, "Mr. Roberts, we are going to continue your case until Thursday morning for sentencing. $500 bail." Charles Roberts walked dejected from the courtroom.

In the months to come other patients would follow like a steady stream going from the treatment center back to skid road, picked up there by the paddy wagon, and taken back to the drunk tank. I knew I could never sit in court again as a detached observer; I would never again see only faceless drunks pleading guilty and receiving their sentences. I could not view these men as merely candidates for an alcoholism treatment center. From now on they would stand there as individuals, men I had listened to, laughed with, shared meals together. Most important, now I knew some of the conditions they would suffer as they took their sentences, turned away from the judge, and walked back into the jail in quiet desperation. As I left the courtroom that day I wondered more than ever about the sign that had stared down at me for months from high over the judge's bence: EQUAL JUSTICE FOR ALL UNDER THE LAW.

V

Almost a year had passed when, one warm September afternoon in 1968, I returned to my office to find a message: "Call Dr. Fred Anderson, Associate Dean of the Medical School." I dialed the number and a secretary answered. "This is Jim Spradley in Psychiatry," I said, "I'm returning Dr. Anderson's call." She sounded as if she expected my voice and said, "Oh, yes, Dr. Spradley, could you come in tomorrow morning at 9:30?" "Yes," I said, "I probably could, what is it about?" She said she would check if I could hold a moment. I'd never met the Associate Dean and I thought it must be some general meeting or perhaps a committee. The secretary's voice came back on the line, "It's about the problems with the police department." I hung up the phone, leaned back in my chair, and picked up an old issue of the Seattle Post-Intelligencer that lay on my desk. "I wonder what he'll have to say?" I thought to myself as my eyes scanned the three-week-old headlines: SEATTLE'S DRUNK TANK: A PLACE OF FILTH, STENCH, HUMAN DEGRADATION. I started reading again that paper of August 13, 1968.

"Seen through the eyes of a Skid Road alcoholic, Seattle's City Jail is an overcrowded jungle of concrete and steel.
   It is a place of filth, stench, sleeplessness and human degredation.
   It is a place where you are lucky to get enough to eat or adequate medical attention.

It is a place where the poor stay longer and suffer more.

This is the sordid picture drawn in an 88-page report just completed by Dr. James P. Spradley, assistant professor of psychiatry and anthropology at the University of Washington.

The report is based on interviews during the past year with 101 Skid Road men who have been arrested at least once for public drunkenness.

Spradley undertook the research project to find out if there is any therapeutic value in arresting an alcoholic and throwing him in jail.

He found that the men he questioned looked on their jail experience as much more detrimental than therapeutic. Of the alcoholics he surveyed:

—83 percent said they had spent at least one night in the jail's drunk tank when it was so crowded they couldn't lie down.

—93 percent reported that there is only one cup in the drunk tank from which those confined there may drink.

—98 percent said they had never been given a receipt for money or property taken from them when they were booked into the jail, and 40 percent said police had taken money from their effects while they were in jail.

—56 percent rated medical care they received in jail as very poor and 46 percent said they had not been able to get medical attention they needed while they were in the drunk tank. . . ."

The article continued with more statistics and quotes from the men interviewed. I skipped to the second page of the paper and scanned the other stories: POLICE ABUSE ON SKID ROAD? read one. Another said, SOME ALCOHOLICS THINK POLICE ARREST THEM TO GET TRUSTIES. At the top of the page a small item gave me the most satisfaction. It read,

NEW EMPHASIS ON REHABILITATION:

"The survey of Skid Road alcoholics by Dr. James P. Spradley was made public yesterday only four days after the City Council's Public Safety Committee recommended establishment of a detoxification center for handling public drunks.

Councilman Tim Hill said the purpose of the proposed ordinance is to change the handling of indigent alcoholics from a police matter to a public health procedure.

The new emphasis," he said, "is on treatment and rehabilitation."

I folded the paper, placed it with a stack of others at the back of my desk, picked up my briefcase and headed for my car, thinking all the while about Dr. Anderson and my appointment the following day.

It was shortly after nine o'clock the next morning when I drove into the staff parking lot at the University Hospital. As I headed for the Dean's office I thought about the repetitious courtroom drama being enacted at that very moment in downtown Seattle. I wondered how many of the men I would recognize if I had been there this morning. I smiled to myself as I thought about Judge James Noe's recent comment: "Immediately following the news story of your research report the number of drunks on the court docket dropped off significantly," he had said, and then added with a twinkle in his eye, "Maybe that was the only way they could keep the jail clean enough for all the visitors coming through."

Dr. Anderson's secretary showed me to his office and he rose to shake my hand; a soft-spoken physician in his middle fifties, he seemed friendly and interested. "Well," he said, getting right to the point, "I'd like to discuss with you your study of the alcoholic. I've read it and I think it's quite a good study, but I'd be interested in discussing with you how this might be handled in the future to prevent this kind of thing that took place." My pulse quickened and I asked him, "What do you mean, *prevent*?" I tried to appear calm and unconcerned but I was beginning to feel warm and my voice sounded defensive. "Well," he answered, "I mean, perhaps there is some other way it could be handled that might have made it better, perhaps it would have been better to have it delivered at a scientific meeting and then it would have gotten out that way."

By this time I was angry but I tried not to show it. "I can't agree," I said, my voice rising slightly, "If I'd presented the report at a scientific meeting or published it in some journal hardly anyone would have read it and it wouldn't have done much good." I could see the next question coming. "By the way, how did the papers get your report?" Calmly, without hesitating, I looked directly at him and said, "I gave it to them." His mouth dropped open and he looked at me in disbelief.

And so I told him how I had been a member of the Ad Hoc Committee for the Indigent Public Intoxicant set up by Councilman Tim Hill who wanted me to contribute the perspective of the Skid Road Alcoholic. We had met for months to plan a detoxification center as an alternative to jailing men found drunk in public. Judge James Noe was a member of the committee; so was an inspector from the police department, one or two physicians, and others involved in work with alcoholics. We had met for months to plan a detoxification center as an alternative to jailing men found drunk in public. I explained how the committee had been under the pressure of a possible Supreme Court ruling, the case of *Powell* v. *Texas*, how everyone expected the decision would make all drunk laws unconstitutional, and how they agreed that Seattle should set up a detoxification program prepare for the coming change. Then, early in the summer, the Supreme Court had ruled against Powell, leaving all the state and local drunk laws intact. When our committee had met after that, many members voiced the opinion that now we did not have to plan a detoxification center. Even the physicians on the committee agreed; one man from the University Medical School had said, "I find it hard put to think that any other facility is going to be able to offer better care, other than the bar bit, than the jail." That meeting had convinced me that I should finish up my report and release it. I gave copies to the members of the committee, sent one to the Mayor of Seattle, to the Police Department, to the criminal court, and to members of the Seattle City Council. I had then called the editor of the Seattle Post-Intelligencer and gave him a copy.

He listened with interest to my long explanation and then zeroed in on the report itself. "I read the report and I used to work in King County emergency ward. I know the conditions, a lot of men dying in the drunk tank, and I learned quite a bit from your paper, especially about the bail system, and that sort of thing. But I noticed you always commented, even though the statistics might be that only 20 percent experienced some negative feature, you still make a comment in your paper. The bias is toward the negative side of the picture."

By now I was more relaxed and I agreed with him. "That very likely is true," I said, "But no one can do scientific research completely free from bias. I attempted to be impartial but I certainly don't feel that I achieved it fully. I'm willing to take the responsibility for that. But you have to understand that this report was prepared to shed light on a specific issue. The argument today is over whether the jail is therapeutic or not; the Supreme Court decision was based, in part, on the view that jailing a drunk has a therapeutic value for him. In view of this opinion and the fact that many people contend that jails *are* therapeutic, I felt we should hear from those who had repeatedly experienced being jailed for public drunkenness. I presented my data in terms of this issue and I say that in the report."

We talked on for some time about the report and the problem of alcoholics. Dr. Anderson said he was sympathetic with my approach in many ways and that it had not been his idea to call me in. As we drew near the end of our discussion I asked him, "How do you think it might have been handled differently?" He thought for a moment and then said, "Well, perhaps not releasing it to the press as you did. If you could have allowed it to slip out to the press through the subcommittee, then you would have preserved your own kind of scholarly identity in the University."

VI

"As people who devote their professional lives to understanding man, anthropologists bear a positive responsibility to speak out publicly, both individually and collectively, on what they know and what they believe as a result of their professional expertise gained in the study of human beings. That is, they bear a professional responsibility to contribute to an 'adequate definition of reality' upon which public opinion and public policy may be based."

**—Principles of Professional Responsibility
American Anthropological Association**

3
RIGHTS, RESPONSIBILITIES AND REPORTS: AN ETHICAL DILEMMA IN CONTRACT RESEARCH

CAROL J. PIERCE COLFER

Carol J. Pierce Colfer is currently employed by Abt Associates, Inc., doing ethnographic on a rural American village and school. She has written "Bureaucrats, Budgets, and the B.I.A.: Segmentary Opposition in a Residential School." She has done fieldwork among the Northern Paiute in Burns, Oregon and at a BIA Indian School in Oregon. Although trained in Middle Eastern studies, her interests have broadened to include the contemporary United States, with special emphasis on women's studies.

RIGHTS, RESPONSIBILITIES AND REPORTS: CONTRACT RESEARCH 33

Our first hint of trouble came in the fall of 1973.[1] My husband, Mike, and I were standing on the school grounds with two officials from Washington, D.C., waiting for the school principal to join us, when one of the men turned to me and said, "Well, how *is* this project doing?" I remember my confusion and dismay as I stammered, "uuuh, well, uuh, fine, I guess." He looked at me aghast and said, "What do you mean, "you guess"? It's your job to know!" He seemed completely unaware of our company's agreements with his Bureau: a prohibition on information flow (and most particularly evaluative information!) between us and members of the Educational Research Bureau.[2]

This prohibition had been necessary in order for us to gain the confidence and trust of the local people in the community and school we were studying; and we had reassured the people repeatedly over the course of the year that we had *no* communications with the Educational Research Bureau that funded the special project in their school. We were not there as "spies", and we had to keep reminding people of that fact.

Later that day, Mike had to refuse point-blank a request by the same official to meet alone with him. We were aware of possible wide-ranging ramifications of such a refusal; after all, our own research funds ultimately came from this same Educational Research Bureau. But we were confident that we had abided by the agreements between our company and the Bureau, and by our commitments to local people. Our hopes that Mike's refusal marked the end of the controversy were short lived, however. Indeed, the controversy was destined to blossom over the subsequent months and require a great deal of our attention.

I had been excited and optimistic in the fall of 1972, when Mike and I had gotten a job with Crex Research Firm. We both had always wanted to work on an interdisciplinary research team, and studying education in rural America appealed to us. We were also anxious to begin the experiment we had suggested and Crex had accepted; splitting one job between us. Our academic training and experience hardly prepared us for the complex and ever-changing world of business and government that we were innocently entering. At the time we took the job, the likelihood of ethical problems seemed remote. Now, as I write in the midst of doing field work, ethical dilemmas impinge from every side. But in order to understand the major one that dogged our footsteps for many months in 1974, one must understand the genesis of the total research effort.

---

[1] I express my gratitude to Dr. A. Michael Colfer for creating this title and for his patience throughout this write-up; and to Abt Associates, Inc., for supporting me during this same period.
[2] Educational Research Bureau and Crex Research Firm are fictitious names.

THE BUREAUCRATIC GENESIS

In March, 1972, a governmental agency in Washington, D.C. announced a competition among small rural school districts, for large grants from the federal government. Announcements were sent to all small schools in the nation, and those who wished to enter the competition sent a "letter of interest" to the agency. The few successful competitors would receive relatively large sums of money to experiment with their educational systems over a five-year period. Although the grants were billed as "no strings attached," there were certain guidelines for the use of the money. First, attempts at change were to be holistic, or *comprehensive* in nature, as opposed to the more "piecemeal," or individual component approach used so often in American attempts at educational change. Second, rather than impose experiments designed externally by "experts," projects were to be "based on local conditions and local desires for schooling." Finally, the projects were to use any uniqueness that derives from the smallness of the schools. That is, any advantages that inhere in a small school were to be enhanced and utilized.

Now, if the governmental agency had stopped here, my husband and I might be suffering in San Bernardino, or doing research in Afghanistan. But, in funding these rural school districts, the Educational Research Bureau wanted to know what would happen. In short, they looked on these school districts as experimental laboratories. They were asking the following question: "What will happen if we give lots of money and free rein to a rural school district?" So, in addition to the above constraints, each of the schools that received the grants would be the subject of an intensive interdisciplinary research effort to document and evaluate each individual project and the overall attempt at educational change. Our ethnographic research was to be one part of this intensive effort at documenting the experiment. Although the successful small schools had not yet been chosen, a "request for proposal" was sent out to various research institutions in the spring, 1972, in order that the documentation and evaluation could begin at the same time that the rural schools were given their grants.

In June, the agency chose six sites from over 300 applicants, and promptly transferred the total program to the new (and incompletely organized) Educational Research Bureau. Some people have blamed the subsequent problems of this program on the shift to the Bureau; but I see it as merely our first encounter with the eternally shifting sands of bureaucracy. The problem, as I see it, derives from the overall instability of the system; not from a specific shift.

THE DOCUMENTATION EFFORT

Crex, a research firm on the East Coast, won the competition for the documentation and evaluation effort, and began assembling its research team. The original governmental agency had specified that the team should be composed of three to five senior social scientists working from one location, and a researcher residing full time at each local site. By November, 1972, the team included several sociologists (one being the Director of Crex's overall research effort), social psychologists, an educational administrator, and anthropologists, with various part-time support personnel from other fields where required. The overall research strategy was to be twofold. First, some personnel called "on site researchers," were to live "on site" and do a case study (in our case, an in-depth ethnography), of the community and school in their vicinity. This was designed to capture the uniqueness of each site and present a narrative that would be comprehensible and useful to a wide range of readers. The second part of the research effort involved other personnel ("core staff"), who were to remain in the home office and conduct standardized, cross-site studies, using questionnaires, expert informants (usually the on-site researchers), and standardized pupil test scores. Vast quantities of data were to be collected for the cross-site studies, and processed by computer.

Gradually, as we became enmeshed in this project, we became aware of the very real differences between this kind of research and the traditional kind of anthropological study. In addition to doing participant observation, we would be required to deal with a large number of people intimately connected with an alien business and governmental world. Besides developing our own set of field notes in our isolated rural village, we would be involved in amassing data for other members of the research team. The complexity of this kind of research can be seen in the development of what was called the "Information Management System." Two concerns motivated the development of this system: *maintaining confidentiality for informants,* and *reducing contamination of the experiment.* Each datum or report received in the home office was to be coded according to who would have access to it, and in what form.

The necessity to protect the privacy of individuals who answer personal questions on questionnaires, who agree to fill out instruments designed to measure their attitudes, values, and cognitive skills, and cooperate in a large scale research effort of this kind in a variety of ways, is hardly subject to debate. The likelihood of obtaining honest answers to personal questions is also enhanced when one can guarantee the confidentiality of the answers. All members of the Crex research staff indicated a commitment to maintaining the confidentiality of the data gained.

The Educational Research Bureau's perception of the local projects as true "experiments" also necessitated rather careful management of information regarding the research. The Educational Research Bureau wanted to know, "What happens if the government gives small schools large amounts of money over a five-year period and lets them do whatever they want with it (within the constraints that the attempted change be holistic in scope and acceptable to the community at large)?" Crex Research Firm was to document and evaluate what actually did happen. However, all parties concerned agreed that the school would very likely make use of any information they learned from the research efforts of Crex, and thereby nullify, or certainly alter, the course of the experiments. The results and experience would not, then, be transportable to other small schools, since small schools do not usually have the kind of expertise provided by a sophisticated research team available to them. The field-workers like us, who were living in the rural communities, were to write their case studies and submit them at the *end* of the local project. The case studies would then become public documents to be disseminated in whatever way seemed most reasonable, efficient, and feasible.

In the interim, however, the Educational Research Bureau, which funded our research, would have the right to refuse permission to publish anything written on the basis of this fieldwork.[3] The Project Director, for whom Mike and I worked, would have the obligation to read manuscripts and decide if they might endanger the progress of the research effort. If he determined that they would not present any problem if published, he would give permission to publish. If he sensed a possible problem, he would refer the manuscript to the Educational Research Bureau for a final decision. At the conclusion of the project, of course, all researchers would be free to publish whatever they wished.

Aside from these few agreements, the Bureau's role in the conduct of the research was not clearly defined. Although their staff interviewed each prospective member of the research team, in our case the interview seemed like a formality. Our impression at the time was that this federal agency would not directly concern us. They seemed interested in negotiating and corresponding with our research director in the home office, but expressed little interest in on-site personnel, such as Mike and I, or our research.

THE RESEARCH TEAM

In January, 1973, relations between the Educational Research Bureau and on site researchers were far less problematical than were relations within

---

[3] We needed permission to publish anything except "Papers...or articles,..which deal primarily with methodological or substantive issues not specific to any of the ten rural projects or to the [governmental] program." Quoted from Crex's contract with the Educational Research Bureau.

the research team. The research firm had had very little experience with either anthropologists or with the ethnographic method. Considerable effort was expended by core staff members and candidates for field work positions to develop an adequate role definition of what an on-site researcher should do. We attempted to ensure the autonomy necessary for an adequate ethnographic analysis, as we worked out the definition of our roles. Some field-workers expressed concern for the maintenance of rapport between researcher and community members, in light of our connections with the not-always-welcome activities necessary for the standardized studies. A great deal of learning was to take place as core staff struggled (successfully) to acquaint themselves with the alien nature of the ethnographic approach, and as Mike and I, as well as the other field-workers, tried to mesh personal styles with the corporate reality.

Our own role involved two components. We had complete autonomy in the conduct of our case study (in this case, an ethnography). We knew it had to directly concern the school and its experimental project. But the ethnographic part of our study was planned to occupy only half of our time over the five-year period. In the remainder of our time we would facilitate the research of the core staff. We had obligations to act as expert informants, edit correspondence with local project personnel and the Educational Research Bureau, collect data for standardized studies, critique prospective research instruments, alert core staff to possible problems, and so on. Core staff and on-site researchers recognized the fine line between our roles as independent professionals conducting our own research and as glorified, highly paid "messenger boys" for other people's research. The home office had opted for the preeminence of the former role, by selecting field-workers who were highly trained and antagonistic to the messenger boy alternative; but, given our two functions, it seemed inevitable that a certain tension would continue to exist between these two options.

In return for the inevitability of such tensions and the anticipated drudge work of collecting other people's data, we hoped to gain a number of things. We felt that looking at the same phenomena from so many different perspectives would tell us a great deal about the phenomena themselves and/or the various research strategies. We felt that the disciplinary boundaries among the social sciences were arbitrary and that important results could emerge from an attempt, such as this, to work together on the same problem. We hoped to learn more about the nature of research in the other disciplines, in order to improve the quality of our own research. The fact that the research effort was to be of five years' duration also appealed to us, as a unique opportunity for relatively long-range research. In more mundane terms, the position with Crex gave us a number of benefits, including lavish budgets for office supplies, telephone, duplicating, and other such material luxuries usually unavailable to anthropologists, opportunities to travel frequently, high salaries, medical and insurance advantages, access to a variety of support personnel and computers where needed or wanted, and, in our case, the chance to split one job and work together. The combination of these advantages and the chance to live and work in the Pacific Northwest were far more compelling than our other option of returning to the rather stultifying academic setting to which my husband could return (to work alone). We accepted the position.

In December, 1972, we moved to our site and began our research. The local educational project that we were employed to document involved two towns and three foci: the environment, basic skills, and career awareness. These foci had been determined by the citizens of the area in a workshop the preceding summer, and had been refined by a special steering committee of elected citizens. When we arrived a director for the local project had already been appointed and the schools were well into the planning year (1972-1973). We began our research by immersing ourselves in community activities. There was considerable interest, apprehension and suspicion about our actual role in the towns. People laughed nervously as they asked us if we planned to write another *Peyton Place*. Others compared our case study to the book *The Egg and I,* a bitingly sarcastic account of rural life in this area, in the 1930s. The Watergate scandal was much in the news for our first year here, and we were constantly teased about the tape recorders we had allegedly hidden in our clothing, or the secret reports we must be relaying to Washington, D.C.

Since the federal presence was very much felt in the area (via a large Forest Service contingent), some community members saw us as federal "spies," there to make certain the school did not mismanage or abscond with the federal funds. Others feared us as "evaluators" who would tell the world of the shortcomings of the towns and schools. Even the most sympathetic community members had difficulty understanding exactly what it was we were doing. But gradually, through much repetition and reassurance, we were able to explain to most people that we could not *evaluate* a community, that our world view required that we accept a community and merely describe it.

As we became aware of the concerns and fears of local people, we also realized that if we hoped to be able to describe their lives and their communities accurately, we had to overcome such negative feelings. So when people asked us what we did (which was often, at first), we were quick to explain our lack of involvement with the federal government, the inaccuracy of their perception of us as spies. We reassured people that we did not report to the funding agency.

In the beginning, during this period of reassurances we became aware of periodic visits to our site by a "project officer" from the Educational Research Bureau in Washington, D.C. A project officer monitors each local project to ensure and facilitate compliance with the contract between the local school district and the Bureau. On several occasions the project officer asked us questions that might well have had impact on the local project. We were able to field the questions; but other on-site researchers had similar, and more serious problems with questions from the project officers for their sites. It became clear that a projectwide policy on the interactions between on-site researchers and project officers would have to be agreed on. Extensive interactions between field-workers and project officers would undoubtedly have heavy impact on the course of the various experiments. In our case, such interaction would also have had extremely adverse effects on our community rapport, considering the already described suspicion that we might be federal spies. In the spring of 1973, the Crex Project Director was able to negotiate, after considerable telephoning and memo-writing among on-site researchers, core staff, and Washington, D.C., an agreement with the Educational Research Bureau that shielded field-workers from contact with project officers (except at the discretion of the field-worker). We now felt that we were off the hook, when the project officer came to town.

But our euphoria didn't last long. In the fall of 1973, the high official mentioned earlier, from Educational Research Bureau, visited our site. He immediately began asking us questions requiring evaluative answers, apparently unaware of the relevant agreements between our company and his Bureau. We were taken completely by surprise. Initially we were able to field his questions (albeit in a rather unpoised manner), but later in the day when he expressed the need to talk alone with Mike, point-blank refusal seemed the only possible course of action. The official had asked us to act in a manner contrary to all the agreements between Crex and the Bureau, and between us and the people on our site.

THE SHIFTING SANDS OF BUREAUCRACY

It was about this time that we began to realize the significance of changing personnel and structures within the federal bureaucracy that funded both our research and the school district we were studying. Living far from Washington, D.C., we were shielded from much of the turbulence of a bureaucratic organization in flux; but eventually the repercussions could be felt even in our isolated village.

The following diagrams indicate our perceptions of relations within our company and in interaction with the various actors in the Bureau at two times. Let me stress that these diagrams represent *perceptions,* rather than accurate organizational charts. Indeed, our exact knowledge of organization within the Bureau was hindered by the fact that "a succession of internal reorganizations had led to eight new organization charts in less than two years." (Miller, 1974:62)

During most of 1973, we saw the significant interrelationships as something like this:

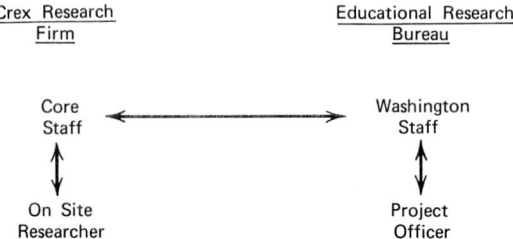

Arrows indicate lines of communication. We considered ourselves effectively protected from communication with the employees of the Bureau by the frequent communication that occurred between core staff and the Bureau, by the Information Management System, and by the fact that we submitted periodic reports to the core staff about our activities.

However, in late 1973, not long after our incident with the visiting official, the internal organization of the Educational Research Bureau began to firm up, and new roles and lines of communication began to emerge. Crex, like the local projects, has a contract with the Educational Research Bureau, which requires monitoring. The project officer for Crex, who had maintained a very low profile, resigned; and the new project officer explained the new structure, and the new rules of the game. The new 1974 reality came to our sites something like this:

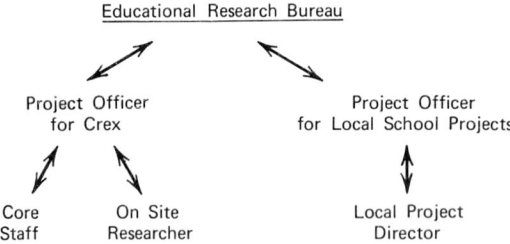

The Educational Research Bureau's project officer for Crex explained that his job was to monitor Crex's adherence to the contract, and that since case studies were such an integral part of the overall research strategy, he needed to know that satisfactory progress was being made. He felt that he could not be satisfied with the assurances of core staff that were based on preliminary drafts available only to members of the research team. When he understood our concern for the confidentiality of our preliminary data, the probability of our information affecting the natural course of these educational experiments, and our commitments not to report to the Educational Research Bureau, he volunteered to keep the information secret. But he insisted that he needed reports from us to do his job adequately.

Further complicating our situation was the fact that implicit in the overall research design was the necessity that our research results remain unavailable to local people until the termination of the "experiments," in order to minimize formative feedback from our analyses. Naturally the project officer also wanted us to maintain our commitment to this research strategy.

We were therefore confronted with a serious ethical dilemma. On one hand, we had repeatedly reassured community members and school personnel that we were not required to report to the federal government until the end of the project. We had even gone so far as to eschew casual interaction with employees of the Bureau, so that appearances would confirm that reality. On the other hand, Crex' Project Officer was now requiring a written, annual report from us, *and* he was requesting that it not be made available to local people. If we complied with the government demands, we compromised our promises to community members. If we held stringently to our commitments to the people and refused to make any reports, we could well be fired.

At this point we felt we had three options: (1) we could quit our job; (2) we could make the requested secret reports; or (3) we could make public reports. No option was without important disadvantages. It is interesting to note that in each case there were *both* ethical and practical disadvantages. Let us look at each briefly.

The first option was to quit our job. We would, of course, experience the usual financial hardships if we did this. But we also felt ethical constraints to remain on the job. At the outset, we had made commitments to Crex, the Educational Research Bureau, and local people to remain on the job for five years. We were very much aware of the difficulties inherent in personnel turnover in an ethnographic endeavor. Even if our notes were not personal and confidential, another researcher would have great difficulty using them (cf. Barth's attempt to make use of Pehrson's field notes, Pehrson, 1966). We felt that the loss of our (or any other on-site researcher's) knowledge of the local project and towns would be extremely detrimental to the overall research effort. And we have strong professional commitments to the value of the research we are conducting. So we did not want to quit our job.

The second option was to make secret reports as requested. If we agreed to make secret reports to the Educational Research Bureau, as requested, we would be violating the AAA Ethics Code, which says:

> *"In accordance with the Association's general position on clandestine and secret research, no reports should be provided to sponsors that are not also available to the general public, and, where practicable, to the population studied." (1971:1)*

and

> "He [the anthropologist] should not communicate his findings secretly to some and withhold them from others." (1971:1)

and, finally,

> "Specifically, no secret research, no secret reports or debriefings of any kind should be agreed to or given." (1971:2)

We would also be betraying the trust of the local people, and we knew that that was never really an option. In addition, we were not convinced that the project officer for the Crex contract *could* keep the reports confidential. The funding agency was under fire from Congress and was seeking evidence of work well done. We felt that if the Bureau were faced with imminent demise, such assurances of confidentiality would go by the boards. Similarly, Crex's project officer seemed to be a very capable and ambitious man, and we predicted his rapid rise in the bureaucracy.[4] If he rose to a level where he supervised local school project officers, it would be difficult for him to avoid making use of what he learned from our "secret" reports. In short, from a purely pragmatic standpoint, we doubted that either the existence of our "secret" reports or the contents thereof could remain undisclosed for long. Such a disclosure would have been fatal for our community and school rapport.

Our last option was to make public reports, available to local people. This option's disadvantage was the probability of very directly influencing the local school's project, and thereby affecting the "experiment" in an undetermined way. We had promised our employer and the Educational Research Bureau at the outset to eschew influencing local events to the greatest degree possible. Another more practical disadvantage to this option was the certainty that some community members would not like what we wrote, and the probability that the quality of our life on site and our relations with community members and school personnel might suffer. If local reactions were extremely negative, our research would also suffer.

We discussed these options with each other at great length, in an effort to determine the "right" and ethical course of action. We felt the weight of many and conflicting commitments — commitments to anthropology and the pursuit of knowledge, commitments to our colleagues, our employer and the total research effort, commitments to the initial concerns expressed by the Educational Research Bureau when its experimental program was conceived, and

---

[4] On December 12, 1974, we learned he was being appointed to a position that supervises all experimental school projects, including all project officers (at the moment, temporarily).

most important (we felt), commitments to the people of the communities and schools. We tried to weigh and measure the importance of all the variables affecting the various plans of the Educational Research Bureau, Crex, the local schools and people; we tried to gauge the strength of our diverse responsibilities, beliefs, and commitments; we tried to note all the instances where changing Educational Research Bureau personnel and policies had already affected the nature of the "experiments," as originally conceived and the nature of Crex's research (including our case studies). The great number of variables and the fact that change seemed the only constant in this situation made discussion and thought incredibly complicated and befuddling. And the fact that my husband (Mike) and I did not feel equally the various commitments made the decision-making even more torturous.

Our decision, in the end, was to choose the last option. We wrote our first public annual report in November, 1974, over the objections of the project officer who monitors the Crex Research firm's contract. The core staff also objected. That report contained an introductory chapter of the final case study that explains our *modus operandi,* our world view, and a rationale for using the ethnographic method to study schools. The report also contains an annotated outline of the final case study. We chose to deal with these two topics in an effort to minimize our impact on the local school project, and secondarily to communicate the nature of ethnography to the educators at the Bureau (who continually expressed concern about and ignorance of what ethnographers do). The annual report of 1975, however, will deal with matters that definitely have the potential of substantial impact on the local project. Our hope is that, by then, the project's direction and goals will be sufficiently set that our work will be ignored by its members (from a practical standpoint). The fourth of five years of funding, for the local school project, is 1975-1976.

Since our decision to write public reports at the expense of probably influencing the local project, we have had other, less harrowing dilemmas caused by the increased communication among ourselves and the Educational Research Bureau. In September, 1974, for instance, lines of communication were opened between us and the local project officers against our expressed wishes. It seems inevitable that such problems will continue to arise throughout the duration of the research effort.

CONCLUSION

In sum, then, in late 1972, my husband and I took a job that promised to be exciting, rewarding, and pleasant. We had always wanted to work on an interdisciplinary research team, and we now had that chance. Educational research seemed among the most devoid of ethical dilemmas one could conceive. After exploring the few ethical concerns we had, we were given reassurances by honest people, on the basis of information then available to them. As our research has progressed over the past two years, we have been confronted with one ethical dilemma after another, the most glaring and disturbing of which has been presented in this article. As noted earlier, the active project officer who requested secret reports has risen in rank within the Educational Research Bureau, and now supervises the entire experimental program. In January, 1975, the core staff and the Bureau official had agreed that Crex should retain the annual reports until some other review mechanism could be found. But the man has retained his old position as our project officer, as well; and I am quite certain that Crex employees have not seen the end of such requests.

We are very glad that we made the particular compromise we did, making our report a public document now, because we need no longer concern ourselves with what is done with it. And yet, we may suffer other kinds of consequences on site, because of public distaste for certain things we have written, although no displeasure has been evinced so far. Furthermore, it seems probable that all parties will have to abandon the notion that the "experimental" projects in the school retain the original conception of experimentation.

The responsibility for the ethical dilemmas that have recurred with such regularity throughout this project lies with no particular individuals; no malice created our problems; the intentions of all parties have appeared to be good throughout. The problem derives from the fact that federal bureaucracies are constantly in flux. Personnel are constantly changing; programs are always being altered; bureaus and institutes change functions and responsibilities. With each change, whether in program, personnel, or organization, the priorities and understandings change. My experience, both in this situation and another research situation at a BIA Indian School (Colfer, 1974; 1975), lead me to conclude that it is extremely difficult to behave ethically when one is closely affiliated with a part of the federal bureaucracy, unless one is in a position of such minimal authority and control that one's actions have little impact. My position as an instructional aide at the BIA School was among the lowest hierarchical levels in the school: I therefore met with few ethical dilemmas during the course of the research. In this position, however, where Mike and I are funded, indirectly, from the same source as the local project, where we have a rather prestigious job and group of colleagues, where we are not free agents in the same sense that I was as a low-level employee of the BIA, we are constantly confronted with ethical questions and uncertainties.[5]

[5] See Everhart, 1975, for a similar experience.

But a final word of caution to those who would escape such ethical dilemmas. Abdicating the responsibility to participate in such a potentially valuable research effort because of the fear of such dilemmas is also unethical and certainly irresponsible. Anyone contemplating a research effort such as the one described in these pages, however, should be aware of the inevitable barrage of ethical questions and concerns with which he or she will be faced. I would have difficulty assembling a group of people who are more sincere and dedicated to their research efforts and to an ethical solution to these various problems than those with whom I work; and yet we do not agree on solutions or on what constitutes ethical breaches. We all have great difficulty dealing with the conflicts in what we set out to do, and what we are being allowed to do; what we are asked to do and what we can allow ourselves to do. And I predict similar troubles for anyone who attempts to do research under the aegis of governmental funding, whether direct, or, as in our case, indirect.

REFERENCES

Colfer, Carol J. Pierce

    1974   "An Ethnography of Leaderlong Indian School." Doctoral dissertation, University of Washington.

    1975   "Bureaucrats, Budgets and the BIA: Segmentary Opposition in a Residential School," *Human Organization,* **34**: 149-56.

Everhart, Robert B.

    1975   "Problems of Doing Fieldwork in Educational Evaluation" *Human Organization,* **34** (in press).

Miller, Judith

    1974   "Washington: Scuttling Education Research," *Change,* November, pp. 46-47 and 62.

Pehrson, Robert N. (and Fredrik Barth)

    1966   "Social Organization of the Marri Baluch." New York: Wenner-Gren Foundation for Anthropological Research, Inc.

"Professional Ethics"

    1971   Washington, D.C.: American Anthropological Association.

4
THE UNDERDEVELOPMENT OF ANTHROPOLOGICAL ETHICS

MICHAEL A. RYNKIEWICH

Michael Rynkiewich is Assistant Professor of Anthropology at Macalester College. He received his B.A. from Bethel College and his Ph.D. from the University of Minnesota in 1972. His fieldwork in the Marshall Islands (1969–1970) has resulted in several articles including "The Ossification of Local Politics: The Impact of Colonialism on a Marshall Islands Atoll," "Adoption and Land Tenure Among Arno Marshallese" and, with Robert Kiste, "Incest and Exogamy: A Comparative Study of Two Marshall Islands Populations." Most recently, he coedited a book of readings for classroom use: *The Nacirema: Readings on American Culture.*

DAILY LOG #3 SATURDAY, AUGUST 16, 1969

After another song LiKijal gave a speech.[1] She said they were sorry they were late, but they were working on Marshallese time and some people weren't ready, and it took a while, and that this food was for us because it was Marshallese custom that when a newcomer was here they were brought food. Then LaMun indicated that I should give my speech. It went all right except that it was too long and I said too much. After I had said "thank you" for the food and that we were going to live here for a year and a half, etc., I said something that I probably shouldn't have. I repeated what I had said in the council meeting, that I was not able to help them much because I was just here to study, not like the Peace Corps or Government. The way that came out (in Marshallese) was bad. The woman who works with MCAA stood up and made another speech and several of her words stood out: that she was sorry that I was not willing to help them, but they would still help me anyway. So I stood up again, sweating, and tried to explain what I meant. LaMun said it turned out OK, but I'll never use the phrase ("I'm not here to help you") again. From now on I'll use "I'm not here to tell you what to do."

Linda (my wife) and I went to bed that night feeling terrible, especially me because of the grave mistake I thought I had made.

That was the end of the most depressing day of my year and a half on a Marshall Islands atoll. Earlier that week I had gotten into an argument with an American artist who was visiting the atoll briefly. He accused me of using the people there to get my Ph.D., of intervening in their lives for my own gain instead of to help them. I agreed that I had not come to help them directly but argued that I had no intention of intervening in their lives.

He was not satisfied with my answer, and neither was I. All week long I worried about what I was doing there. The misunderstanding at the welcoming party occurred because I wanted to clarify an issue that probably did not bother the Marshallese. At the very least, I did not want to deceive them about the nature of my presence. In attempting to present myself honestly,

---

[1] Fieldwork on Arno Atoll was carried out between June, 1969 and December, 1970 under a grant from the National Institutes of General Medical Sciences, GM01164, administered by E. Adamson Hoebel and the Department of Anthropology at the University of Minnesota. Earlier drafts of this paper were read by Gary Rubin, Linda Rynkiewich, Robert Kiste, Jennifer Grismer, Jill Levinson, and Jane Patrick, to whom I am thankful for criticisms.

All Marshallese names in this chapter are ficticious. The events, such as this slightly edited selection from my diary, are accurate.

I offended the people by saying that I was not willing to help them. I found out later that willingness to help is a very important value.

During those first few weeks of fieldwork I had just about convinced myself that my presence posed no ethical problems. I avoided the danger of ethnocentricism by keeping my value system separate from the Marshallese system. I avoided the danger of disturbing the social order by not intervening. Still I had an uneasy feeling that I was fooling myself. I was trying to put into practice what I had learned in both undergraduate and graduate schools, and it was not working out very well.

PREPARATION FOR THE FIELD

One of the lessons I learned in school and took to the field with me was the distinction between pure and applied research. Clearly, the object of the graduate program was to turn out anthropologists who, through research, publication, and teaching, would contribute to the growing body of anthropological theory. The course offerings dealt with the methods, theories, and findings of anthropology. Ethics were mentioned only in the context of an occasional discussion of applied anthropology. Pure science meant, among other things, that the research was not directed to solving practical problems. Applied anthropology, on the other hand, involved intervention in other people's lives, and thus raised complicated ethical issues. Such work also seemed to be considered second class because it did not contribute to the growth of theory and because it did not fit the value of cultural relativism. If, as an extreme cultural relativist would assert, what people do is to be evaluated only in its cultural context, then why would any anthropologist feel it appropriate to make changes?

In sum, my graduate training led me to believe that most traditional anthropological fieldwork did not involve significant ethical issues. I felt strongly that knowledge of method and theory would be all the preparation I would need to do a good job as a field anthropologist.[2]

Only when I reached the last step before leaving for the field did a question arise that I thought was relevant to my situation. In my preliminary oral examination I was asked what right I had to disturb other people just so I could get my Ph.D. I sidestepped the issue by asserting that social interaction anywhere involved using other people and being used. I would be acting in the Marshalls as I would in the United States. This question continued to

[2] My training was typical, not unusual, so I am not chastising my teachers. For the most part, they, like me, have become much more concerned with ethical issues in the field and are discussing them with their students.

MAP 1. Trust Territory of the Pacific Islands (Micronesia).

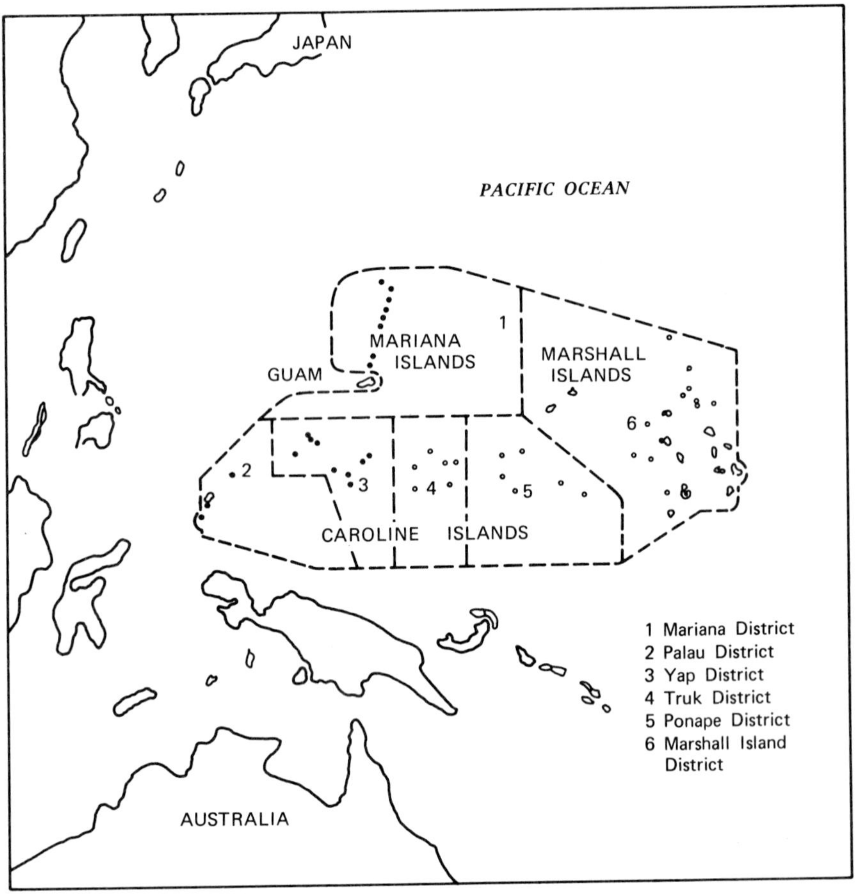
JAPAN
PACIFIC OCEAN
MARIANA ISLANDS
GUAM
MARSHALL ISLANDS
CAROLINE ISLANDS
AUSTRALIA
1 Mariana District
2 Palau District
3 Yap District
4 Truk District
5 Ponape District
6 Marshall Island District

haunt me, as can be seen in my fumbling attempt to be honest with the Marshallese about my intentions.

In the rest of this chapter, I want to examine some of the consequences of not training students how to recognize and deal with ethical problems. My sense of anthropological ethics went through three stages of development. Before leaving for the field, I anticipated few, if any, ethical dilemmas. Instead, I concentrated on learning method and theory. During the fieldwork period, I began to recognize an ethical aspect in some situations, but I generally responded in a paternalistic manner or refused to become involved at all. After completing my fieldwork, I became convinced that my very presence and that of other Americans, particularly the military, constituted intervention that

THE UNDERDEVELOPMENT OF ANTHROPOLOGICAL ETHICS 51

MAP 2. Marshall Islands

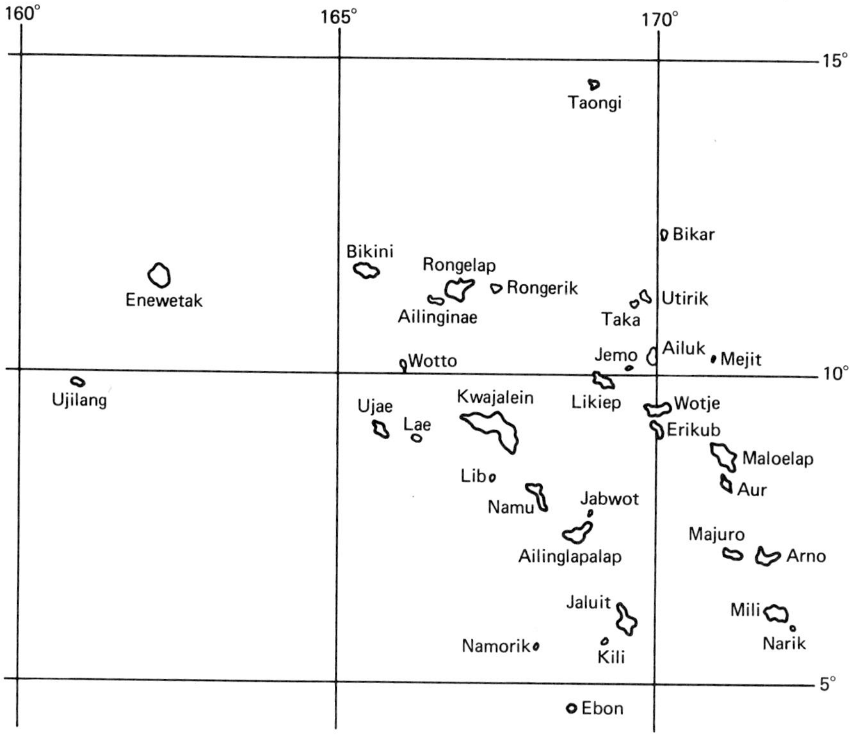

called for a more positive and helpful response on my part. The Marshallese were right to expect my help.

PATERNALISM IN THE FIELD

Early in the summer of 1969 my wife and I went to live on a coral atoll in the middle of the Pacific. Of the 12 trust territories created by the United Nations after World War II, only one remains—the Trust Territory of the Pacific Islands that makes up most of the culture area known as Micronesia (see Map 1). The Marshall Islands compose the easternmost district of the Territory (see Map 2). Arno Atoll, our new home, is in the southern Marshalls.

We settled into one of the 17 communities on Arno. The whole atoll included 1200 Marshallese and 6 Americans, all Peace Corps volunteers. My object was to discover how the people held rights to land, how those rights were transferred from generation to generation, and how the pattern had changed in the last 100 years. First, I asked who lived in each of the 155 houses on the atoll, then I determined how land was divided. Finally, I gathered the history of land rights ownership for each of the more than 700 plots of land.

The work that I had planned went well. What I had not anticipated was that I would be perceived and used in a way that I found objectionable. The desire for Western and Japanese goods is long standing among Marshallese. Although the people still have the knowledge of gathering and preserving vegetables, fruit, and fish from their atoll environment, and although they still know how to build houses and canoes out of local materials, their wants have made them largely dependent on goods from the outside.

The Marshallese have been in regular contact with western and Asian countries since the 1850s. While Spain nominally held the area from the 1600s, her influence was felt only in the islands far west of the Marshalls. Germany declared a protectorate over the Marshalls in 1885 and continued to develop the trade in dried coconut meat called copra. Rifles, steel tools, and cloth were among the first trade items. In 1914 the Japanese forcibly replaced the Germans. Japanese colonization was more intense in that many more colonizers came to the islands, the pressure on the Marshallese to produce copra increased, and the Japanese eventually required land and labor to fortify the islands. Clothes, footwear, bicycles, lumber, lanterns, kerosene stoves, and tinned foods from Japan provided an added incentive to copra production. The Japanese made sure that each atoll had a well-stocked store, and soon many Marshallese preferred rice, flour, sugar, tea, and canned fish to some of their traditional, and locally available, foods.

During World War II the Americans landed on several Marshallese atolls and bypassed the rest. Food was in short supply and many isolated Japanese became harsh in their treatment of Marshallese. Thus, the Americans were welcomed as liberators. The United States attempted to revive the coconut economy after the war, but the world demand had shifted to soybeans as a source of vegetable oil. The Marshallese were stuck with a single item of trade and a trustee nation that was interested only in the strategic position of the islands. While there was little economic exploitation by the United States, there was also little economic development.

I accepted the situation as it was in 1969 when I arrived. I bought the foods and goods that were available to all residents at the local stores and used them both for myself and for others as they desired. When I knew people preferred imported rice to local breadfruit, I served rice. Though I wished they would not be so dependent on the outside world whose economy was known to undergo dramatic changes, I could not have presented myself as a person to the Marshallese if I did not share the available imported foods and goods with them as they did with me.

THE UNDERDEVELOPMENT OF ANTHROPOLOGICAL ETHICS   53

About a month after the disastrous welcoming party, I got my chance to assist someone. Lekman and Ineril came to the house to talk. While we sat on the floor drinking tea, Lekman's eye caught my Sears and Roebuck catalogue. I had brought it along to order some supplies not locally available. He picked it up and began to leaf through it. I thought he was just idly looking at pictures, but when he came to cameras, he asked me to order some film for his Polaroid. Since he already had a camera, I saw no harm in doing so. Soon the two other men on the atoll with Polaroids were also asking me to order film, and I did. A few months later one of them came and asked me to order him a photo album. I complied and soon had to order albums for the others as well.

One day I was clearing leaves and grass from my part of the public road when Lekman stopped by to visit.

"What are you doing?" he asked.

"Cleaning the road."

"Why aren't you fishing?"

"Are you going?"

"No. I can't yet. I haven't finished painting my boat."

"Like some tea?" I asked.

"All right. I want to look at your catalogue anyway."

We walked inside and sat down. He flipped through the pages until he found what he wanted.

"I want you to help me order a suit," he began.

"A suit? What do you want a suit for?"

"To wear to church. To look nice," he grinned with mock embarassment. We sat facing each other, each wearing only bermuda shorts. Our Japanese sandals rested on the stoop outside the door. All the men dressed as we did. The most formal occasions, church and parties, called only for the addition of a shirt. Pastor Langi and deacon Mejton both had well-worn suits that they donned but twice a year, Christmas and Easter.

While he continued to look through the catalogue, I asked myself why he wanted a suit. Lekman was not even a church member, so it would not improve his position there. He had a small store, a truck, and political ambitions. He had failed twice to be elected to the Marshallese legislature. I wondered if he thought that the suit would give him some respect as a man who knew how to deal with the outside world. There was no way to find out.

"Can you measure me for a suit?"

I thought of his large family and the inappropriateness of a suit in the tropics.

"I don't know how." It was the truth. "Besides, mail-order suits rarely fit right." I hoped that was true because I was really reaching for excuses. Fortunately, he did not ask again.

In my eyes, the Marshallese are becoming increasingly dependent on outside goods. Moreover, they consume from a market over which they have no influence. Expenditures of time and money that seem small to us (e.g., buying a suit) involve several months' labor for them. While we are fully dependent on the market, our salaries fluctuate, more or less, with the fluctuations of the market. Their access to money is relatively limited and fixed. The more dependent they become, the less time they spend on self-sufficient enterprises. While I could not stop the drift toward dependency, I did not want to increase it. The film and albums seemed harmless enough at first since several people already had cameras, but I did not want to foster escalating wants, so I refused to order anything else.

Several weeks before I left the atoll for the last time, Jamij came to me with a request. He described a commercial bingo game he had seen in operation elsewhere. He asked me to buy such a set when I got back to America and send it to him.

"Why?"

"To give the people here something to do. To provide some entertainment. I would set it up in the village and people could come every night to play."

I closed one eye and gave him my suspicious look.

"You would also make money from it, wouldn't you?"

"Yes. A little. But I just want to give the people something to do."

"All right. I'll look for one when I get to Hawaii." Even while I was talking, I knew I was equivocating. This seemed to me to be intervention of the kind to be avoided, helping one man exploit others by bringing in outside resources. I looked for a set in Hawaii, but not very hard. Then I sent a letter back saying I could not find one.

In retrospect, especially in light of the problems to be discussed below, the matter of access to outside goods seems relatively unimportant. My heightened sense of being a gatekeeper who could decide what goods to let in and what goods to keep out is clearly paternalistic. While I felt compelled to refuse to bring in goods that would increase dependency, or to provide one man with the means to exploit others, I also did little to help the people understand the dangers of dependency. If, as I believe, the ultimate decisions about changes should be in their hands, then a less paternalistic and more prophetic role would have been appropriate.

UNINVOLVEMENT IN THE FIELD

During my last few months on the atoll, the Congress of Micronesia, the legislative body for the Trust Territory, began negotiating with the United States for a new political status. The Trust Territory has a High Commissioner appointed by the President of the United States and responsible to the Department of the Interior. Members of the Congress of Micronesia are all Micronesians, the High Commissioner has always been an American. A special committee of the Congress of Micronesia had undertaken a study of the political options open to the Territory. The President of the United States appointed a negotiating team from the departments of Interior, State, and Defense.

The Congressmen brought the issue home to their separate districts at the end of session. The Marshallese Congressmen canvassed public opinion in person or through representatives. The local representatives on Arno began to go from house to house discussing the options. The Marshallese radio station also provided information about the issue.

People began discussing among themselves what the options meant and soon many of the conversations at places where people meet along the road were on this topic. I had ample opportunity to overhear both the questions and the explanations.

"Well, what do you want, commonwealth, free association, or independence?"

"We don't know. What do they mean?"

"Commonwealth means that we throw away Marshallese customs and keep the Americans, both money and customs. Free association means that we keep Marshallese customs and keep the Americans. They watch out for us and help us with money. Independence means we throw away the Americans and keep Marshallese customs and go it alone."

"Well, what shall we do?" a man asked.

"It's your decision. You tell me what you want."

"We don't want to throw away Marshallese custom," said one man.

"And we don't want to get rid of the Americans, or at least their money," said another.

The discussion continued for a few minutes longer, then the questioner moved on down the road.

"Well, what do you think, Mike? What should we do?"

I had been sitting quietly, but I was not ignored.

"I don't know," I said. "I can't tell you what to do. It's up to you. Its your choice, not mine."

"But, what happens if we choose free association?"

"The Cook Islands are in free association with New Zealand, and it means that the Cook Islanders take care of all their own internal affairs and the New Zealanders take care of the external affairs, like military and trade agreements."

"What about commonwealth?"

"I don't know for sure what that means." And I didn't.

I tried to stay out of the discussion as much as possible over the next few months. I was busy finishing up my study of land tenure. And, like the cases of the suit and the bingo game, I did not want to intervene in their lives with outside information. Then a sequence of events occurred that showed me this was not a simple matter of a bingo game.

At about the time I had arrived in the Marshalls, military construction crews (Navy Seabees and Army Civic Action Teams) were arriving in each of the districts of the Trust Territory. Their pattern was to establish a camp, then help a community build schools, roads, causeways between islets, and other projects.

In the spring of 1970 a crew arrived on one of the islets of Arno, not the one on which I normally resided. The people there had asked for help in building a school, so the team was filling a felt need. Many people on the atoll were excited by their presence because they remembered the time right after World War II when there were many benefits to be gained by living around a military installation. The people talked about the big machines and the skills of the men. They enjoyed watching the free movies that the military personnel shared most evenings. People on other islets of the atoll were jealous of the community where the military stayed.

Still, there were Marshallese who argued that something is never given for nothing. They were suspicious, and so was I. Why had the military returned after 20 years absence? Was there any connection between their work and the fact that the Micronesians were trying to decide how close their future political ties to the United States would be? To my mind it represented a peacetime version of "winning the hearts and minds of the people." I did not want to speak up at first about my doubts, but then I had a conversation that changed my mind.

I sat one day talking with an old woman who was the manager of her lineage's estate. She was commenting on how nice it was that the military came to help them build things. I was worried that the military eventually wanted land several places in the Trust Territory.

"What would you do if the army came in here and told you that they want to use this piece of land?" I asked.

Without hesitation, she said, "I'd ask them where I was supposed to live?"

I tried to clarify the answer. "What if they told you to go over to ocean side and live there?" I choose that location because people go there to relieve themselves.

"I'd go there to live."

"For how long?"

"Until they came and told me I could come back."

Though her words are no sure indication of what she would really do, her attitude disturbed me greatly. From that point on, when the occasion arose, I reminded the people of the actions the Japanese military had taken in 1939 and 1940 and warned them not to put their land in jeopardy again by being overly impressed with the military teams.

Whether there was intentional intervention or not, I felt that there was a definite threat that the opinions of the people would be affected by the military teams. I therefore felt justified in trying to counterbalance that effect. I said I was in favor of free association because I thought that arrangement gave the most economic security while giving full protection over land.

I am not sure how much weight my opinion carried or what difference it made that I told too few Marshallese too late what I thought. In time the initial impact of the military teams was counterbalanced by the behavior of the teams themselves and by nature. The longer the men stayed, the more rumors grew about their social and sexual abuse of Marshallese people. The causeway they built was washed out twice by storms and high tides. The school and road they constructed remain as tributes to the humanitarian side of their intentions.

In sum, the people of Arno Atoll could have used some help in discussing their political options and in responding to the presence of the military construction teams, but because I was busy with my work and did not want to intervene, I responded slowly to their needs. By the time I left it was clear to me that it was not my own government that needed help, but rather the people whom they were trying to manipulate.

AFTERMATH

Five years after completing my fieldwork I can see some of the issues more clearly, but I continue to be perplexed by others. After I left the field, I became aware of developments in the talks between the Congress of Micronesia committee and the U. S. negotiating team that have led me to see that I evaded my responsibility to the people by not trying to get more information about the political alternatives that they faced and by not investigating the objectives and impact of the military teams. Subsequent events have further clarified these issues.

First, during negotiations in 1970 the U.S. team and the Congress of Micronesia committee came to an impasse. The United States proposed that the Trust Territory be converted into a commonwealth. This status would give the United States the right of eminent domain over Micronesian lands and would prohibit Micronesians from ever dissolving the union on their own initiative.

The Congress of Micronesia's committee responded in two ways. They defined the basic principles which they would not negotiate: "the rights of sovereignty and of self-determination, the right to structure a Micronesian government and constitution, and the right to terminate the compact of association unilaterally" (Mason, 1974:215). They also decided to take a closer look at independence since it was clear that the United States would argue for a closer union than most Micronesians wanted. Had I known that the United States was so interested in retaining the right of eminent domain and the right to terminate the agreement, I would have argued that the people consider independence, if only to increase their bargaining power.

Second, during further negotiations in 1972, the United States military finally defined its plans for the use of land in Micronesia. Their needs did not include Arno Atoll, but they did include land in the Marshalls, Palau, and Mariana districts. The right of eminent domain now loomed even larger as an issue since land (strategic position) was all the Micronesians had to bargain.

Third, during the same talks, the Mariana District representatives asked to be allowed to bargain separately with the United States. Marianas people have had more intensive contact with foreigners, particularly the Spanish, than other Micronesians. The more the Congress of Micronesia explored independence, the more the Marianas people wanted to terminate their association with the Territory.

The request was granted, the United States exploited the split and negotiated a covenant spelling out the terms of the proposed commonwealth. The covenant was signed in January, 1975, and was followed by a plebiscite in June, 1975.

The talks with the remaining five districts of the Territory continue. Meanwhile, the United States is busy rebuilding the big air base on Tinian Island in the Marianas.

I think I would have recognized these possibilities in 1969-1970 if I had taken more time to examine the information available about the alternative political statuses, and if I had paid more attention to the military teams. At that time, my position was to stay out of the argument, if I could. Now, I feel that a more responsible position would have been to find out as much as I could to help the Marshallese in making their decision.

CONCLUSIONS

I can now recognize three stages in the development of my sense of ethics in anthropology.

First, my undergraduate and graduate training concentrated on the methods and theories of anthropology to the exclusion of ethics. Ethical problems were relevant only to cases of intervention, and cases of intervention only occurred in applied anthropology.

Second, during the fieldwork period I developed some principles that were an extension of what I had learned in school about the integrity of cultures. Over the months I slowly became aware of the falseness of the concept of nonintervention. My very presence was intervention. The presence of the United States administration and military was massive intervention. Still, my behavioral responses were based on the ideas of intervening as little as possible (uninvolvement) and shielding the Marshallese from adverse influences (paternalism). These postures may have blinded me to the more serious problems.

Third, in the five years since I left the Marshalls, I have become more aware of the economic and political impact of the United States overseas. It is now obvious that the United States' presence in Micronesia has been calculated to secure land for military bases.[3] The interests and needs of Micronesians are far down the list of U.S. priorities. The relocation and mishandling of the Bikini Marshallese should have been ample evidence of America's values in action (Kiste, 1974). In light of this observation, my actions should have been more helpful on the issues of political status and the presence of the military on the atoll.

In sum, I began with an underdeveloped awareness of ethical issues, something not uncommon for anthropologists of the past. In the field I developed some principles that I would now call uninvolved paternalism. I am now moving toward a more positive fraternalism. I see my responsibility to the people I study to be to deal with the problems that concern them as well as with those that interest me.

Some anthropologists would still argue that ethics and the methods and theories of anthropology should be kept separate. I would argue that they never were nor could be separate. I never considered, for example, studying the American administration in the Marshalls instead of the Marshallese themselves. As my sense of ethics develops I find myself much more concerned about relations between the United States and the Marshall Islands. Fortunately, my data on land tenure allow me to ask questions about the impact of colonialism on local political and legal structures (Rynkiewich, 1972; 1974). I am not arguing here for a particular ethical standard or even asking for agreement about the choices I made. My point is that our sense of ethics guides our fieldwork choices and behavior, no matter what that sense of ethics is.

---

[3] "The main push behind the acquisition deal came from the Pentagon, which had planned to make the flat-topped volcanic island of Tinian into a modern air-naval base at a cost of $300 to $400 million" (The Roanoke Times 1975:A-7).

REFERENCES

Kiste, Robert C.

    1974   *The Bikinians: A Study in Forced Migration.* Menlo Park, Cal.: Cummings Publishing Co.

Mason, Leonard E.

    1974   "Unity and Disunity in Micronesia: Internal Problems and Future Status" in *Political Development in Micronesia,* D. Hughes and S. Lingenfelter (eds.). Columbus, Ohio: The Ohio State University Press.

Rynkiewich, Michael A.

    1972   "Land Tenure Among Arno Marshallese." Ph.D. dissertation, University of Minnesota.

    1974   "The Ossification of Local Politics: The Impact of Colonialism on a Marshall Islands Atoll" in *Political Development in Micronesia,* D. Hughes and S. Lingenfelter (eds.). Columbus, Ohio: The Ohio State University Press.

The Roanoke Times

    1975   "U.S. Acquires Remote Pacific Island Group," February 9, 1975: A-7.

5
THE PEOPLE OF ENEWETAK ATOLL VS. THE U.S. DEPARTMENT OF DEFENSE

ROBERT C. KISTE

Robert C. Kiste took his graduate training at the University of Oregon where his Ph.D. in anthropology was awarded in 1967. In the same year he moved to the University of Minnesota where he now is Associate Professor of Anthropology. While on sabbatical leave during the 1972–1973 academic year, he taught at the University of Hawaii. Dr. Kiste's specializations and interests include social and cultural change, the history of anthropology, and Oceania, particularly Micronesia. He has published several articles and, most recently, a book, *The Bikinians: A Study in Forced Migration,* which appears in the Kiste-Ogan Social Change Series in Anthropology.

Like many anthropologists, my major research efforts have been with populations that belong to the Third World, that is, they have been colonized by the more powerful industrialized societies. In 1963, 1964, and 1969, I conducted fieldwork with the peoples who formerly inhabited Enewetak and Bikini Atolls in the northernmost regions of the Ralik (Western) chain of the Marshall Islands. Both atolls are quite isolated from others (see Map 2), and after World War II, the United States considered them to be excellent sites for military and scientific experiments with nuclear bombs. The inhabitants of both atolls were removed and resettled elsewhere. The Bikinians' initial relocation occurred in March, 1946 and ended in disaster. The islanders were resettled two more times in 1948 (Kiste, 1968; 1972, 1974; Mason, 1950; 1958). The Enewetakese were resettled on Ujilang Atoll, also located in the northwestern Marshalls.[1] They have remained there since December, 1947.

This article is primarily concerned with events and issues pertaining to the Enewetak people. First, the relevant historical background of the population is provided. Second, the values and attitudes that representatives of American society have manifested in their dealings with the islanders are examined. Third, my own involvement with certain recent events affecting the lives of the Enewetakese is discussed. Finally, the paper is also a comment on the role of the United States in the one area of the Pacific over which it has hegemony.

HISTORICAL BACKGROUND

It has been well documented that the expansion and dominance of the so-called "civilized" societies of the world has occurred only at great expense to smaller and less powerful ones (Bodley, 1975; Diamond, 1974). While the Enewetakese are no exception to this obvious fact of human history, they were spared early contact with Europeans in the Pacific. Enewetak and the rest of the Marshall Islands are part of a larger cultural area known as Micronesia. Most of Micronesia falls within the political boundary of what is now the United States Trust Territory of the Pacific Islands (see Map 1).

As early as the sixteenth century, Spain established a port of call in the Mariana Islands in western Micronesia, and the Spanish presence there resulted in the depopulation of the indigenous people and a rapid destruction of their traditional culture. Spain never had more than nominal control over the more

---

[1] On most maps and in the literature on the Pacific, this is commonly spelled "Eniwetok." The people of the atoll prefer "Enewetak," which is a more accurate rendition of their pronunciation. I follow what they believe is correct except when quoting from other sources. Similarly, Pacific maps and literature usually refer to "Ujelang" whereas the Enewetak people prefer "Ujilang."

eastern islands. Germany was able to declare the Marshalls a protectorate in 1885. With the exception of Guam, Germany acquired the remainder of Spain's Micronesian interests after the Spanish-American War in 1898 and soon established firm control over the island empire. Japan seized the islands with the outbreak of World War I. Both Germany's and Japan's interest in Micronesia was primarily commercial and focused on the copra trade. In the late 1930s, Japan fortified some islands in the series of events that culminated in World War II.

In 1943, the American invasion of Micronesia began, and, within two years, the islands were under American rule. The Marianas provided the base from which the atomic bombings of Hiroshima and Nagasaki were launched. The United States had no economic interest in Micronesia, but its military was determined to retain control of the islands because of their strategic location. Military interests were served when Micronesia became a strategic Trust Territory within the framework of the United Nations in 1947. According to the trusteeship agreement, the United States is entitled to establish military bases in the Territory while promoting the general health and well-being of the islanders.

Although the Germans had visited Enewetak periodically to encourage the people to expand their plantings of coconut trees for the copra trade, the Enewetakese had remained mostly to themeslves until the Japanese era. The islanders were divided into two very small communities of about the same size that were located on the two largest islands of the atoll, Enewetak Island in the atoll's southeast quadrant, and Enjebi Island in the northeast. In the 1920s, a Japanese trader arrived and effectively gained control of all other islands of significant size in the atoll. (The 45 islands comprising Enewetak have a land area of only 2.26 square miles that are situated on a reef that encloses a lagoon area of 388 square miles.) The trader falsely claimed that the Japanese government had granted him permission to develop coconut plantations on the atoll. Out of fear and ignorance, the people did not resist and worked to establish the plantations for modest rewards in trade goods.

In the early 1940s, Enewetak became one of Japan's military bases. An air base was constructed on Enjebi, and its people were forced to move to a small corner of the island. Military personnel were also stationed on Enewetak Island.

The American invasion wrought massive destruction. The two main islands were bombarded from sea and air, and many of their palms and much of their top soil was bulldozed into the sea. The cataclysmic scope of the American's arrival was overwhelming to the islanders. In all, 2661 Japanese and 169 Americans were killed (Hines, 1962:85). The people of both Enjebi and Enewetak numbered only about 140 at the time, and 17 of them were killed.

After their victory, the Americans developed Enewetak Island as a support facility for the push further west. All of the islanders were moved to two small islands in the northeast quadrant of the atoll where they did not interfere with military operations. They remained there for over three years at which time the military requirements of a foreign power again intervened in their lives. After the initial nuclear tests at Bikini in 1946, the U.S. plans called for a larger test site, and Enewetak was selected. The islanders did not believe that they could have resisted, and with haste and little planning, they were moved to Ujilang just before Christmas in 1947.

Ujilang had been a commercial copra plantation, and at the end of World War II, it was uninhabited. A village was constructed on Ujilang's largest island, and the people were left on their own.

The years on Ujilang have been extremely difficult. Ujilang is much smaller than Enewetak. Collectively, its 21 islands amount to only 0.67 square mile, and the small lagoon covers 25.5 square miles. Largely as a result of a modest health effort provided by the Americans, the Enewetakese have grown in number from 141 in December, 1947 to about 400 by the early 1970s. Ujilang's resources have not always been sufficient to support the population, and the islanders have experienced periods of hunger. Ujilang is quite distant from the American administrative center, and ships that carry imported foods and trade goods have routinely failed to make the journey to Ujilang. The islanders have often not been able to market the small amounts of copra that they can produce, and the situation has prevented them from supplementing local resources with the imports of rice and flour that are mainstays of Micronesian diets today. Because of the deprivation suffered at Ujilang and a deep emotional attachment to their ancestral homeland, the islanders have always harbored a fervent desire to return to Enewetak, and they have made numerous appeals over the years to do so.

The situation of the Bikinians has been far worse than the Enewetakese since relocation, and they have been much more vociferous and demanding in their pleas to return home. After years of frustration, the Bikinians met with some success. The Atomic Energy Commission (AEC) determined that radiation levels were low enough so that most of Bikini could be reinhabited and, in August, 1968, it was announced that the atoll would be cleared of radioactive debris and the people would be returned.[2]

The announcement caused deep resentment among the Enewetakese, and they protested the fact that they could not also return to their ancestral home. In a move that can only be interpreted as an effort to pacify them, "undisclosed agencies" of the United States government provided them with $1.02

---

[2] As of 1975, and for a variety of reasons, the program to return the Bikinians to Bikini has encountered many delays and the Bikinians remain alienated from their ancestral home.

million in compensation for inconveniences suffered. The sum was invested to provide the people with an annual income.

The attempt to placate the Enewetakese failed. In December, 1971, they declared their intention to return home, and they placed a notice in the Marshall Islands weekly newspaper:

THE WAITING IS OVER

"We, the representatives and leaders of the dis-placed people of Eniwetok, are making public notice of our intent to return to our island of Eniwetok before the end of 1972.

"A group of our people will be coming to the District Center of Majuro in April of 1972 to meet with representatives of the United States Department of Defense to work out the details of our return."

(Micronitor, Vol. II, No. 40, December 28, 1971)

By early 1972, the Enewetakese took advantage of the newly created Micronesian Legal Service Corporation (MLSC), an agency funded by the Office of Economic Opportunity, which offered legal services to Micronesians. Apparently after their decision to return home, the islanders appointed MLSC lawyers as their official counselors and representatives to assist them *(Micronitor,* Vol. III, No. 2, January 18, 1972). In February, American officials were notified that unless the Enewetakese were granted permission to return home, they would indeed institute legal action. Two months later, it was announced that the United States would surrender Enewetak by the end of 1973 after the completion of certain "unspecified activities" currently underway on the atoll.

THE PACE PROJECT

In May, 1972, five Enewetakese leaders and their lawyers were permitted a brief visit to Enewetak. The islanders despaired at what they saw. Between 1947 and 1958, more than 30 nuclear tests had been conducted on the atoll. Afterwards and until 1969, it had been used as an impact area for Inter-Continental Ballistic Missiles launched from California. Three islands had been completely obliterated; hugh craters scarred the reef and portions of other islands. Where coconut trees had stood before the blasts, useless brush now proliferated. A large portion of Enewetak Island was covered by a concrete airfield (see photos in Hines, 1962:116, 119). Junk, debris, and old abandoned military structures dominated the landscape. Some islands could not be visited because of radioactive contamination. The Enewetakese were particularly disturbed when they learned that one-half of a 40-acre island had recently been stripped of covering soils and sands in preparation for the Pacific Cratering Experiments (PACE), the initial phases of the "unspecified activities" that were already underway.

PACE was sponsored by two components of the U.S. Department of Defense, the Air Force Weapons Laboratory, and the Defense Nuclear Agency. PACE had commenced with relatively small explosions, but it was planned that the project would culminate in several 5-, 20-, and 100-ton detonations of high explosive charges and one final 500-ton blast. These detonations were referred to as "events" and were to occur for the purpose of monitoring ground motion. The 500-ton event would simulate the magnitude of one of the 1958 nuclear tests. Ground motion studies of such an event in the well-known geological structure of Enewetak would enable scientists to determine how American missile silos would be affected by nuclear missiles launched by an enemy force.[3]

The Enewetakese, through their counsels, asked if an environmental impact statement as required by the National Environmental Policy Act (NEPA) had been prepared. NEPA required that PACE's potential impact on Enewetak be thoroughly investigated. Furthermore, it had to be determined that there would be no long-term damage to the environment and that there would not be any adverse effect on the Enewetakese. It was learned that a draft of such a statement had in fact been filed with the Council on Environmental Quality the previous month. No effort had been made to explain PACE to the islanders, and only on the insistence of counsel, did they receive a copy of the statement.

By September, 1972, the Enewetakese filed suit in the U.S. District Court in Hawaii to halt all activities associated with PACE until a final environmental statement was completed. They charged that several of the provisions of NEPA had been violated. PACE had been initiated before the environmental statement had been filed. The current draft was both incomplete and incomprehensible to the layman. The Enewetakese had not been informed of the project. They had requested but had been denied public hearings that would explore the consequences of PACE.

On October 6, 1972, a federal judge ruled that the draft of the environmental statement was inadequate and issued an injunction that terminated all PACE activities until a full court trial (*Honolulu Advertiser* October 6, 1972). PACE planners retrenched and took their statement back to the drawing boards.

---

[3] The United States ended above-ground testing of nuclear devices in 1958 (see Hines, 1962:291-292). Thus, PACE could only simulate a nuclear detonation with the 500-ton event of high explosive charges.

EVALUATION OF PACE

Fortuitously, the beginnings of these legal proceedings in Hawaii coincided with my sabbatical leave from the University of Minnesota. In the fall of 1972, my family and I arrived in Honolulu for a year. I was a visitor at the Department of Anthropology, University of Hawaii, and was scheduled to teach a course on the Peoples of Micronesia in the spring semester. Soon after our arrival, I was contacted by the Micronesian Legal Services Corporation staff and was asked if I were willing to serve as a witness during the proceedings.

I gladly volunteered. In my own view, it was clear that the Enewetakese had suffered enough at the hands of foreigners and the detonation of tons of high explosives on their atoll was a definite threat to their future well-being. The ecology of a coral atoll is extremely fragile, and it was obvious that PACE would inevitably add to the destruction Enewetak had already sustained. Furthermore, I feared that a continuation of the project against the expressed wishes of the islanders would damage their morale and add to their long-standing frustration.

I observed but was not called as a witness during the October court proceedings. Indeed, no witnesses were called other than the principle figures involved. PACE officials made a painfully obvious attempt to cover up the fact that one-half of an island had already been stripped of topsoil, and the judge quickly ruled in favor of the Enewetakese. Not long afterward, I was contacted by the director of PACE, and my own first-hand education with the representatives of at least one segment of the Department of Defense began. The director was intent on pursuing PACE and had a great personal investment in the project. He indicated that he did not understand the recalcitrant stance of the Enewetakese and complained that he had contacted three other anthropologists with experience in the Marshalls, but they had provided him with no assistance. I noted that my primary concern was with the welfare of the Enewetakese and was met with the response: "You anthropologists all sound alike."

A second version of the environmental statement was prepared by February, 1973. Public hearings were scheduled to be held at Ujilang in March and Honolulu in April. A description of PACE, complete with illustrations, was translated into Marshallese. The hearings were to provide both the Enewetakese and other interested parties the opportunity to offer opinions or raise questions about the impact of PACE. An Air Force attorney with no direct connection with PACE was appointed presiding officer, and the results were to be incorporated into the final environmental statement.

I was again contacted by the director of PACE. He was not pleased with the prospect of the public hearings and indicated that he did not believe

68 ETHICS AND ANTHROPOLOGY—DILEMMAS IN FIELDWORK

that he and his colleagues would receive a fair reception at Ujilang. The audience there would consist of the Enewetakese, their lawyers, and observers from the Trust Territory administration, one of whom, anthropologist Dr. Jack A. Tobin, had gone on record as being opposed to PACE. At this point, I agreed to attend the Ujilang hearings in the capacity of an outside observer if the project paid my travel expenses and if it was understood that I was free to draw my own conclusions about the fairness of the proceedings. Considering my earlier expression of sympathy for the Enewetakese, I was somewhat surprised that the director accepted the conditions under which I would attend the hearings. He did not fully comprehend that his fellow countrymen would oppose a project initiated by our own government, and he extended another invitation to attend the Ujilang hearings to Dr. Leonard Mason, Professor Emeritus, University of Hawaii, one of the three anthropologists who had rejected an association with PACE.[4] My 1963 and 1964 research with the Bikinians and Enewetakese had been done in collaboration with Mason, and he was thus quite familiar with the people.[5] He declined to travel to Ujilang, however, because of other commitments.

The Ujilang Hearings

In late March, a party composed of seven military and civilian personnel associated with PACE, the hearing officer, a court reporter, and me, flew from Honolulu to Kwajalein Atoll in the Marshalls. Kwajalein is a military installation involved in the same missile program that used Enewetak as an impact area. There we joined four lawyers of the MLSC staff, two interpreters, four observers from the Trust Territory administration, the editor of the weekly Marshall Islands newspaper, and several members of the Enewetak community who were temporarily away from home and were employed at the military base. Our party flew to Enewetak where we viewed the conditions of the atoll and the proposed sites for the PACE tests. The Enewetakese were excited by their return home but were obviously disturbed by what they saw. The trip from Enewetak to Ujilang was made by ship.

During the entire journey and the proceedings at Ujilang, I conceived my

---

[4] The other two anthropologists who had refused to assist PACE were Dr. Saul H. Riesenberg, Smithsonian Institution, and Dr. Alexander Spoehr, Department of Anthropology, University of Pittsburgh.

[5] The 1963-1964 field work was conducted within the framework of a larger research effort, *The Project for the Comparative Study of Cultural Change and Stability in Displaced Communities in the Pacific.* The project was directed by Dr. Homer G. Barnett, Department of Anthropology, University of Oregon, and was funded by the National Science Foundation. My collaboration with Mason has been partially described elsewhere (Kiste, 1974:8-9).

role to be that of an ethnographer, observing and conducting interviews (all informal) in a style not different from that I had employed in my earlier research. This time, however, I was focusing on Americans as well as Marshallese, and several things were made immediately clear. The majority of the PACE group viewed the entire effort as a necessary formality. They did not expect to encounter any serious opposition from the Enewetakese. They did not seriously entertain the notion that the values and wishes of the islanders were of any significance for future decisions because ". . . local opposition is a fact of life in so many military projects." The journey was a lark, a fun jaunt into an exotic area of the world for some of them fresh from stateside. I was informed by one member of the group that one thing that I did not understand is that we ". . . start with the assumption that when the United States deals with minorities in our own country and people from other parts of the world that we will fuck it up. After you start with that basic assumption, you go out and do your job."

We arrived in the lagoon at Ujilang shortly after noon on March 26. The community was well organized and prepared for our visit. Men from the village came in small boats to meet the ship; all of them wore cardboard signs with the message *Enana Pace* "PACE is bad (evil)." We were courteously ferried ashore where a large arch made from palm fronds had been erected. A sign at the top of the arch proclaimed "Welcome to Ujilang-Yokwe" (*Yokwe* "love" or "hello" much as Hawaiian *Aloha*). We visitors were escorted through the arch to face and shake the hands of the entire community (Tobin 1973). Everyone was polite, and many of the islanders, including children, wore the *Enana Pace* signs.

Everyone proceeded to the community's council house. Introductions were made, and the purposes of our visit were explained. That evening, the PACE group commenced their explanations of their project with a color slide and movie presentation portraying the proposed events and similar ones elsewhere. The following day, PACE personnel showed more slides and with the aid of a large map of Enewetak Atoll described what would occur where.

The descriptions of PACE were often cast in the scientific jargon of Western culture, parts of which were unintelligible to me and at least some of the other Americans present who were not specialists in the physical sciences. (One of the PACE group later wrote to me: "I will grant you that we didn't do the world's best job of explaining what the seismic refraction and core drilling phases of PACE were all about.") Military code names such as David, Elmer, and Fred and not the indigenous terms of Muti, Merren, and Enewetak were used to refer to islands in the atoll, and most of the time, the people never knew which islands were being discussed. Ironically, the slides and movie showed massive detonations of high energy explosives and only further convinced the people that PACE represented a terrible threat to them.

An attempt was made to ensure the people that all land forms would be restored and that no permanent damage would be done. It was also argued that the tests would help protect the free world and was thus in the best interest of all present. (A similar argument was advanced when military officials persuaded the Bikini and Enewetak peoples to abandon their homes in the 1940s. The Enewetakese, however, were no longer swayed by the notion that what is best for Uncle Sam is necessarily best for them.)

During the entire presentation, the islanders listened patiently and asked few questions. They provided fresh coconuts to drink during the long day, and afterwards they indicated that they would make their response on the following (third) day of the hearings.

The next morning's meeting was brief. The elected magistrate (head) of the community made an impassioned speech. He emphasized that his people had listened carefully but knew that bombs were destructive, and that they wanted no part of PACE. He reported that the people wanted to return to the home of their ancestors, and if PACE was necessary, it had to be conducted elsewhere. He suggested that if PACE would cause no lasting destruction, then that fact should be explained to President Nixon and the High Commissioner of the Trust Territory (a presidential appointee and the chief executive of the Territory's administration), and then PACE could stage its events near the White House and the Commissioner's residence. He indicated:

> "I do not know if you have made an attempt to compare your sense of values, you who live in America or elsewhere, with ours. You live with gold and money and we have to depend on land and whatever life we can find on land and in the water. Without these we are nothing. We do not have to explain further that Eniwetok, with whatever land resources and whatever marine resources it has, is our homeland, and seeing that you understand this, we do not know why you continue to insist to do these things on Eniwetok, when for us there is really nothing else to look forward to. For this reason we must continue to ask that you refrain from proceeding with this program. PACE is no good.
>
> Those of you here today have been to Eniwetok, as I have and some of our people have, and we all know that Eniwetok has undergone severe damage. There are islands that are missing. There is a considerable amount of land that has been destroyed. The question then comes: Has not Eniwetok done enough for your testing? We do not know who you will take this message to — perhaps you will take it to Washington or to the Department of Defense — but, the point still remains that we feel that Eniwetok has done enough. We have sacrificed enough and

> PACE should not be continued because it will only mean further damage and further destruction of our homeland"
>
> (Department of the Air Force, 1973b:5-6).

The magistrate reiterated that PACE officials should inform their superiors that the Enewetak people were vehemently opposed to the project. "My people and I . . . do not like PACE; we do not want PACE to continue, and we want you to take this message to your people." Throughout his speech, the magistrate paused occasionally, and the people responded in unison with a resounding "PACE is bad (evil)."

Several other members of the community spoke briefly to emphasize the magistrate's points. It was indicated that if their wishes were not respected, they would sail to Enewetak and be killed with the bombs. As one man phrased it:

> "I would like to ask the director of the program in Eniwetok another question. The question or parable is: Suppose a cargo ship were to be sailing in the Pacific Ocean — I do not know where it is going or what it has in it, but it's a cargo ship — and as it goes along — it's an American ship — a Russian airplane comes and bombs it and destroys it. What would be the reaction of the Americans to such an incident? If your answer to this is would be war, then we, the people of Eniwetok, because we do not have military weapons would have to react in this way: That would be to return to Eniwetok to be there when you explode those bombs"
>
> (ibid.:16).

The morality of PACE was questioned by several. To give one example:

> "Today we meet to discuss actions by the Air Force which they had taken on Eniwetok on their own. I now wish to cite an example: If I had some belongings, and Mr. _____ (the director of PACE) has his own belongings, and I went over and took his belongings without his knowing, would that be all right with him? It is the same thing with Eniwetok today"
>
> (ibid.:10).

The magistrate concluded by thanking the visitors for coming and taking the trouble to explain PACE. The visitors were presented with gifts of handicraft, and the people sang three songs, one of which was entitled "Oh How I

Love My Atoll." The scene was charged with great feeling. Some people wept, and one of the Marshallese interpreters left the meeting overcome with emotion. Most of the Americans were stunned and puzzled; one of the PACE group asked: "What the hell is going on here?"

Our ship departed Ujilang the same day and arrived at Enewetak the next where we boarded a plane for Kwajalein and Honolulu. The hearings had two effects on members of the PACE group. Three or four understood the islanders' point of view and questioned the morality of continuing the project. Others were obviously annoyed at their reception at Ujilang, and one indicated: "To hell with them, we'll go ahead anyway."

One (and perhaps others) of the representatives from the Trust Territory administration was angered by his role in the affair. He was a member of an administration that was pledged to protect the well-being of the islanders, yet he and his colleagues had only been sent along in the passive role of observer.

The Honolulu Hearings

The public hearings were continued in Honolulu on the evenings of April 4 and 5. The scene was staged in a large auditorium at a military installation. At the front of the audience and on one side of the room was a lectern equipped with a microphone that PACE officials used to make their presentation and respond to questions. On the other side of the room, a similar facility was provided for those who wished to question or raise issues pertaining to PACE and its environmental impact statement. Of the party that had traveled to Ujilang, the seven members of the PACE group, the head of Micronesian Legal Services Corporation (MLSC), the hearing officer, court clerk, and I were present. Others in attendance were students, including Micronesians, from the University of Hawaii, representatives of several environmental groups, Dr. Leonard Mason, and other interested parties. A brief description of PACE was given and a short film on the proposed project was shown. The hearing officer opened the proceedings to questions and opinions.

Being unfamiliar with legal proceedings and not wishing to interfere with the efforts of the MLSC staff, I had previously consulted with the MLSC lawyer to determine how I might play an active role. In my own mind, the time for playing the passive role of ethnographer had passed. It was far from clear that PACE would not result in further permanent damage to Enewetak, and even if that were not the case, the purpose of the project certainly did not justify ignoring the desires of the Enewetakese and adding to their anxieties and fears about their future. Their history had been tragic enough. Aware of the direction of my sentiments, the lawyer felt that any challenge to PACE that I wished to make would not adversely affect the way in which he and his colleagues would handle the case.

The revised environmental impact statement of February, 1973 contained what I thought were obvious attempts to mislead and conceal the truth. In my judgment, it was just those areas that had to be challenged. My questions led to a confrontation with two PACE officials.

First, the environmental statement implied that Runit Island, the island in Enewetak Atoll that had been selected for the 500-ton event, had a radioactivity level that was approximately the same as that found at Albuquerque, New Mexico (Department of the Air Force, 1973a:Section 3-21). Our recent survey of Enewetak had suggested a quite different state of affairs. We had not been allowed to visit Runit because of radiation levels, and personnel at Enewetak had reported that the island's soils were heavily contaminated with the highly dangerous plutonium. At the hearing, I asked if the radiation levels described in the environmental statement were correct, and if the island were indeed as "hot" as suggested at Enewetak, would not a large explosion scatter radioactive debris over other portions of the atoll. The question never received a direct response. The director of PACE informed the audience that to indicate ". . . what the exact radiation levels are and what they mean would take a radiological expert, which I am not" and "The proper time to respond to those questions would be in the final (environmental) impact statement" (Department of the Air Force, 1973b:51-53).

Second, the environmental statement provided in table form a list of 30 "Specialists Consulted in Planning PACE" (Department of the Air Force, 1973a:Section 2-10). The list included the three anthropologists who had refused to cooperate with PACE. The actual text of the statement repeatedly referred to the opinions of specialists, but, in most instances, it did not identify which ones provided what data, advice, or opinions. Thus, the document gave the clear impression that the three anthropologists had been involved in PACE's planning. In reality, two of the three had refused affiliation with the project when contacted by phone. The other one had had a few face-to-face conversations with PACE personnel, but also provided no assistance.

I asked the director of PACE to clarify ". . . what kind of input did these three specialists, these anthropologists, have in planning PACE?" His response was: "Well, in actually planning PACE, very little" (Department of the Air Force, 1973b:46). I made the point that they in fact had had *no* input, and I suggested that the technique of providing a list of specialists and then referring to unnamed specialists in the text of their document was an attempt to give it a credibility that was false (ibid.,:48).

Third, the environmental statement claimed: "The effect of PACE activities on the Eniwetokese people has been considered and is recognized throughout the impact statement" (Department of the Air Force, 1973a:Section 4-3). Certainly the accuracy of this claim had to be questioned. The people had only been consulted very recently and only after the revised environmental statement of February, 1973 had been published. I reported that I saw little evidence during the Ujilang hearings that PACE personnel gave serious consideration to the concerns of the people and I questioned the veracity of all statements that purported to consider the results of PACE on the welfare of the Enewetakese. These comments were challenged by one of the PACE group; he indicated that the purpose of the Ujilang survey was ". . . to understand the Eniwetok people. We were there for that purpose and that purpose alone. Any comments that were made on that trip did not mean we were not trying to understand these people. It's purely something of his (Kiste's) interpretation; something we should not want to elaborate on" (Department of the Air Force, 1973b:80-81). My rebuttal was to quote the statements by those associated with PACE that Americans should pursue their own ends while disrupting their relations with others and that the Enewetakese could go to hell as far as PACE was concerned. Such statements, I suggested, clearly expressed the real attitudes of some of the PACE group.

Finally, one obvious point had to be made for the public record. I indicated that PACE officials did not understand why anthropologists had not been willing to affiliate themselves with the project. I suggested that essentially, anthropologists had only been asked to provide advice that would help accomplish the goals of PACE and perhaps convince the Enewetakese of its inevitability and/or necessity. No one had asked what would be best for the Enewetakese future well-being, and I suggested: "Until the right questions are asked, in terms of Micronesian welfare and the welfare of the Eniwetok people, I doubt very seriously that you will get the cooperation of anthropologists" (ibid.,:70).

Dr. Leonard Mason also expressed his opinions of PACE. He affirmed that he had had no part in its planning. He indicated that he was not in sympathy with the project and appropriately suggested that perhaps PACE did not need to consult professional anthropologists to learn about the people. The Enewetakese, he noted, had clearly expressed themselves: "They gave you a flat negative" (ibid.:58). Mason also entered into the public record a copy of a letter he had received from Dr. Jack A. Tobin in the Marshalls. The original letter had been sent to an Air Force official. Without his permission, PACE planners had used Tobin's Ph.D. dissertation, "The Resettlement of the Enewetak People: A Study of a Displaced Community in the Marshall Islands" (1967), as a resource document for preparing the environmental statement. Tobin's letter indicated:

> "I did not give you permission to do this and it is protected by copyright as clearly indicated in the early part of the dissertation. Parts

> *of this work that would have helped the people of Eniwetok against the PACE program were not quoted in the draft environmental statement.*
>
> *I am biased against the PACE program as I have told Mr. _____ (the director of PACE) as I feel that it is against the best interests of the Eniwetok people and is against their expressed wishes.*
>
> *Do not use my name as a consultant to the program as you have other anthropologists. Do not indicate that I have helped you or assisted you in the preparation of your inadequate and misleading statement. I will take legal action against you if you do so"*

(Department of the Air Force, 1973b:56).

The head of Micronesian Legal Services Corporation provided a clear summary statement of his clients' views. Other individuals questioned the morality of imposing PACE on the islanders and further challenged the claim that the project posed no threat to the environment of Enewetak Atoll. Mason later prepared and circulated a position paper on PACE. U.S. Representative Patsy T. Mink of Hawaii, who has long been concerned with the American administration of Micronesia, entered the paper in the *Congressional Record* along with her own objections to PACE (*Congressional Record,* Vol. 119, No. 89, 1973).

After the formal hearings were concluded, those members of the PACE team whose views had been altered by their experience at Ujilang and I moved to my favorite pub in Honolulu and talked long into the night. They had not expected the strong reactions of the people, and they were disturbed by the entire affair. I suggested that perhaps it was time for them to speak out, and I encouraged them to do what the Enewetakese had asked them to do — inform their own superiors in Washington, D.C. of the feelings of the Enewetakese and argue that PACE should be ended. I later learned that two of them indeed followed just such a course of action. Some Department of Defense officials realized that Enewetakese opposition to PACE was firm, and that as a result, litigation to remove the court's injunction could extend over two or more years. On June 8, it was announced that PACE would not be continued. (*Honolulu Advertiser* June 9, 1973; *Pacific Islands Monthly* Vol. 44, No. 7, July, 1973).

Unfortunately, the victory of the Enewetakese in the PACE affair represents only one of several obstacles that the people must overcome in their quest to return home. The results of a study conducted by the AEC released in the fall of 1974 indicate that the islands in the northern half of Enewetak Atoll are too heavily contaminated by radiation and may not be reinhabited for perhaps 30 years. Thus, the people who once inhabited Enjebi Island cannot be returned to their ancestral land, and all of the islanders will have to be resettled on the southern half of the atoll (*Honolulu Advertiser,* September 9,

1974; Holmes and Narver, Inc., 1975). As late as the spring of 1975, the U.S. Congress had shown little interest in appropriating the funds required to restore and make safe from radiological dangers those portions of Enewetak Atoll that may be reinhabited.

OTHER ISSUES

The termination of PACE would never have occurred without the dedication and substantial efforts of the Micronesian Legal Services Corporation lawyers over many months; it was mainly their skills and experience that were required for the successful prosecution of the case. Since the PACE affair, the MLSC lawyers have continued to work on behalf of the Enewetakese, and in the spring of 1975, they were representing the people in Washington, D.C. at congressional hearings pertaining to the funds necessary to rehabilitate Enewetak.

As for my own involvement, I was only one of a number of individuals the MLSC staff contacted; specialists in other disciplines were consulted for relevant information and professional opinion. With regard to my role in the Honolulu hearings, I am not comfortable in situations that involve emotionally charged public confrontations, especially when one is questioning the basic intentions and honesty of others. At the same time, I never felt that there was any great decision to be made. The facts were clear. I was obligated to the Enewetakese. They had befriended me, tolerated by inquiries into their lives, and had thus made my own fieldwork possible. When an issue that had significant consequences for their future was being contested, I felt I had no choice but to help challenge those who represented a threat to their well-being.

The Enewetak case illustrates two remaining points. First, within areas controlled by the United States, the anthropologist can certainly play an active role when events occur that are detrimental to a population with which he is familiar.[6] At the same time, the anthropologist is unlikely to possess the skills required to operate effectively within our legal system. Also, the anthropologist, like other single individuals, is unlikely to have any significant impact upon the decisions of government and other institutions when operating alone. Thus, it seems necessary to ally ourselves with those relatively few members of the legal profession and those interest groups which are concerned with the rights, dignity, and well-being of others and which have the vision to see beyond the values and goals of our own society. The National Environ-

[6] Anthropologists working in areas outside those controlled by the United States are visitors in other nations (or their territories and colonies), and they face a quite different set of circumstances (e.g., see Diamond, 1974:49-92).

mental Policy Act which provided the basis of the Enewetakese legal action certainly has implications for the protection of the interests of other peoples within the United States and its possessions.

Second, the Trust Territory government's failure to even attempt to protect the interests of the Enewetakese is indicative of America's basic stance since World War II. As suggested by the strategic trusteeship agreement with the United Nations in 1947, military interests have consistently been given priority over other concerns. Communities other than those of Bikini and Enewetak in the Marshalls have been resettled because of American nuclear and missle programs. In western Micronesia, the Marianas have been used for activities of the Central Intelligence Agency (see Hines, 1962; Kiste, 1974:193-198). After the PACE affair, the High Commissioner of the Territory attempted (albeit unsuccessfully) to terminate the efforts of the MLSC in the islands.

Further, since the late 1960s, Micronesians have been attempting to negotiate their future political status with representatives of the United States. Like the Enewetakese, Micronesians as a whole desire to gain greater control over their own destinies and are calling for some form of self-government. For an area with very few natural resources, the islanders' strongest strategy would have been to maintain a united front and grant the United States *limited* sites for military bases in exchange for financial support and internal self-government (see Heine, 1974; Mason, 1974). The United States, however, has encouraged separatist sentiments in the Marianas, and it appears that those western islands will become a Commonwealth of the United States and satisfy American military requirements. The remainder of Micronesia will thereby have lost most — if not all — of its bargaining power. The prospects for Micronesians do not appear very promising.

With regard to PACE, I believe that other anthropologists took the only defensible courses of action when they either publically opposed the project or rejected any affiliation with it. As events progress in Micronesia and as Americans continue to manipulate the islanders for their own ends, I suggest that a greater number of us in the profession will not easily escape the obligations we have to those who have made our work in Micronesia possible. The point may be self-evident, and it was brought home by several Micronesian students at the University of Hawaii who expressed their appreciation of my appearing on behalf of the Enewetakese. They also indicated that they would have questioned my silence if I had remained the uninvolved ethnographer.

REFERENCES

Bodley, John H.

    1975   *Victims of Progress*. Menlo Park, Cal.: Cummings Publishing Co.

Congressional Record

    1973   Vol. 119, No. 89, Washington, D.C., June 11.

Diamond, Stanley

    1974   *In Search of the Primitive: A Critique of Civilization*. New Brunswick, N. J.: Transaction Books. (Distributed by E. P. Dutton and Company.)

Department of the Air Force

    1972   *Draft Environmental Statement, Pacific Cratering Experiments (PACE)*. April.

    1973a   *Draft Environmental Statement, Pacific Cratering Experiments (PACE)*. February.

    1973b   *Transcript of Testimony Environmental Hearings "Project Pace."* Office of the Judge Advocate Pacific Air Forces. Honolulu.

Heine, Carl

    1974   *Micronesia at the Crossroads: A Reappraisal of the Micronesian Political Dilemma*. An East-West Center Book. Honolulu: The University Press of Hawaii.

Hines, Neal O.

    1962   *Proving Ground: An Account of the Radiobiological Studies in the Pacific, 1946–1961*. Seattle: University of Washington Press.

Holmes and Narver, Inc.

    1975   *Enewetak Atoll Master Plan for Island Rehabilitation and Resettlement* (2 Vols). Anaheim, Cal.

Honolulu Advertiser

    1972   October 6

    1973   June 9

    1974   September 9

Kiste, Robert C.

    1968   *Kili Island: A Study of the Relocation of the Ex-Bikini Marshallese.* Department of Anthropology, University of Oregon, Eugene.

    1972   "Relocation and Technological Change in Micronesia" in *Technology and Social Change,* H. Russell Bernard and Pertti Pelto, (eds.). New York: Macmillan Co.

    1974   *The Bikinians: A Study in Forced Migration.* Menlo Park, Cal. Cummings Publishing Co.

Mason, Leonard

    1950   "The Bikinians: a transplanted population," *Human Organization,* Vol. 9, No. 1.

    1958   "Kili Community in Transition," *South Pacific Commission Quarterly Bulletin,* Vol. 18, April.

    1974   "Unity and Disunity in Micronesia: Internal Problems and Future Status" in *Political Development in Micronesia,* Daniel T. Hughes and Sherwood C. Lingenfelter (eds.). Columbus, Ohio: Ohio State University Press.

Micronitor

    1971   Weekly newspaper published in the Marshall Islands (now called *The Micronesian Independent*). Vol. II, No. 40, December 28.

    1972   Vol. III, No. 2, January 18.

Pacific Islands Monthly

    1973   "Peace not PACE in Eniwetok," Vol. 44, No. 7, July.

Tobin, Jack A.

    1967   *The Resettlement of the Enewetak People: A Study of a Displaced Community in the Marshall Islands.* Unpublished Ph.D. dissertation, University of California, Berkeley. (Available through University Microfilms, Inc., Ann Arbor, Mich.)

    1973   "Pacific Cratering Experiments (PACE) Program Hearings on Ujilang Atoll March 26-28, 1973." Typescript, Majuro, Marshall Islands, April 3.

6
THE AMERICAN INDIAN MOVEMENT AND THE ANTHROPOLOGIST: ISSUES AND IMPLICATIONS OF CONSENT

FAY G. COHEN

Fay Cohen was educated at Radcliffe, Harvard, the University of Minnesota, and in fieldwork with the American Indian Movement. She has taught at the University of Puget Sound in Tacoma, Washington and is currently employed as an anthropological consultant in Seattle. She recently coedited a special issue of the *Law and Society Review* in which her article "The Indian Patrol in Minneapolis: Social Control and Social Change in an Urban Context" appeared.

The American Indian Movement — AIM — is very much a part of America's current scene. The Trail of Broken Treaties March to Washington, the occupation of the Bureau of Indian Affairs, and the siege at Wounded Knee: all these events put AIM into the headlines and thus into the national consciousness.

AIM was just getting started when I began my fieldwork with them in January, 1969. The previous summer, a small group of Indian men and women in Minneapolis had organized themselves as the Concerned Indian Americans (CIA). They had hoped to improve the condition of Indians in the city and to provide social services that they felt were neglected by other Indian and non-Indian organizations. Realizing the implications of their newly chosen acronym (CIA), they quickly changed their name to the American Indian Movement (AIM).

AIM's new members were men and women in their twenties and thirties who were friends and relatives of each other. Most had been born on one of the several Ojibwa reservations in northern Minnesota, but they, like many other Indians, had migrated to the urban center of Minneapolis-St. Paul. They congregated in the East Franklin Avenue area of Minneapolis, although some also lived on the Near North Side. AIM members, however, were not brand-new migrants unfamiliar with urban life; most had lived in the Twin Cities for at least five years.

Many AIM members knew all too well the problems faced by urban Indians. For example, Clyde Bellecourt, one of AIM's leaders, never attempted to hide the fact that he personally had encountered discrimination, unemployment, and repeated incarceration. Others had had similar experiences that led them to be ill at ease in the white-oriented city.

The Indian Patrol was one of the first projects adopted by AIM members. They conceived of it as a means of combating what they saw as police misconduct in their community. They felt that police did not treat Indians fairly, and asserted that the paddy wagon arrived promptly when the bars closed on East Franklin Avenue in order to round up the Indians. Non-Indians drinking in fashionable bars in wealthy neighborhoods, they said, were rarely subjected to such indignities or to the legal procedures that followed them.

In addition, AIM members felt that there was an unjustifiably high concentration of police squad cars in their area. Some members even felt that the roughest officers were avoiding the black neighborhood because a black patrol had been established. In AIM's view, these officers needed to be watched, not only for the blatant uses of unnecessary force, usually called "brutality", but for the more subtle forms of mistreatment, such as the use of insulting language.

The planners of the Indian Patrol hoped that by stationing Indian Patrollers to observe police-citizen encounters, they would decrease the possibility of mistreatment. Also, they hoped that by instructing the Indian patrollers to remove drunks from the street, they would reduce the number of arrests. The patrol was planned for weekend evenings because activity on the avenue was greatest then.

The patrollers worked on foot from late August, 1968, until the cold Minnesota winter set in in November. Then they took to their cars to observe the action around the bars in the area. The Indian Patrol also operated at AIM-sponsored powwows. The project continued, with varying degrees of intensity, until June, 1970.[1]

When I became interested in AIM and the Indian Patrol, I was beginning my second year of graduate study in anthropology at the University of Minnesota. I had had only a minimal academic indoctrination into the field, and thus had very few preconceptions. I did, however, have a small amount of practical experience. As a college undergraduate, I had been one of a group of Harvard and Radcliffe students hired by the Ute Tribal Chairman, Francis McKinley, to work at a summer camp for Ute children. That summer on the Ute reservation introduced me to cultural differences and to some of the problems faced by Indian people.

Working with the Utes also alerted me to the ways in which Indian people were attempting to become more self-sufficient in running their own economic and educational lives. Perhaps for the same reason, I became interested in AIM's ideological focus on "self-determination." The Indian Patrol seemed to be AIM's way of placing Indians in a more self-sufficient (and perhaps even powerful) position vis-à-vis the legal system.

I also saw the Indian Patrol within the context of general trends in the United States during and after the urban riots of the early 1960s, when many cities witnessed increasing citizen involvement in law enforcement in response to disorders. This citizen participation frequently took the form of citizens' patrols (Knopf, 1969). Thus the Indian Patrol seemed to represent the convergence of several important issues that were well worth studying.

With these thoughts in mind, I first talked with the leader of the Indian Patrol, Harold Goodsky, at an AIM meeting in early January, 1969. His reply to my request to ride along was hardly cordial. "Sure you can come along — we don't have anything to hide," he said. Then he added a sentiment that I was to hear again and again: "We Indians have been surveyed too much, and we never see the results."

I quickly learned that there was a general feeling among AIM members

---

[1] The Indian Patrol continued to operate at powwows and protests after its street operations declined. Also, AIM has since operated patrols in other cities besides Minneapolis; for example, in 1972, the St. Paul chapter of AIM had a patrol.

(shared, no doubt, by many other Indians as well), that the relationship between anthropologists and Indians usually was an unethical one, with anthropologists exploiting Indians for their own professional, if not financial, gain. They felt that anthropologists, like the countless commissions formed to study the "Indian problem," had produced few results that tangibly benefited the Indians. Indeed, many believed that the government and foundation money spent on research and commissions would be better spent directly on Indian programs.

Vine Deloria's immensely popular articles (first in *Playboy* magazine, then in *Custer Died for Your Sins* 1969: 78-100) expressed these views precisely, painting the anthropologist as a curse visited on the Indians. Many AIM members read Deloria's work before I did.

My own views tended toward those recently expressed by the American Indian anthropologist, Alfonso Ortiz (1972: 11): although the anthropologists may not have always been the best friends of the Indians, they did not have the power to be the Indian's worst enemies. That power was vested in the legislative, executive, and administrative structures overarching the total system, a system that had rarely been friendly to Indians.

Still, I felt that anthropologists have a responsibility not only to avoid harming people but, also, to make some contribution in return. One way to meet these responsibilities is to obtain clear consent to do the fieldwork, so that people do not participate against their will. That they understand the research and its goals, and that they have opportunities to accept or reject it are important considerations.

In my view (which is admittedly based on my own cultural background and values), people have a right to privacy, which includes the right *not* to be studied if they so choose. When a social scientist asks for consent to work, she (he) is, in effect, asking the individuals and the group to weigh their desire for privacy against the possible benefits of the study, either to themselves or to society. I feel that it is important that they have this choice. If, at any point, consent had not been granted, I would have given up my plans for writing about AIM and the Indian Patrol. I probably would have continued to work with the group because of the friendships that later were formed. But, lacking consent, I would have looked elsewhere for a dissertation research subject.

I also felt that the Indians' reward for consenting to the presence of an anthropologist (and thereby "contributing to knowledge") should be more than a thesis, bound in black, lettered in gold, and ready to catch dust. The anthropologist should also try to do something in return for the people — something that they consider useful.[2]

See footnote on following page.

The processes of gaining consent to work and of developing a useful role in AIM evolved over a period of about one year. At first, I sought consent by the simple and direct means of requesting permission to be present at certain times and places.

The first permissions that were given were tacit ones. AIM leaders allowed me to ride on patrol and "become a member," to attend general membership meetings and other AIM activities. When I first submitted a brief research proposal, no action was taken — a sure sign that full acceptance was not yet appropriate. A few months later, when I was preparing to give a seminar to share some of my experiences with other students in my class, I wrote a brief article about the Indian Patrol, and asked Clyde Bellecourt, who was AIM Chairman at that time, if we could talk about it.

"You're going to write about *your* opinions of *our* patrol?", he asked. "Who gave you the right to talk about AIM?" On this discordant note, we made arrangements to go over the half-written manuscript the next morning.

When Mr. Bellecourt saw the seminar paper, he made several suggestions, but he liked the paper and saw a use for it. He became a coauthor, and had several hundred copies printed up. AIM frequently received requests for information; the paper provided a handy response. It was distributed widely. Later, I was asked to update the first report, and I also wrote some additional ones. This role, as minor as it was, filled a need in the organization, and gave me a definite way to reciprocate for their help.

About six months later, I asked the AIM Board of Directors for formal permission to do a thesis using the knowledge I had gained in association with AIM. I sent a copy of my proposal to each board member. My request was considered at the end of a long meeting in early February (1970).

Dennis Banks, then the Chairman, introduced me and my proposal, and stated that "She's stuck with us through our ups and downs for over a year now." "Now she wants to do the unthing — a study." The board then discussed the whereabouts of patrol equipment and the status of the patrol, which was then in a state of decline. "Well, you could call your report 'The Rise and Fall of Indian Patrol,'" said one board member. But, when the laughter subsided, the continuing concern was voiced — would I neglect my

---

[2] Golde (1970:10) suggests that reciprocity is so deeply ingrained in anthropological fieldwork that it is almost an unconscious process. In my opinion, this process is becoming increasingly conscious and explicit. A recent report in the **Newsletter of the American Anthropological Association** (October, 1974:5) shows just how explicit the process can be: it describes how Clare Farrer, a graduate student fellowship recipient, and the Mescalero Apache Tribal Council agreed that "in exchange for the opportunity of working and studying on the reservation, the folklore she collects and her observations on contemporary life as well as historical documents will be made available for use as the base for first through sixth grade supplementary reading materials she will develop for reservation schools."

writing for AIM in my zeal to do the dissertation? Reassured that I would continue to do reports for AIM, the board unanimously voted to allow me "to do my thing."

Throughout this period of gaining consent, AIM was a small local group with a close-knit membership (although this situation was changing). The active members all knew about whatever was going on. Gaining permission to work with AIM meant getting to know a small group of people and letting them know about me.

My role in AIM, as it evolved, centered on documenting the growth and development of AIM and the Indian Patrol through my short papers. From the beginning, AIM members had a keen sense of themselves as a group engaged in an important struggle at a specific time and place in history. My reports of their activities (and indeed my dissertation as well) thus would have seemed valueless to them if I had referred to their organization only as some nameless or renamed example of anthropological processes. Instead, the usefulness of my role centered on providing a "factual group history." How then could I follow the long-hallowed anthropological tradition of disguising the name and locale of the group and the identity of its members?

The tradition protects the anonymity of sources of information; it shields individuals from having their private lives suddenly made public information. In addition, a coded data file and a well-disguised written presentation may give some protection if individuals later were accused of illegal acts. This last concern did not loom large during my fieldwork with the Indian Patrol, because patrolling was a relatively quiet operation that did not result in violent confrontations with police. But it did become important later when I considered additional fieldwork with AIM. Thus there are good reasons for giving the studied group a fictional name and locale. Nonetheless, under the circumstances I felt that AIM's desire for a factual group history should be honored.

AIM leaders and members had already consented to allow me to work with and write about the Indian Patrol and AIM. This consent would permit the factual use of locale and organization. Before I prepared the final draft of the thesis or wrote articles for publication, I sought additional, written permission from individuals who were likely to be key figures in my writings. The permission forms are shown in Figure 1.

Most people chose to sign the upper portion of the form. A few preferred pseudonyms. Some individuals left town or were otherwise inaccessible — I felt that I had to assume that they preferred pseudonyms. Thus while the permission forms alleviated some ethical problems, they caused problems of stylistic inconsistency. In the thesis (Cohen, 1973a), there were so many important individuals that I used real initials for those who did not want their identity disguised, and pseudoinitials for the others. In a recent article in the

FIGURE 1
PERMISSION FORMS

I, _____ , give Fay Cohen permission to use my real name when referring to me in her writings about the American Indian Movement and the Indian Patrol.

Signed _____

Witness _____

Date _____

I, _____ , prefer and request that Fay Cohen use a pseudonym when referring to me in place of my real name in her writings about the American Indian Movement and the Indian Patrol.

Signed _____

Witness _____

Date _____

Law and Society Review (Cohen, 1973b), I presented an overview of the development and meaning of the Indian Patrol; no names were necessary to that discussion. At a presentation to the American Anthropological Association (1972), all of the key figures except one could be designated by name. None of these methods of presentation are totally adequate. There is always the small chance that, within the factual context, readers will guess the true identity behind the pseudonyms or pseudoinitials. Also, the use of the factual context may raise another dilemma — it makes it very easy for those who oppose the group to utilize the data in undesirable ways, such as to contain the group and prevent its further development.

The possibility that AIM's "enemies" might attempt to utilize my data occurred at two rather different points in my relationship with AIM. In the fall of 1969, a young woman, whom I will call Susan Jones (since she left town before the consent forms were prepared), began to attend AIM meetings and local Indian conferences. She rode along with the Indian Patrol, and talked with teenagers at the Youth Center.

Susan was a tall, pretty young woman in her early twenties, light-skinned with long light brown hair. She usually dressed in an old shirt or sweatshirt and baggy, faded jeans, and resembled more closely the hippies at the University of Minnesota than the Indians in the East Franklin area.

Susan said that she had come to Minneapolis from a Northwest Coast state, where she had worked for Indian fishing rights. In Minneapolis, she worked in a church mission, then became a carpenter's apprentice in hopes of gaining enough skill to teach that trade to Indian youths. She said that her ancestry was one-quarter Indian of a Southeastern tribe.

One of the most unusual things about Susan was that she seemed to have no relatives in town. New people came into AIM all of the time, but most were brought into the group by relatives or by friends of relatives. In contrast, Susan seemed to have no ties. By December, people half-jokingly called her "the FBI," and noted that "she sure does ask a lot of questions."

I suspected that Susan's new appellation was the result of some emerging group paranoia. New people entering small groups are often thought to be spies.[3] Being somewhat naive, I didn't fully believe at that time that the FBI would have any interest in AIM. Although I didn't like seeming unfriendly to Susan, I avoided her nonetheless and hedged when she tried to engage me in conversation. However slight the possibility, I didn't want to take any chances, because I felt then — and still feel — that the government should not spy on its own citizens.

The possibility of government spying on AIM may not have been as slight as I thought at the time. It is now clear that the FBI did use informers to infiltrate AIM at the Bureau of Indian Affairs in Washington in 1972 and at Wounded Knee in 1973. It is even possible that an FBI informer may have infiltrated the Wounded Knee defense team. Maybe the covert surveillance began long before the major confrontations.

I still wonder about Susan Jones. I later heard a rumor that Susan had been labeled "FBI" after she incurred the wrath of the wife of one of AIM's leaders. According to this account, Susan had been talking with the leader at a party following a powwow. The wife saw them talking and became very jealous; the following day she supposedly began telling people that Susan was an FBI agent. This story has some plausibility. But it isn't altogether convincing, because the wife didn't spread rumors about other women her husband happened to speak to. Also, why did she choose this particular rumor?

When I moved to the Northwest Coast in 1971, I casually inquired around about Susan Jones. Maybe I asked the wrong people — but nobody knew her. Recently, I spoke with an Indian woman who remembers somebody who fits with Susan's description, but with a different last name. I am following up this lead. At the present time, however, Susan's affiliation with AIM is still unclear, and it is probably wise that I treated her the way that others in AIM did: guardedly.

[3] Anthropologists have also been considered to be spies. For a description of one such case, see Weidman (1970:255).

The timing of Susan's first appearance in AIM — fall 1969 — was perhaps significant. After slightly over one year in operation, AIM was at a crossroads in its development. Its members were beginning to reach out to other Indian organizations throughout the country. While some members flew off to national conferences and to protests such as the Alcatraz occupation, other members stayed home and tended the local shop. During that winter, the internal debate on priorities grew. Some people felt that AIM's chief purpose was to work on local problems. "We should settle it here first," they said. Others asserted that AIM needed national political action and should demonstrate on the larger issues affecting all Indians. "Get at the basic problems," they said.

The leaders of AIM opted for the latter approach. In March, 1970, AIM staged its first occupation of a building when its members took over the Minneapolis area office of the Bureau of Indian Affairs. AIM's occupation was done in support of a similar action in Littleton, Colorado the previous week. Both occupations, and others that followed in later weeks, were protests against the Bureau of Indian Affairs leadership, exclusion of Indians from key positions, and handling of funds.

AIM's evolution from a small local group with local goals to a nationally oriented group with an emphasis on political protest raised additional ethical problems. It had taken a whole year to get consent to work, and, when I thought that I had permission, I found that the group context had changed. There were new people, changing patterns of leadership, and more controversial forms of protest. These changes seemed to require new consent if I wished to extend my research range beyond the local group and the Indian Patrol.

Events during the occupation of the Minneapolis BIA office made these changes and their implications clear. I was notified of the protest during its planning stages. I anticipated no problems in attending. When I entered the BIA building, however, I quickly noticed the many unfamiliar faces and, at the same time, I missed many more familiar ones. I soon learned that many of the participants had come from other Upper Midwest cities and towns to support AIM. I also learned that some long-standing AIM members had decided not to participate because they did not agree with occupation as a form of protest.

After two days of the occupation, AIM's demands had not been met. The Minneapolis police had made some arrests, but only after police officials and AIM leaders had established a nonviolent arrest plan.

By the third day, I could feel considerable tension, which grew when an off-duty Indian police officer was asked to leave. I was not surprised when someone turned toward me and said, in tones of anger and distrust, "There are still some of THEM in here!" I left quickly. The few remaining non-Indians left shortly thereafter.

Later, there were apologies all around, but the issue remained clear. The consent that the original group had given extended only to that original situation. The consent that the leaders had implied when informing me of the protest did not have the support of the new, more amorphous gathering typical of protests. The relative neatness of gaining permission to study AIM the local group stood in clear contrast to the ambiguities of working with AIM the national movement.

After this episode, I continued to work with the Indian Patrol until I completed the study in the summer of 1970. In the press of writing up the material, I did not frequently think of the problem raised by the BIA occupation. However, the issue arose again in the fall of 1972, when I returned to Minneapolis for a visit.

In October, 1972, Indian people from all over the country gathered in Minneapolis-St. Paul on their way to Washington, D.C. They were participants in the caravan called "The Trail of Broken Treaties," a second Trail of Tears to dramatize the historic and present injustices suffered by American Indians. When Clyde Bellecourt casually suggested that I go along because I was a "good observer" and could "document what happens," I began to think about extending my research. The suggestion raised — or rather, raised again — important questions for which there were no easy answers. The same questions could be raised concerning anthropological work at Wounded Knee or at any other confrontation between a social action group such as AIM and the authorities.

First, there was the ever-present problem of consent. Gaining consent locally was possible because of the continuous and relatively stable nature of the locale and organization. Gaining consent from a group recently assembled to augment the local group, such as occurred at the BIA office, was more problematic, because of the influx of new personnel and the brief duration of the situation. Gaining consent from the caravan to Washington seemed nearly impossible. Minneapolis AIM members performed some key roles, but they comprised only one segment of a large group whose members came from all over the country. Both the situation and the personnel were thus very fluid.

The caravan leaders hardly had the time (or, it seemed, the inclination) to sit down and discuss research. Polling a significant number of participants on the spot seemed absurd. Furthermore, as I had learned in March, 1970, consent given before the fact might slip away in the face of the tension of unfulfilled demands, arrests, or struggles for leadership. Consent to write about my observations in terms of real events and real people might raise grave legal difficulties should arrests follow the protest.

Second, there is the potential physical danger of confrontations. Anthropologists traditionally have placed the value of their fieldwork above personal risks to health and safety. It is, however, an important consideration.

Third, as AIM increased the intensity of its protests, I feared once again that my data might be usurped for nonresearch purposes. This time the possibilities seemed much more imminent. Suppose, for example, I had observed various occurrences at this, or another confrontation, which resulted in criminal charges against the participants. Or, suppose that I had gathered descriptions of such events from the participants. As a trained social scientist, my observations and interviews might carry considerable weight in legal proceedings. Legally, it is not established that I would have any right to withhold my data even if I felt that it might harm the research group or that, on general principles, social science data should be used only for their intended purposes.

This contradiction between ethics and law is more than hypothetical. In November 1972, for example, Samuel Popkin, a political science instructor at Harvard, was sent to jail after he refused to cooperate with a federal grand jury investigating the Pentagon Papers. Popkin was held in civil contempt because he would not disclose the names of the confidential sources whom he interviewed as part of his research. Although social scientists are not routinely hauled into court or sent to jail because of their work with militant groups or unpopular causes, the number of such cases (and related cases involving journalists) is increasing and the problems remain. The social scientist (or journalist) can hold to ethics, keep the data, protect his sources — and possibly face a long court battle or a jail term for contempt. Or, he can accede to the powers that be, forget about ethics, and hand over the goods.[4]

In college and in graduate school, we tend to think of social science data as sacred. They are not. It is not certain that the anthropologist has any special legal privileges either as an observer or as a participant. An anthropologist observing a confrontation involving trespass may be charged with the same violations of law as the group being observed. Being an anthropologist probably confers no special defense. Thus the anthropologist has no personal protection against legal involvement, just as she can offer no definitive legal protection against disclosure of material from the research group.

In conclusion, the problems of ordinary fieldwork are magnified and complicated when studying a group that is involved in protest and confrontation. In my own case, the seriousness of these problems was largely responsible for my decision not to "go along and document" AIM's march to Washington, D.C. Other reasons, such as family obligations and lack of time and funds also played a significant part in my decision. Even without these per-

---

[4] Three recent articles discuss in more detail the complex and changing law in cases involving social scientists and journalists. The reader is referred to Boness and Cordes (1973), Goodale (1975) and Nejelski and Finsterbusch (1973).
Legislative remedies ("shield laws") are one possible method by which the current ethical dilemma might be resolved. Some writers believe that researchers must make a strong effort to encourage such legislation.

sonal considerations, however, it would have been difficult, if not impossible, for me to go with a clear conscience, feeling as I did that my presence potentially could result in more harm than good.

REFERENCES

Boness, Frederick H. and John F. Cordes

    1973   "Notes: The Researcher-Subject Relationship: The Need for Protection and a Model Statute." *Georgetown Law Journal,* 62: 243-272.

Cohen, Fay G.

    1972   "Unofficial Legal Proceedings as Social Drama: An Urban Indian Case." Paper presented at the annual meeting of the American Anthropological Association, Toronto.

    1973a   "The Indian Patrol in Minneapolis: Social Control and Social Change in an Urban Context." Unpublished Ph.D. dissertation, University of Minnesota.

    1973b   "The Indian Patrol in Minneapolis: Social Control and Social Change in an Urban Context." *Law and Society Review,* 7: 779-786.

Deloria, Vine Jr.

    1969   *Custer Died for Your Sins.* New York: Macmillan Co.

Golde, Peggy

    1970   *Women in the Field.* Chicago: Aldine.

Goodale, James C.

    1975   "Branzburg V. Hayes and the Developing Qualified Privilege for Newsmen." *Hastings Law Journal,* 26: 709-743.

Knopf, Terry Ann

    1969   "Youth Patrols: An Experiment in Community Participation." Waltham, Mass.: Brandeis University.

Nejelski, Paul and Kurt Finsterbusch

    1973   "The Prosecutor and the Researcher; Present and Prospective Variations in the Supreme Court's Branzburg Decision." *Social Problems,* **21**: 3-21.

Newsletter of the American Anthropological Association

    1974   "Grants Given to Study Eskimo Music and Apache Folklore." Vol. 5, column 2, October.

Ortiz, Alfonso

    1972   "An Indian Anthropologist's Perspective on Anthropology" in *The American Indian Reader: Anthropology,* Jeannette Henry (ed.). San Francisco: Indian Historian Press, pp. 6-12.

Weidman, Hazel Hitson

    1970   "On Ambivalence and the Field" in *Women in the Field,* Peggy Golde (ed.). Chicago: Aldine. pp. 239-266.

7
THE ETHICS OF FIELDWORK IN AN URBAN BAR

BRENDA J. MANN

Brenda Mann is a graduate student at the University of Minnesota. Her major fieldwork, on which this chapter is based, was the study of a midwestern college bar. This resulted in an article, "Bar Talk," and a book she coauthored with James Spradley, *The Cocktail Waitress: Woman's Work in a Man's World.* Her special interest is the anthropology of work.

It was 5 P.M. but the heat of the midwestern summer day was just reaching its peak.[1] I had driven downtown, through rush hour traffic, for a job interview at Brady's Bar. A casual acquaintance of mine had just begun working as a waitress at Brady's and she told me they were still looking for some "girls" to work a couple of evenings a week and, although I already had a full-time research position for the summer, I wanted and needed an extra evening job. So, I called Brady's the next day and spoke with the night manager, Mark Brady, who told me I would have to come for an interview.[2]

Hesitantly, I pushed open the double doors leading into the bar. Outside, the sun was glaringly strong and my eyes adjusted only slowly to the dim, air-conditioned coolness of the room. As I stood self-consciously in the doorway, I could feel people watching me. Indeed, several of the men seated at the bar had turned and were openly staring. As I was to discover later, I was an unusual spectacle. Not only was I a lone female appearing at a time of day when the bar was usually occupied only by men, but I was also a stranger. I walked to the bar and told the bartender that I wanted to see Mark Brady. He pointed to a table and told me to have a seat and wait. I sat down. Half a dozen men were seated at the bar but I sat alone in the middle of the room, surrounded by 12 empty tables.

The men turned back to their talking and drinking, but a few turned occasionally to take a second look. I couldn't hear their discussion from the bar, but scattered bursts of laughter emanated from the group. I felt uneasy, but concentrated on waiting, glancing impatiently at my watch and staring at the walls and table top in front of me. In a few minutes a man emerged from a door in the rear of the room and headed toward the bar. The bartender pointed at me and smiled, "She's waiting to see you, Mark." Mark sat down across from me, "Well, what can I do for you?"

"I'm Brenda, the girl who called about the waitress job. . ."

"Oh, yeah. Did you ever waitress before?" I shook my head. "Well, we'll start you on a Saturday, that's our slow night. Give you a chance to learn." Mark was talking a mile a minute. "You get $10 bar money from the bartenders. You pay the bartender for drinks out of that, then collect from the customers. You just wait on the tables and that's about all there is to it. Can you work Saturdays and Thursdays to begin with?"

"Yes."

"Okay. Then we'll see about putting you on a regular schedule later. Okay?" He didn't wait for my response. "Well, that's about it, Brenda. Just

---

[1] This article is based on research conducted from July, 1971 to July, 1972. See also James P. Spradley and Brenda J. Mann, *The Cocktail Waitress: Woman's Work in a Man's World,* New York, Wiley, 1975.
[2] The name of the bar as well as those of all employees and customers are pseudonyms.

be here on Saturday night, around seven. Oh, one other thing. No jeans. You can wear a pantsuit if you want, but no jeans. We don't like our girls to look messy. Any questions?"

"Is that all? You mean I'm hired?" I couldn't believe the interview was finished.

"Sure. We mainly call you down here just to make sure you aren't too ugly for the job. You know, make sure you don't have buckteeth or anything." Mark laughed as he stood up, "See you on Saturday night." Then he turned to the bar, "Hey, Steve. This is our new girl, Brenda, so be nice to her." Steve smiled broadly at me as Mark left me standing alone in the middle of the room and joined the other men seated at the bar. I nodded to Steve, picked up my purse, and left.

It had taken me 20 minutes to drive across town for the interview, but only 5 minutes to get hired. It was difficult for me to believe that I was actually going to work at this place, and the days preceding my first night at work heightened this feeling and increased my anxiety as I discussed my new occupation with friends and contemplated what was for me, a decidedly novel role.

Brady's Bar represented another cultural world, one with which I was totally unfamiliar. I had just turned 21 and my own experience with bars, though not with drinking per se, was extremely limited. Most of my drinking to this point had taken place at home or in the college dorm and involved not professionally mixed cocktails, but a bottle from the local liquor store, purchased and shared by many. Adding to my anxiety were the preconceptions that my friends and I shared about bars. The idea of working in such a place conjured up pictures of serving beer to inebriated and aggressive men. My friends did little to disabuse me of such notions, each of them warning me of the perils ahead. As a consequence, I was convinced that this new job would not only be an excursion into another cultural world, but might also prove to be a more difficult undertaking than I had originally anticipated.

The next day I related these thoughts and my interview experience to James Spradley, the anthropologist with whom I was working, and we discussed the fact that my new occupation might well present a unique opportunity to do research on a facet of American culture that few anthropologists had explored. Many studies have been done on drinking behavior cross culturally, but few had examined the culture of an American bar, and none from the viewpoint of the women who worked there — the cocktail waitresses. Although our commitment to a formal research project was only tentative at this point, as we were not yet certain that the bar would offer the rich source of data that it eventually did, we made the decision to begin recording my experiences at Brady's.

My own socialization into the role of cocktail waitress provided the opportunity to learn the cultural rules and categories of this institution. Each night on the job was a lesson in how to behave appropriately as a cocktail waitress: learning how to make sense of the world at Brady's Bar, how to interpret the language of bartenders and customers, how to identify people in the social structure, and, in particular, how to behave appropriately as a female in this small male-centered world. In short, in acquiring the training and knowledge necessary to my new occupation, I was simultaneously discovering much of the culture of Brady's Bar. Beginning with my first night at work, I began to systematically record my observations of life at Brady's. In addition, I would meet several times each week with James Spradley and we would informally discuss these experiences. These sessions were tape recorded and transcribed for later analysis.

As the months passed and as the project took form, it became clear that I was assuming not one new role, but three rather distinct yet interrelated ones. In addition to my initial role of *cocktail waitress,* I was also acting as an *informant* in this cultural scene. And with time, I increasingly assumed the more detached role of *participant-observer.* The assumption of these additional roles, however, created two basic kinds of problems: the first one largely methodological, the second one ethical.

First, there was the methodological problem of objectivity, a problem associated with the very nature of anthropological inquiry, whether conducted at home or abroad. Because the anthropologist is herself a major research tool and an important reservoir of data, it is essential that she retain some measure of detachment while simultaneously submerging herself in the customs and daily life of her informants. Therefore, much depended on my own self-awareness and understanding, not only of the role I was playing at any given time, but also of the effects of the socialization processes to which I was being subjected as I learned the job.

For example, as an employee I had more than just a casual investment in the ongoing social life at Brady's. Because I wanted to do my job well and to be accepted by my fellow employees, I conformed, though at times only outwardly, to most of the group values and norms. In particular, this meant I had to learn to act appropriately within the confines of a system that definitively places women in a subordinate role and that requires passivity and deference to the male in most matters. Initially, much of the behavior required of me seemed alien and distasteful, yet there was one entire stage of my fieldwork where I largely accepted the group's definition of "femininity," and this greatly affected my perspective of bar culture. For these reasons, team fieldwork was invaluable. Spradley provided a consistently more objective view of life at Brady's Bar, contrasted to my own shifting perspective as it was affected by my socialization into the culture and my attempts to balance the triad of roles I had assumed.

While this methodological problem was resolved relatively easily, a particular ethical dilemma followed us throughout the entire period of the investigation, the essence of which was how to communicate the aims of the research to those at Brady's Bar.

The anthropologist's primary responsibility is to those she studies and this responsibility entails at least two aspects: (1) protecting the privacy of informants, and (2) communicating the aims of the research to informants. There was no question that the identities of all the individuals at Brady's, as well as the actual name and location of the bar itself, would remain anonymous. But the second issue, that of informing people at Brady's of the research, was more complex. The ethics statement of the American Anthropological Association states simply: "The aims of the investigation should be communicated as well as possible to the informant" (1971). But what does this relatively ambiguous statement mean in the context of my particular research setting?

First, there was the question of just who my informants were. Bars are public places, frequented by large numbers of people, many of whom are transient. Although my role as waitress allowed me to interact with and to observe everyone in the bar, it was obvious that it would not only be impossible, but incongruous in terms of bar culture and my role in it, to attempt to inform every individual who came into Brady's of my special interest in them and their activities. This same problem faces the anthropologist who does fieldwork in a more traditional setting. Does she attempt to offer an explanation to everyone in the village and to gain everyone's permission? Or just her primary informants? In my case, did this mean I should tell all the customers? Just the employees? Or, because I was studying the perspective of cocktail waitresses, need I gain only their permission? Or, furthermore, should I keep this information entirely to myself?

Another issue is the question of what constitutes an adequate explanation to my informants. Does it mean I must teach them anthropology in order for them to understand the project more fully? For even in one's own society, simply telling someone you are an anthropologist does little to clarify one's identity or purpose. Or is it sufficient to say, "I want to observe and to study your customs"?

A third issue further complicated the situation in my case: my role as an employee and the fact that the research project was initially secondary to this role. This problem is becoming more frequent as anthropologists turn to their own society for study and as research funds become increasingly scarce, compelling graduate students to take jobs, both as a means of support and as a place for research.[3]

---

[3] See Footnote on following page.

Communicating the aims of the research to one's informants is a complex task affected by many variables, some of which are not always controlled by the anthropologist. I can best explain my approach to this ethical problem by examining the progression of roles I assumed during the course of my work at Brady's and the evolution of the research project.

BECOMING A COCKTAIL WAITRESS

The first couple of months at Brady's posed few problems in the way of research, but they were awkward and tiring nights nonetheless as I worked at learning all that I had to know in order to fit into the group, to be what every woman who works at Brady's strives to be: "a good waitress." I was definitely an outsider and every aspect of my behavior indicated this to others. The way I talked to bartenders, my ineptness at handling customers, and my ignorance concerning the contents and prices of drinks were just a few indicators of my marginality. This lack of knowledge made work difficult and almost every encounter, whether with a fellow employee or customer, was cause for anxiety. The people at Brady's seemed more like complex objects that I had to learn to understand and to maneuver simply in order to do the job and to make it through each grueling night of work. Although we kept detailed notes during this period and held regular debriefing interviews, I made no attempt during this period to explain to anyone my involvement in a research project. This decision was related not only to the tentative nature of the research at this point in time, but to other reasons as well.

First, my primary role in the research project at this time was as an informant. The job and my relationship with fellow employees was of major importance, the research only secondary. Second, throughout these first few weeks at Brady's I was continually on the verge of quitting. The work was much more difficult than I had originally anticipated and my numerous nightly mistakes made me question my ability to handle the job. Each night at work reinforced these negative thoughts as well as increased my feelings of being an outsider. And each evening I would return home exhausted, depressed, and determined to quit. But gradually the job became a challenge and I was learning to cope. There was still much I didn't understand and I was very much on the periphery: I did not yet feel comfortable in my role as waitress nor did I wholeheartedly embrace the role of researcher. I was simply trying

[3] See Christina Milner and Richard Milner, *Black Players: The Secret World of Black Pimps,* New York, Bantam, 1972. This ethnography is based on data collected during Christina Milner's employment while in graduate school and contains a brief account on the manner in which she and her husband dealt with the double role of employee-researcher.

to learn a new and difficult job. I occasionally wondered how the people at the bar would react if they knew about the research, but most of my notes and my interviews with Spradley during these weeks dealt primarily with my own feelings and observations in adjusting to a new situation.

But as the weeks passed and as I came to know and become involved with people at Brady's, and as it became increasingly clear that there was indeed an abundance of interesting data to be gathered, the research began in earnest and major ethical questions were raised.

BECOMING ONE OF BRADY'S GIRLS[4]

I had been working at Brady's approximately three months when my feelings about the bar, the people, and the research changed radically. By this time the job had become almost second nature to me and I found that I no longer had to concentrate so intensely on the mechanical aspects of waitressing. One of the bartenders had even complimented me at the end of a particularly long and hassled night: "You did a good job. You're a good waitress." I felt secure in my ability to perform my new role. The crowds of customers who jammed themselves into Brady's each night were no longer just tiring hassles for me, most became recognizable faces, each with an individual personality and history. I now participated in the ever-constant joking behavior between bartenders and waitresses, and I stayed after work most nights to drink and discuss the events of the evening with other employees. In short, I was becoming one of "Brady's girls." But other, more subtle changes in my status took place, and this brought the ethical issues to the foreground.

An an insider, I had access to all sorts of new information about Brady's and the people who both worked and drank there regularly. I served free drinks in the kitchen to on-duty policemen, I knew which underaged individuals were to be allowed to drink, and I heard all the gossip about customers and employees. My now close-working relationship with other waitresses and bartenders was the main channel for this information. Since bars are places where intimate relationships are formed, discussed, and often rapidly dissolved, I heard details of these relationships as well as of the personal antagonisms and conflicts that arose among employees. But I was not merely listening and recording all this information. I was also, to a greater extent than before, part of it. If a bartender was angry with one of the waitresses, I heard about it. And if for some reason the waitresses were upset with the bartenders, I took sides with the women. Like other employees, I also had gripes about

---

[4] Bartenders at Brady's affectionately refer to waitresses by the terms, "Brady's girls" or "our girls."

certain aspects of the work and there were some people, both customers and employees, with whom I did not get along. This new kinship raised the delicate question, "How much of what goes on at Brady's should I tell?"

My discussion with the other researcher often included accounts of quibbles among employees, barroom liaisons, and gossip. Up to this point, I had been relatively candid in these interviews, supplying details of these incidents as well as the names of the individuals involved. However, since I now had access to the more intimate details about people, this altered the situation and I hesitated to relate this information in full. And so when I observed or heard of incidents that exposed more private facts about individuals and their relationships, I did not discuss them with Spradley nor did I include them in the field notes. I felt at that time, and still do, that these data were not crucial to the study.

It was shortly after this change in my status that it also became apparent that some explanation of the project and my involvement in it was necessary. We were now fully committed to the project and were ready to begin interviewing the other waitresses. Before contacting the women for the interviews, however, we discussed alternative methods for disclosing the investigation. My rapport with fellow employees at this time was excellent. I was enjoying both the work and the people I worked with, and I hesitated to do anything that would alter this situation. We finally decided that an informal approach would be best, allowing word to pass from one individual to another and answering questions as they arose rather than making a formal announcement about the project. I contacted the waitresses at work, asking if they would be willing to participate in an interview with a professor studying bars. I told them I had already been interviewed by this person about Brady's and asked if they would mind coming to school one afternoon to discuss their work. The response was enthusiastic and some of the waitresses questioned me about the upcoming interview: "Did I know this professor very well?" and "Why does he want to talk to us?" were the two questions asked. I explained I was working for him this summer as a research assistant and that he was interested in studying drinking behavior. These explanations were sufficient for the time being.

At the first interview I was present and participated as one of the waitresses. Spradley explained the research project and explained that he had been talking with me previously. He added that he had been doing some studies on alcoholism and that he wanted to know what it was like to work as a cocktail waitress. A tape recorder was sitting in plain view and he announced that he would be taping the discussion if no one had any objections. Although I did not explain all aspects of my role in the project at this time, I was sure that most, if not all, of the waitresses knew of my interests. I had previously told one of them about my involvement in the study and was certain that employee gossip, the informal "grapevine" that normally carried information *to* me, also operated to circulate information *about* me to the other employees.

The grapevine worked quickly. Almost as soon as I walked in the door for work that night, Dave, one of the bartenders, brought up the subject of the interviews. He was dating one of the waitresses and she had evidently told him all about the session that had occurred that afternoon. It was also obvious that I was considered the main source of information on this subject and all questions concerning the project were directed at me. "Hey," said Dave, "I hear you've been spending the afternoon with the other waitresses, tearing all us bartenders down." He was kidding, but I knew some explanations would be in order.

Throughout the project, I operated on a "filter-back principle." That is, the type and the amount of detail in my explanations depended, in part, on the kinds of reactions I received from my informants. The more interested they seemed, the more detailed information I gave them. If they seemed disinterested, as I found was often the case, I would let the matter drop, giving information only in response to direct questions. This strategy was, in a very large sense, a reaction on my part to the tacit rule in bar culture requiring avoidance of serious discourse of any kind, and to what I knew was a rather extreme sensitivity on the part of males in the bar towards "scholarly" women.

But Dave's reaction was positive. I could tell, however, that while he was interested, he also found the matter amusing, "What did you broads find to talk about all afternoon?" I continued the discussion in the joking context in which he had placed it: "But Dave, we said such nice things about you. We all agreed that we girls are here to serve you." "Oh, go away," was Dave's response. And for the time being, the discussion was closed.

As I ran into each of the waitresses, I tried to thank them for coming to the interview but they demurred: "Oh, no. It was really a lot of fun." They asked if they could arrive early the next time in order to listen to the first tape and I told them they could. One of the bartenders overheard the conversation and kiddingly suggested I destroy the tapes, so I reassured him: "But Steve. We said so many good things about *you*." His response was, "Keep it." Nothing more was said until after work that evening.

Almost all the waitresses and bartenders had gathered around the bar to drink. It was after 2 A.M. and we were having our usual after-work employee party. John Brady, one of the owner's nephews, began taunting me: "Miss Anthropologist. Oh, Miss Anthropologist." Although everyone knew months ago that I was an anthropology major, just as I knew such personal trivia about each of them, John's mode of address was an indication that the grapevine had recirculated this information and that it was now considered a significant detail.

"Yes," was my only response.

"I hear you've been sitting around all afternoon discussing bartenders. Now which one of us did all of you decide was the worst one — he's going to get a raise!" The interview, as everything else in the bar, was going to become an issue in the battle of the sexes. The other waitresses and I hedged the question. We all knew long before the interview which one of the bartenders we unanimously disliked, but none of us would say. Yet it really did not seem to matter. As John had said, he "wanted to give a raise to the one we disliked the most." In fact, most of what women in the bar do or think has little significance for the bartenders and the reality that "women's work" has little status in the bar, as do the waitresses, rendered the whole affair almost totally insignificant in the eyes of the bartenders — except as a brief subject for jest and only as it related to them. John was laughing now, "All these sociologists running around here." I corrected him, "I'm not a sociologist. I'm an anthropologist."

"Whatever. I don't see what use this study will be." And the subject was dropped by his dismissal.

Although little more was said in the months that followed, it was generally accepted from this point on that Brady's Bar was being studied and that I was involved in the research. We continued interviewing the waitresses in the same manner as before, but the interviews soon lost their original fascination for the informants. Because interest declined among the waitresses and because we felt we had sufficient information, we did not pursue the interviews further.

My rapport with people at the bar continued to be good, and occasionally individual waitresses or bartenders would ask how the project was progressing. When this occurred, I attempted to answer all their questions as completely and honestly as I could. And since many of these people were college students like myself, my answers often emphasized the sociological aspects of the study. More often than not, however, I found that people preferred to keep the discourse on a superficial level, relegating it to a humorous context or to the form of polite inquiry. This was notably the case with bartenders, all of whom refused to treat the subject seriously. And in accordance with their expectations of female behavior, I was often forced to remain coy and demure in response to their jests and inquiries. This necessity to conform to the dominant male standards, a situation often faced by female researchers (see Daniels, 1967), greatly hampered my ability to communicate in a completely open way with informants and often gave me little control over the role I played. To a great extent, my role and manner of communication with informants were defined by them in a manner congruent with their expectations of proper female behavior.

REJECTING THE ROLE OF COCKTAIL WAITRESS

My romance with Brady's lasted only a few short months. I had begun work in the bar in July, 1971, but by the end of the following March my perspective again shifted, leaving me thoroughly disenchanted with what I saw and knew of life at Brady's Bar. This malaise stemmed not only from my aversion to the job itself, which I now perceived as stupefying, but was also associated with my complete familiarity with the people and activities at the bar. Much of what I knew, for example, about the social organization at Brady's and the values on which it was based, I found personally distasteful. I objected to the rigidly traditional definitions of masculinity and femininity which my informants accepted as "natural," and which dominated every facet of social activity in the bar, and which compelled me, as a waitress, to play a subordinate and passive role vis-à-vis the men in the bar. I also found that beyond the work situation, my informants and I had little in common, and I knew that my dislike for many aspects of bar life was shared by few other than myself. Unlike my earliest conceptions of the bar, however, these negative reactions were now tempered by a degree of understanding as I attempted to play the role of participant-observer, placing my observations into a more objective, anthropological framework. Despite this more detached perspective, I still retained affection for many of the people at Brady's and outwardly, I continued to play my role according to their rules.

As time went by, however, I found this role increasingly difficult to assume. In May, I finally quit. Several weeks later I began working at Brady's again on a substitute basis, and an incident occurred on my first night back at work that made me realize the extent of my shift in perspective toward the bar and the people there. I arrived early for work that evening and was sitting at the bar with Mark and his girl friend. I quote here from the field notes from this particular evening:

> *"Mark and Laurie were engaged in a semiargument about what kind of work she was going to do now that she had graduated. Laurie was dissatisfied with her home economics major — she felt she really hadn't learned all that much. I suggested graduate school as a possibility or maybe looking into Betty Crocker or something like that. Mark thought she should be an airline hostess. Everytime Laurie or I tried to talk about what it would be like, Mark would break in and say how glamorous it was and how it was the best-paying job for a female, etc. We couldn't get a word in. Mark knew all about women's jobs. He wouldn't listen to me when I tried to talk about the hassles inherent in being a stewardess or a waitress.*

> *I was just getting over this frustration, stifling my urge to tell Mark to shut up and listen when John took a break. He fixed himself a drink and sat down next to me at the bar. He hopped right into the conversation, not only overriding what Laurie and I were trying to say but advancing the discussion into the roles of bartender and waitress: 'Of course, the bartender has it the roughest. It's the harder job, more to cope with, more complicated. Sure waitresses work hard, but bartenders. . .' Mark and Laurie left. Then John started explaining marriage, divorce, etc., to me. I was being bombarded with advice and descriptions of reality. I just gave up. No one, absolutely no one, was interested in anything I had to say. And if I wanted to say anything, it would have required me to be rude, telling the men to shut up and please listen. I just smiled and nodded and let my mind wander to other things. It was a relief to finally start working. By the time the evening drew to a close, I had had it with listening. The attitude of the men upset me. They accepted their right to talk, to instruct, to order, so completely that they were totally insensitive to the women sitting at the bar with them. They were totally oblivious and uninterested in hearing anything I had to say. They perceived my role as that of the gracious listener and proceeded to talk, talk, and talk."*

My first night back at work was indeed a disappointment and served to emphasize my feelings of isolation from the group. I worked at Brady's only a few more nights until finally, I found the required role playing too oppressive. At the end of July, I quit for good.

Although we had been analyzing the data on Brady's as it accumulated, it was not until after I quit work at Brady's that we began to seriously attempt writing up the mass of data that had accumulated during the year of research. We began working on an ethnography that we planned to publish, and this raised the final aspect of the ethical problem, that of protecting our informants' rights to privacy. We attempted to do this in several ways.

First, in order to get some idea of how our informants would react to seeing life at Brady's analyzed, I gave one of the waitresses, whom I knew would circulate it, a copy of a paper I had written on one aspect of bar culture. I asked her to read it and to give me her reactions. Although I know she read it, as well as discussed it with others in the bar, there was little substantive comment or criticism from anyone, and I was able to elicit only a few brief, but largely favorable, comments.

The major strategies for protecting informants involved both the omission of certain kinds of data as well as disguising all of the people and some of the events that were to be included in the published material. In writing up data, the anthropologist must seek a delicate balance between presenting the most accurate picture of her field experience and protecting the people involved in the study. In every case, the anthropologist must rely on her own judgment and sensitivity to her informants' needs. In this case, it often meant that sensitive decisions had to be made concerning the inclusion of certain material. We found, however, that most data could be used, particularly through the use of pseudonyms and by changing minor details of certain events. However, some data were omitted altogether, especially where it might have reflected negatively on an informant or informants, and where it would have been impossible to disguise the situation and participants.

The third way in which we were able to further protect our informants was through a delay in the publication of the ethnography. It has been over two years since I worked at Brady's and all of the women who were our informants have graduated from college, many have married, all have moved on to new cities or new jobs. The same can be said for most of the bartenders as well as the vast majority of customers. This delay serves to prevent or to minimize any possible repercussions of our study for the people involved.

CONCLUSION

Each field situation is unique and presents a multitude of problems for the researcher: theoretical, methodological, and ethical. One thing common to all anthropological inquiry, however, is the necessity for personal involvement of some sort with one's informants. The anthropologist deals with people and, because of this, fieldwork is subject to all the complexities, ambiguities, and unpredictability inherent in any form of social interaction. Thus, it is seldom possible to anticipate, or to completely control, the types of problems that arise in a given research situation. However, it is the task of the anthropologist to maintain a constant awareness and sensitivity to the needs and rights of her informants as they relate to her involvement with them. Two most basic responsibilities are the communication of research goals and the protection of informants' anonymity.

Communicating the aims of the research is a complex task that takes different expressions depending on the public nature of the research setting and the kind of involvement and rapport achieved by the anthropologist. In this case, it was a continual process, a gradual explanation that   several months. As my role in the bar changed and as the project   did my ability and the necessity to communicate with informants.

In the first stage of the fieldwork, in my role as the "new girl," I made no attempt to disclose my interests in studying the bar because of the tentative nature of the project and because the job itself was of primary importance to me. As weeks passed, however, I entered the second stage of fieldwork as an insider in bar culture, and the project began in earnest. I was able, at this point, to effectively utilize the grapevine at Brady's, not only to gather data about the bar, but also to alert people to my interests in them and their activities. It was only during the end of this stage and the beginning of the final stage of investigation, when my rapport with informants was quite good, that I used a more direct explanation. Even then, however, my low status as a female prevented completely open and serious discussion of the topic, and my informants, particularly males, expressed little interest in the details of the project, preferring to keep such discussion in a superficial and humorous context.

Subsequent to my departure from Brady's and in preparing for the publication of the data, several precautions were taken to protect the anonymity of the bar and all the individuals involved in the study. This entailed the use of pseudonyms, the alteration of minor details and events, and the omission altogether of some data that might have proved damaging or embarassing to informants. A delay of over two years in the publication of the ethnography also served to further protect the anonymity and privacy of informants.

REFERENCES

American Anthropological Association

    1971   "Principles of Professional Responsibility."

Daniels, Arlene Kaplan

    1967   "The Low-Caste Stranger in Social Research" in *Ethics, Politics, and Social Research,* Gideon Sjoberg (ed.). Cambridge: Schenkman.

Milner, Christina and Richard Milner

    1972   *Black Players: The Secret World of Black Pimps.* New York: Bantam.

Spradley, James P. and Brenda J. Mann

    1975   *The Cocktail Waitress: Woman's Work in a Man's World.* New York: Wiley.

8
STUDYING ELITES: SOME SPECIAL PROBLEMS

BARBARA HARRELL-BOND

Barbara E. Harrell-Bond received her D. Phil. from Oxford University in 1972. She is a senior research fellow of the Afrika-Studiecentrum, Leiden. She has conducted fieldwork in an urban housing estate in Britain and has done a study of marriage and family life in Sierra Leone. She has written a number of articles and a book, *Modern Marriage in Sierra Leone: A Study of the Professional Group.* Most recently she has led a team study of family law in Sierra Leone. Dr. Harrell-Bond resides in Oxford, England and is a member of St. Antony's College, University of Oxford.

Participant observation requires the personal involvement of the investigator with the people whose social behavior is being studied. Although anthropologists have always relied heavily on participant observation, they have rarely reported on their personal experiences and the problems that arise from this kind of research. In part, this may be due to the fact that participant observation raises certain moral and ethical questions that, at least in my own case, have yet to be resolved.

The ethical problems I discuss here developed during research on marriage and family life among the Western-educated elite of Sierra Leone.[1] They were problems that might be encountered in the study of a professional group in any society. The following issues stand out: (a) gaining entree into an exclusive, elite group in an honest way even though the members did not always wish to accept me as an equal; (b) convincing informants that I would maintain absolute confidentiality and then *keeping* that promise; (c) cutting social ties with informants when I left, especially after I had taken the initiative to create those ties in the first place; and (d) writing and publishing a final report that most members of the informant community would read.

THE NATURE OF THE RESEARCH

My research in Sierra Leone was complicated by the nature of the topic I was investigating: marriage and family behavior. Although this topic is a sensitive one in any society, I anticipated that it would be especially difficult in Sierra Leone because the professional group (among other groups) of that country has adopted what they perceive to be the western form of monogamous marriage.[2] Almost all of the professionals were married in the church under statutory law. In Sierra Leone, the law is based on English concepts of Christian ideals regarding the companionate marriage. High social status for both men and women among the professionals is very clearly bound up with

---

[1] This research was supported by the Department of Anthropology, University of Edinburgh where I was employed as a research fellow. The fieldwork began in November 1967 and was completed in June, 1969. The research was broken by a five-month period during which I made a preliminary analysis of the data collected thus far. The writing of the research was supported by the Institute of Mental Health, Bethesda, Maryland (National Institute of Mental Health Fellowship No. 1 PO3 MH 34, 176-01 (CUAN) and a Fellowship from the American Association of University Women, Washington D.C. I have conducted further research in Sierra Leone (1970–1972) on family law supported by the Afrika-Studiecentrum, Leiden, Holland. However, the problems I discuss in this paper refer to the first period. My acquaintance with the elites greatly facilitated the later study that was not restricted to any particular social group.

[2] See Little and Price (1967) for a bibliography of most previous work.

outward conformity to the standards of Western ideas concerning marriage.[3]

At the same time certain traditional values persist among men and influence marital behavior. These include the importance of large numbers of children and the acceptance of extramarital sexual relations. Professional husbands frequently become involved in both short-term liaisons and permanent relationships with women who have come to be called "outside wives."[4] These extramarital unions and the children born to them impose a serious burden on the professional's income and, more to the point, threaten the legal wife's security and social position. As a result, there are complicated rules a man must follow in order to maintain the appearance of acceptable public behavior.

It would have been impossible for me to understand the structure of family organization and marital behavior without learning a good deal about these and other aspects of professional couples' lives. They, of course, had a considerable stake in keeping much of this information private.

THE PRESENTATION OF SELF UPON ENTERING THE FIELD

Before going to Sierra Leone I sought advice on how to describe the research to my informants. Several of my colleagues who had experience in West Africa believed that if I were explicit about my research topic, no one would agree to cooperate. One of them even suggested that I conceal my true aims and behave as a kind of lighthearted academic tourist.[5] I could not accept their advice. Instead, I decided to adopt a straightforward approach to this matter.

I explained to the informants that my research was part of a wider comparative study of marriage and family organization which the University of Edinburgh was launching. One scholar had already begun work in Ghana and another would commence soon in Scotland.[6] Most of my informants had achieved a high level of education, and it was necessary to discuss with them some of the theoretical background of the research. I referred to the common assumption in sociological literature that the extended family in Africa would

---

[3] For a full discussion see Harrell-Bond, 1975.
[4] See Baker and Bird, 1970; Izzett, 1961; Jellicoe, 1955; and Little and Price, 1967.
[5] Indeed, the official letter (for which I was not responsible) introducing my research to the university, pointed out that, although I would be doing a study of marriage, I would not be doing it among the Creoles, the group having the longest tradition of western education, implying that they were far too sophisticated to permit such research to be conducted in their midst. The special significance of the Creole group is described below.
[6] For a report of the Ghana study, see Oppong, 1973. The Edinburgh study has not yet appeared in print.

not survive the processes of modernization and industrialization. I explained that my study was, in part, an attempt to test this concept by finding out to what extent the patterns of family life among professional people in Sierra Leone had changed from the traditional mode. In contrast to the people living in remote villages, my informants were knowledgeable about and interested in such research. One man questioned me for more than an hour regarding the methodology I was adopting. In the course of our discussion he pointed out that his own thesis at Oxford had been a survey of the methods used in the social sciences, and he wanted to be fully assured that I was aware of the special problems of research in Africa. Only after he was satisfied on these points would he consent to be interviewed.

GAINING ACCEPTANCE AND ESTABLISHING RAPPORT

The task of gaining acceptance by persons in the upper echelons of Sierra Leone society presented some special challenges. To begin with there were difficulties simply because I was known to be an anthropologist conducting a study of elites. Had I been doing a village study I would have been introduced to the local population under the aegis of the local administrative officer and the village chief. They would have been officially encouraged to give me support by the Ministry of Interior representing the national government. The villagers would have had little or no opportunity to express an opinion about my presence among them.

These elites, on the other hand, were perfectly free to accept or reject my presence among them. If I were to have any informal social contact with them, it required that *they* invite me, since their social gatherings were both private and exclusive. Moreover, the problems of establishing rapport were even more complicated by the composition of the professional group, which can only be understood in terms of Sierra Leone's colonial history.

Freetown was a colony founded in 1787 for the resettlement of freed slaves from Britain, Canada, the United States, and the West Indies. They were later joined by others taken off slave ships captured on the high seas. These early settlers, later called Creoles, were given the benefits of western education and religion through the auspices of the philanthropists who had founded the Colony.[7] These people very early achieved high educational standards. Today, although Creoles number less than 2 percent of the population, they represent 64 percent of the professional group. Around the turn of the century, "Provincials," persons from indigenous tribal groups, began to compete educationally and now they also make up a significant proportion of

---

[7] For an excellent study of Creole society, see Porter, 1963 and Spitzer, 1974.

the professional group. Strong antagonisms exist between Creoles and Provincials. In addition, the indigenous population is divided into tribal factions. As if these problems were not enough, the research was conducted during a period of military rule that followed two coups. Another coup occurred while I was there (1968), and since then a state of emergency has been in force. Thus, it was necessary for me not only to succeed in becoming acquainted with this group of persons but also to keep on good terms with people who were competing politically with one another in a period of considerable stress.

It is seldom that the anthropologist has the opportunity to choose his first informants. Usually *they choose him,* in the sense that they are the first individuals to show friendliness or the willingness to talk about what interests them. The dangers of relying on these persons as long-term or exclusive sources of information has been discussed over and over among anthropologists. Sometimes they are marginal characters whose own position in the society is not well defined. However, it is quite obvious that the anthropologist conducting a traditional study is initially completely dependent on the assistance of these first willing individuals.

My own situation was quite different. I was faced with the necessity of enlisting the help of informants who would be willing to admit me into one of the more obscure areas of society — family life. Since I had chosen to make a direct approach, I could not slip into the households of these people under some guise and observe their behavior. My aim was to find a sufficient number of couples who would form a pilot group who were willing to endure prolonged, intensive interviews. They were to be selected so that they represented to some extent the composition of the professional group as I had come to know it.

My initial contacts were the Mende, an ethnic group that was out of political favor at the time.[8] One Mende woman agreed to assist me in getting acquainted with professional families. We tried calling on various Mende families, but no one seemed to be at home when we arrived. Later I discovered that as a result of the political tension, these people preferred to open the door to me, a stranger, when I was alone rather than in the company of someone, even a Mende, who knew them! I had to reorganize my approach to getting acquainted.

This early experience altered my choice of a location for the early phase of the research. Originally I had planned to begin intensive participant observation in an up-country town where there were only 26 professional families living. While I had thought that conducting intensive interviews in a place where most of the couples lived in close proximity was an ideal situation, this now seemed unwise, as my contacts with individual families would be imme-

---

[8] Professor Little's study of the Mende is reported in Little, 1967.

diately visible to all. The wisdom of this decision was confirmed by the fact that my Mende family friends, whom I came to know best at the outset and who kept track of my movements, often expressed criticism of my friendship with families of other ethnic backgrounds. I decided to center my initial fieldwork in Freetown, the capital of the country where the majority of the professionals lived. I was able to secure the names of possible candidates for the pilot group from doctors, welfare workers, and a lawyer. I began calling on these couples by myself.

HONESTY IN PRESENTING THE RESEARCH

After introducing myself to a couple, sometimes showing letters of introduction, I explained my research and how I should like them to help me. I told them that, although I was to study family life in Sierra Leone, I really knew nothing about it, and that in order to begin this task I wanted permission to come to see them, etiher together as a couple or individually, at least four times to ask questions and learn from them. I felt it was necessary to limit my request to only four formal appointments because of the general wariness that many expressed. One woman quite sincerely wondered aloud what her neighbors would think if this "colored woman" was coming around all the time.[9] In this way I was able to get a group of 14 couples to agree to cooperate. However, this approach presented me with a serious ethical dilemma: "How honest should I be in presenting myself and explaining my aims to informants?"

In the usual anthropological approach, the investigator sits chatting informally before finally getting round (and even then indirectly) to a discussion of his research interests. Because I was a stranger and had asked to visit only four times, it was necessary to give more direction to these sessions in order to justify my visits. It is not possible to ring the doorbell of a professional family in Africa or anywhere and, as a stranger, just sit down and observe behavior. I hoped that after the first four formal interviews had been completed, I would be well enough acquainted to drop in informally. Obviously, if I could become acquainted and trusted by these people it would be during these later informal sessions that I would obtain the most valuable data as a participant-observer rather than as an interviewer who was treated as a guest. Certainly, then, it can be said that my *motives* for these initial interviews were partially disguised, if not dishonest. In order to be a participant-observer among these couples I had to succeed in becoming a friend — or at least they would have to perceive me as a friend.

---

[9] She referred to me in this manner in a discussion with another couple who were her relatives.

I found myself consciously manipulating the situation to gain my hidden goals. Each time I called on a family during the first four visits I concentrated on establishing a close personal relationship. I brought small gifts of fruit or the like. (The "dash" or "shake hand" is a well-established institution in West Africa, and this was understood as the correct behavior for someone hoping to establish an enduring relationship.)[10] Although I had a list of questions and followed them in a semiformal way when necessary, I utilized every opportunity to enter into general discussions in the manner one would adopt in order to become thoroughly acquainted with another person. I told them about my family and showed them pictures of my children. When invited, I remained for meals. I invited couples to my flat and went shopping with some of the women. When I left Sierra Leone for a period of five months, I left my car in the care of one wife who had learned to drive but did not yet have her own vehicle. I also asked all these families what they would like me to purchase for them in Europe, and I kept in contact with them by letters while I was away.

Two of my children accompanied me when I returned for the second 10-month phase of the fieldwork, and they also went along on many of my visits to the families. We were welcomed, fed, and invited to family gatherings. More than once my children stayed with some of the families overnight and their children came to our home to play.

The ethical dilemma was that I was not being fully honest in the presentation of myself as a researcher who wanted only four interviews. I wanted those four interviews, but I intended that the personal commitment of the informants, enhanced by the "dash," would increase to the point that I could continue to drop into the house informally. Of course, this kind of involvement is what participant observation is really about, so I did not let the manipulatory aspects bother me too much. However, my actions led me into deeper waters than I had anticipated.

INTERACTING AS A PERSON

As the research progressed many of the wives came to regard me as their confidante, and all of the couples viewed me as their friend. My second dilem-

---

[10] The "dash" or "shake hand" is a small token gift which is given to establish an obligatory relationship, as in the case of a visit to the chief. An individual arriving in a chiefdom or village presents himself to the chief and offers a gift (the amount being dependent on the visitor's status). By accepting the gift the chief assumes the obligation to offer hospitality and safekeeping to the visitor for as long as he is in the village and to attempt to meet any requests the visitor may have. The dash may also be used to acknowledge some nonmonetary service that has been rendered and to strengthen good relations should the service be required again.

ma arose when confidential information I had received from one person was in danger of being leaked to another, or worse yet, was requested by another person who wanted to know what his/her spouse was doing behind his/her back.

One woman, suffering serious problems in her marriage, asked me to accompany her on a visit to a family counselor in the Ministry of Social Welfare. I found it very difficult, but necessary, to avoid going with her especially since her husband was officially connected with this department.

I was asked to give advice on a whole series of complicated marital and family problems. When one wife packed her belongings and moved out, the husband wanted me to intervene. He hoped that if I would act as the intermediary, he could avoid the traditional method of asking his relatives to settle the argument. Of course, hearing about and witnessing such problems gave me invaluable insights into the topic I was investigating, but the ambiguity of my role became a source of serious personal introspection. For example, a wife might discuss with me her anguish about her husband's extramarital relations and ask me to try to find out whom he was seeing. At the same time her husband would be informing me in quite different terms about his relationships with other women and his responsibilities for his illegitimate children. The attitudes I was forced to assume in these sessions with men and women had to be, because of my research aims, completely hypocritical. I could not express my opinions when talking with a man if I expected to get any information. On the other hand, I could not help but be understanding and sympathetic with a wife who was expressing her insecurity and distress.

I became involved in other ways. I was often asked to loan money. However, my one unsuccessful attempt to collect a loan led me into a fuller appreciation of the workings of the extended family and general attitudes about reciprocity among relatives and friends. On several occasions I was asked to take a child back to England with my own family for education. Some people still assume that there will always be room for one of their relatives to live in my home while he is studying in Britain. On more than one occasion such a young person has resided with us temporarily. I once needed some clerical assistance, and a professional man secured a relative to do this work. When I sought his advice on how much to pay, a rather exorbitant figure was suggested. I realized that he was using me to help lift his enormous financial burden, a burden all the professionals carry for the members of their extended families.

One of the few violent incidents that occurred during the coup in 1968 involved one of the families in my pilot group. Soldiers came to the house looking for one man, and being very sure he was hiding there, had peppered the walls of the interior with bullet holes. The couple had been away at the time, and when they returned to find their house in that condition the husband asked me to photograph every wall, to have the pictures developed, and to return them to him so that he could use them in an official complaint to the government. I shared his alarm over what had happened, particularly because there had been eight children of under 14 years of age and an old woman in the house at the time of the incident. I could not refuse to take the pictures, although had it become known that I had done so the government might very well have interpreted this as interfering with the internal politics of the country. Fortunately, I was able to accomplish this without notice being taken.

LEAVING THE FIELD

During the fieldwork it became increasingly difficult to sustain such intensive relationships with these 14 families. Later, I administered a standardized interview to a sample of the entire professional group (160 interviews), so naturally I was busy with this and other aspects of the research.[11] Some of the families registered disappointment when I stopped making regular visits to their homes. I had so many invitations for meals and social events from them that it was impossible to accept them all.

The anthropologist who does, for example, a more traditional study of a village is, perhaps, largely spared such problems — at least, they are not so forcibly imposed on him. The villagers know at the outset that one day he will leave and that continual communication is usually out of the question. The people with whom I was involved are my educational and social equals. They write letters and expect me to answer them. They frequently travel to Europe and come visit me. Once I had the mortifying experience of momentarily failing to recognize one of the husbands when I unexpectedly met him in London. More than a year after I left the field, one of these families traveled to Britain where the husband was to take a course. The wife suffered a miscarriage. I invited her to stay with our family for a few days to recover. It was discovered that she required surgery, and she remained in our household for five months. In similar ways I am continually faced with the realization that there is no way to "bow out" of such relationships, while at the same time it is humanly impossible to continue so many close friendships.

In order to accomplish my research goals I had spent a lot of time creating friendship bonds with people who initially were not interested in that relationship. Then, after many months of initiating social interaction, and after they had decided to become my friend, I changed the rules of the game, so to speak. First, I began to draw back from the relationships, reduced the amount of interaction, and eventually I left the field altogether. It is true that

---

[11]See Harrell-Bond, 1972 for further discussion of the methods used in this study.

many people took advantage of our bonds, and properly so, to visit and stay with me in England. Furthermore, the course of these friendships was not a great deal different from what frequently occurs in such relationships. However, underlying the entire process was my realization that my intentions were mixed and that I had manipulated the relationships for the purpose of research.

WRITING AND PUBLISHING

The final ethical problem that I still face in my research among these professionals in Sierra Leone is the matter of maintaining confidentiality. The professional group in Sierra Leone is very small. At the time of my fieldwork there were only 754 persons who held professional qualifications and were living and working in the country. While I realized that these people were often closely connected through kinship and that most were acquainted with each other, I was surprised to learn just how much they knew of one another's personal affairs. I often showed a list of the professional group to individuals to see just how many they knew. I was amazed to discover that some individuals could go through almost the entire list and tell me details about the political affiliation, the ethnic background of the spouse, the educational achievements of the individual, and even more personal details. In the first report of my research I used a large number of case studies and verbatim accounts for illustrative purposes. To my horror I discovered that although I had taken great care to conceal the identity of individuals concerned, almost everyone who read the material could recognize who was involved.

For example, I handed one chapter to a woman to read. It contained a case study about a professional who told me that he was the illegitimate son of a retired professional person. He explained the unpleasant relationship he had had with his father's wife and the neglect he and his mother had suffered through the years. He also disclosed other personal information about his own marriage and that of his father. Halfway through her reading she told me the names of all the individuals involved and gave me even further information. I was glad that she was not one of the persons I had interviewed for the research, or she might have been understandably alarmed at how much of her own personal life might soon be in print. As a result of this problem, much rich illustrative material had to be discarded in the final writing of my research for publication. The rights of privacy had to take precedence over the claims of science for well-documented data.

SUMMARY AND CONCLUSIONS

In working with the elite of an African country I encountered several ethical problems of varying severity. The initial problem was that of presenting myself honestly without jeopardizing further and more intensive contact. In the end, I carried out a piece of deception that I am not able fully to justify.

The second problem arose when my first plan succeeded and I became more deeply involved in people's personal lives than I had anticipated. I was under constant pressure to divulge information that had been given to me in confidence. I was successful in resisting the pressure and protecting my sources. At the same time, some of my worries about my earlier manipulating faded as I found myself just as obviously manipulated.

The third problem came when I left the field. I had to cut the bonds that I had so carefully woven with the people, and perhaps in the process hurt the feelings of some.

The final problem continues to plague me. The best information in anthropology is often the most detailed. However, I had to disguise identities and often events just to be able to publish them without hurting my informants. The community was so small, so educated, and so vulnerable to gossip that any other course would have wrought havoc on their social organization.

It would, of course, be more satisfying to you as well as to me if I could conclude this discussion with a report of how I resolved these ethical dilemmas. In short, I have not resolved them. Moreover, I suspect that they are inherent in all the participant observational research conducted by anthropologists. It is simply always a great deal easier to avoid facing up to them when our field research is conducted among a remote and nonliterate group.

REFERENCES

Baker, T. and M. Bird

    1959   "Urbanization and the position of Women," *Sociological Review*, Vol. 7, No. 1, New Series.

Harrell-Bond, B. E.

    1972   "Survey Research in a Study of Marriage" in *Solving Problems of Survey Research in Africa,* O'Barr, Spain, and Tessler (eds.). Evanston: Northwestern University Press.

    1975   *Modern Marriage In Sierra Leone: A Study of the Professional Group.* Den Hague: Mouton.

Izzett, A.

    1961   "Family Life Among the Yoruba in Lagos, Nigeria" in *Social Change in Modern Africa,* A. W. Southall (ed.). London: Oxford University Press.

Jellicoe, G.

    1955   Unpublished London University Diploma in Social Anthropology Thesis.

Little, K. L.

    1967   *The Mende of Sierra Leone* (First Edition 1951). London: Routledge.

Little, K. L. and A. Price

    1967   "Some Trends in Modern Marriage Among West Africans," *Africa*, Vol. 37, No. 4, October.

Oppong, C.

    1974   *Marriage Among a Matrilineal Elite.* Cambridge: Cambridge University Press.

Porter, A. T.

    1963   *Creoledom.* London: Oxford University Press.

Spitzer, L.

    1974   *The Creoles of Sierra Leone.* Madison: University of Wisconsin Press.

9
THE ANTHROPOLOGIST IN THE FIELD: SCIENTIST, FRIEND, AND VOYEUR

JUDITH FRIEDMAN HANSEN

Judith Friedman Hansen received her Ph.D. in 1970 from the University of California, Berkeley. She is currently Assistant Professor of Anthropology at Indiana University, Bloomington. She has conducted fieldwork among Danish-Americans in California (1966–1968) and in Denmark (1968–1969). Her specialties include urban anthropology, symbolic interaction, and social anthropology. She is the author of "The Cultural Analysis of Schooling," "Proxemics and the Interpretive Process," and "The Proxemics of Danish Daily Life."

Our arrival in Copenhagen, Denmark, a city of some one and three quarters of a million people, was greeted by flowers, waving flags, smiles, and the clicking of cameras. No, the fanfare wasn't directed at some celebrity we had followed off the plane; it was indeed for my husband and me. The exuberant warmth of that welcome provided the data for my first field notes, but it also presaged the ethical dilemmas I was to encounter in the course of my year of study.

Like many other anthropologists, my choice of a fieldwork site had been influenced by a variety of factors. I wished to study social networks and interpersonal interaction in a city outside the United States. This was balanced by the fact that my husband's research in classics and folklore required access to a high quality library. My acquaintance with many Danish-Americans and my husband's own Danish ancestry combined to make Denmark a particularly promising place to conduct such research. We anticipated that his family connections and our preliminary familiarity with the culture would simplify entry into Danish society. By the time we actually arrived in Copenhagen, friends and kinsmen of his family had learned of our plans to study there through an exchange of letters. Their response was generous and thoroughly hospitable, from our welcome at the airport, to the apartment they had found for us in spite of a housing shortage, to the advice and assistance they gave us in getting settled in an unfamiliar society. It would be many months before I understood the full significance of these actions and, even more important, the meaning of friendship among Danes. Because these and other friends were later to provide me with crucial data in my research, they themselves became part of a continuing ethical dilemma.

Denmark is a small country, both geographically and demographically. Its population is also rather stable residentially, even in the metropolis of Copenhagen. Kinship is the basis of the most important relationships in an individual's social world and close adult friendships are almost always the result of bonds established long before among childhood play- and schoolmates. Hospitality to strangers is generous but limited in scope: an initial welcome to a foreign visitor is unlikely to be followed up by more extensive informal social contact. Many such visitors have commented to me that, in their view, Danish hospitality is a myth, for they have themselves found their gestures of friendship rebuffed and social contacts outside the formal arena of work kept at a minimum by their Danish hosts. What such visitors rarely understand is that Danes spend most of their leisure time with kinsmen and close friends and thus have little to spare for transient visitors. Furthermore, Danes tend to view friendship as the product of many years of interaction. When, after a year's residence in Denmark several people commented that we were their friends, they spoke with some surprise and even awe that this could be true, given the short time-depth of our relationship. That so many hearts and homes were opened to us during that time, in spite of the relatively closed social networks that surround Danes, was thus a gift for which we were exceptionally grateful.

"WHAT ARE YOU STUDYING?"

This question, one of the first put to us by the friends who received us, was asked repeatedly as our circle of acquaintances widened. Americans? Living in Denmark for a year? Why? Studying? Oh, you're students at the University. No? Well, what are you studying? Every ethnographer must explain his presence, his reasons for being there, to those he hopes to study. Due to the type of research in which I was engaged, I found the question difficult to answer clearly. I wanted to learn about the underlying rules, values, and understandings that Danes take for granted in everyday behavior. Because they take them for granted (as people in any society do), they don't think about them as significant topics of study. Basically, I told questioners I wanted to find out how Danes think about things, how they do things; to put it simply, I wanted to learn how to be a Dane. Though this seemed an odd sort of goal, it was apparently accepted. In fact as my behavior shifted from an American cultural style to a style more closely approximating that of my Danish hosts, I was graciously complimented: "Ah, Judith, now you are becoming a good Dane!" Yet what lay behind this was a complex fabric of perception and interaction, fraught with what I felt to be a fundamental ethical dilemma for me as a participant-observer.

Meanwhile the central members of our adopted social network were busily entertaining us and offering us assistance of every kind. We were both guests from American and honorary members of the extended family. In these roles we were invited to every festive occasion of the kin group (of which there were many, from individual birthdays, weddings, and the like, to numerous annual holiday celebrations) as well as to more casual nuclear family gatherings. We were taken on tours of places our hosts thought might interest us or give us pleasure such as historic sites, pleasure parks, beer factories, homes for the aged. We were counseled as to where to shop and how to handle business transactions. Although some large supermarkets carried a wide range of diverse products, most shops were highly specialized in the goods they carried and one might search in vain at a local "grocery store" for an item such as facial tissue or, in some instances, fresh produce and meat. Even writing a check to pay for a bill involved a different procedure than in the United States. We were provided access to special services one or another of our adopted kinsmen could arrange such as discounted film supplies or camera equipment or a television at wholesale price. Current events noted in newspapers or on television were patiently explained to us and our often-halting attempts to speak coherent Danish were complimented extravagantly. We were even brought into the telephone network of communications whereby extended family members kept up with each other between frequent gatherings. These were but a fraction of our hosts' efforts on our behalf. There was no way to fully repay these kindnesses, nor were we expected to. Our appreciation and our attempts to reciprocate in ways we could were evidence of our goodwill.

At base the personal conflict I confronted rests on a right I value for both myself and others: the right to privacy. There are several facets to this problem but I shall concentrate on two here to point up the issues involved. The first reflects the contradictions inherent in the dual roles of detached observer and participant-friend. The second revolves around information people provided unwittingly, revealing without knowing it far more than they intended to. Before I discuss my Danish experiences in this light, it will be helpful to look at a similar example from a quite different culture that Gerald Berreman discussed in his monograph *Behind Many Masks*.

In studying a mountain village in Northern India that was rather hostile to strangers and sensitive about possible misinterpretation or negative evaluation of legal practices, Berreman found much important data revealed to him as a by-product of local disputes and distrust. Members of one faction would tell him more about their own situations than they might otherwise have chosen to, in order to counteract the "bad impression" of them they assumed he had been given by members of opposing factions. By pooling the data thus gained and using it subtly to obtain still more, the ethnographer succeeded in acquiring a much fuller understanding of the actual daily life of villagers. The reality that lay behind the ideal facade that villagers collaborated to present to visitors was less peaceful and far more complex than a casual observer might have suspected. Berreman, following Erving Goffman, terms these two vantage points of observation "front stage" and "backstage." "Front stage" is behavior that group participants engage in for "public" benefit, the ways of being and doing and thinking that they wish observers to perceive as characteristic of them. Often this entails a playing down of disagreement, hostility, and conflict of interest among group members in favor of a more united image. "Backstage" the cooperative effort at image maintenance relaxes and the rockier terrain of everyday life, complete with bickering, violation of traditional or ideal rules of behavior, and other human weaknesses, dominates the scene.

I began my fieldwork in typical fashion, intent on watching closely and listening attentively to everything that occurred. From the first weary day, exhilarated by the trip but exhausted by jet lag and the anxiety of embarking on a year's research in a strange country, I kept a detailed journal of everything I could remember about actions and conversations, participants, and settings. Note taking was frustrating in the extreme, for I knew I was seeing far less of the detail that makes up any social situation than was there and yet to write up notes of even a couple of hours' interaction with Danes took several hours of careful description at my desk. Nevertheless, I knew from my training that what might now appear to be a trivial bit of data could well prove significant in the light of long-term observation. Information poured in from all sides at a faster rate than I could process it — from newspapers, T.V., and radio, from acquaintances and strangers, from explicit instruction and answers to questions by informants, and from their incidental comments and spontaneous reactions to new situations.

Still, we were guests and outsiders. The backstage of interpersonal conflict, private family problems, and actual as opposed to ideal attitudes and behavior were carefully screened from us by cooperative effort. After all, we would only be there for a limited period of time and it was best that we return to America with a view of Danish life as it *should* be lived, not of the "imperfect" version actually characteristic behind the scenes. As time went on and we got together more often privately with segments of the extended network as well as with the kin group as a whole, the props of the front stage began to tilt. Our company was seen as a valuable commodity and each segment began subtly to vie for our time and loyalty. Concerned lest we be misled (and disaffected) by unsympathetic accounts about them given by another family member, uncertain as to just what we might have already been told by one or another, various members began to reveal to us their versions of the internal dynamics of the family as a whole and "facts" they considered significant about other members. Most often this information was conveyed in confidence in one-to-one or one-to-two-of-us interactions. We respected the confidences and never revealed them to others, but our very silence increased the uncertainty of each segment about "how much we knew" and called forth further counterrevelations and occasional probing questions.

Embarrassed by our role as valued allies, we strove to avoid taking sides or increasing our commitment to one segment at the expense of another. Our position as relatively detached outsiders enabled us to see the validity of each of the versions of the family "script" presented to us. It was at this point that I began to realize the fundamental anthropological dilemma built into the dual role of participant and observer, between the intimate commitment of friendship and the analytic detachment of the scientific observer. The confidential information I received was given to me in my role as friend. Yet I was also an anthropologist and everything I heard or observed was potentially relevant to my understanding of the dynamics of Danish interaction.

ANTHROPOLOGIST OR FRIEND?

At about two o'clock one afternoon, Inge and I sat drinking afternoon coffee together, I on the couch, she across the long, narrow coffee table on a low stool. We had just fetched her son from nursery school and were relaxing with meandering conversation.

"Judith, there is something I want to talk to you about." I looked at Inge with concern; she appeared suddenly tense and troubled.

"Of course, Inge. What is it?"

"There is something I want to explain to you before you hear about it from others. If you haven't already," she added with a bitter note.

I waited, puzzled.

"You know the house Jens and I are going to buy?" I nodded.

"Well, when we first decided to buy it — there just isn't enough space here with only two rooms for the three of us and the fourth we'll soon have, even though the rent is very cheap — anyway, we went to Jens' parents and asked them if they would be willing to lend us part of the down payment. It seemed simpler than going to a bank, and all they had to do was say yes or no. But instead they started in telling us we couldn't afford it, we were irresponsible about money, and they wanted to see our financial records. They berated us for just having gotten a new car when the old one was still perfectly good — Judith, the repair bills were getting so high it made much more sense to get a new one. Don't you think?"

"I'm sure the two of you are the best judges of that. Why do you think they reacted that way?"

"I don't know. They never wanted Jens to be an engineer, they thought he had enough schooling. But he did it on his own anyway. And they never liked me — they thought I wasn't good enough for him."

"Why? I can't imagine your not being 'good enough' for anyone."

Inge smiled gratefully. "Thanks. That's because you're my friend. Another cup of coffee?"

After telling me a little about the history of her relationship with Jens, she went on:

"But about the loan, you know what was worse? After they talked to us and we understood that they didn't want to lend us the money, that should have been the end of it. But then Jens' father got on the phone and called *my* parents and told them Jens was an irresponsible spendthrift, and they should tell us not to get involved in such foolishness."

"What did your parents say?"

"I don't know, they were embarrassed by it and just tried to be polite, I guess. But they were kind of shocked."

"They don't think you're that way."

"No, they like Jens..."

Inge brought this topic up because she anticipated my hearing a very different version from her parents-in-law and she wanted to set the "facts" of the situation straight. She also talked about it because she considered me a friend and she was troubled. As her friend I understood and sympathized. She and I both knew this was the way friendship was; an unspoken contract provided the basis for our shared trust. Later that day I would record this conversation, alone, without her knowledge, in my role as anthropologist. In my role as investigator her conversation became "data." Would she have spoken so frankly about this and other more intimate subjects had she understood that I listened in *both* roles, not only as friend? Would others have done so? True, I had said I was an anthropologist, I had told Inge and other Danes that I was there to study Danish ways of living and thinking. But as we began to relate on a human to human basis rather than merely as American visitor to native Dane, this ceased to be an active factor in people's perception of our interactions and they talked with me as a friend who would respect the confidences they shared with me.

As members of American society, we frequently voice a strong value for the right to individual privacy, a concern for the violation of that right by credit investigators, law enforcement officials, or independent snoopers. Danes, too, hold this value. Moreover they less often find it threatened by investigations of one kind or another because the value is so pervasive in their society as a whole. Between individuals the rarity of friendship which is not based on long association and enduring commitment means that relatively few people have knowledge of the more intimate events of another person's life. In the United States it is not uncommon for two people to meet and exchange rather detailed life histories after a comparatively short period of acquaintance. Bartenders and hairdressers as confidantes are cliches in our society. But how many of us have not met a co-worker or a fellow student or a stranger at a party whom we felt enough liking for that "friendship" rapidly followed? More generally, how many of those individuals we count as friends are people we have known since childhood, and how many are persons we have come to know later in our lives? As I noted earlier, adult Danes are far less likely to make friends and share intimacies on short acquaintance than Americans. Therefore, the gift of personal vulnerability that people such as Inge entrusted to me was a rich gift indeed, one granted in good faith between friends.

THE ANTHROPOLOGIST AS VOYEUR

However, there is another side to this problem one equally fundamental to the study of people's daily lives as private individuals. In addition to all the information that was provided to me directly, whether casually or in confidence, a great deal was revealed unwittingly. Again, let me contrast the United States and Denmark for a moment. In the United States the psychological insights of Freud and many other students of human foibles have become translated into language any layman can understand and widely disseminated in popular books and periodicals. As a result, the "average" person has a working knowledge, though frequently somewhat skewed or stereotypic, of subtle implications of other people's behavior. Dreams are an example. Many people take for granted that dreams have "meanings," that they can be interpreted as clues to the dreamer's personality or internal psychological process. We often talk casually about another individual as being "neurotic" or "paranoid" or suffering from an "Oedipus complex." This generalized awareness of psychology and of the readily observable clues people give as to their own internal dynamics tends to make many Americans somewhat self-conscious about their own behavior. How many times have you heard someone say something they hadn't intended and heard the response — "that must have been a Freudian slip!"? That is, the speaker has just betrayed his private self by his words.

Psychology and psychologizing are much less part of popular culture in Denmark. Danes are not naive about understanding people pragmatically; they are as shrewd in their assessments of others as any other humans. But they make much less explicit use of "lay psychology" in interpersonal interactions, and as a result, are less self-conscious about controlling their self-presentations in this light. As an observer enculturated in the United States and trained to perceive very subtle cues in interpersonal communication, I found myself often feeling as if I were in the midst of a psychological nudist camp — but one in which everyone assumed they were fully clothed. As an American I was accustomed to protective masks on the selves of my fellows, and I felt uneasy, even guilty, about perceiving so much that was not intended for my eyes. From my vantage point as anthropologist, this type of data was very relevant to my understanding the dynamics of Danish behavior. Yet my perception of it, though generally unrecognized by the Danes with whom I lived and worked, constituted a violation of their right to personal privacy. Because they granted this personal space to one another, they took for granted that it was equally operative in their relationships with me.

The following example illustrates one such instance. Grete and Jørgen, a delightful young couple in their middle twenties, had a three-year-old son, Harald. Grete had been born and raised in Norway, but had settled in Denmark permanently on meeting and marrying Jørgen. She was a student at the University and was trying with some difficulty to satisfactorily complete her education and be a good wife and mother. Very sympathetic to her goals, Jørgen provided as much assistance in housekeeping and child care as he could when he was off work, but Grete's own strong feelings about fulfilling all three of these roles to the utmost of her ability created standards that she never, in her own perception, was able to meet adequately. The continual conflicting demands on her energy and involvement sometimes made her irritable and impatient with both Jørgen and Harald. Her husband, understanding the sources of her tension, responded calmly, ignoring or gently teasing away her occasional rancorous remarks and actions. Neither of them, however, seemed to be aware of the impact of her communications on little Harald. An active and curious child, his exploring behavior and general rambunctiousness earned him frequent rebukes from his mother. Indeed, it was toward him that most of her irritation was expressed. It disturbed me to see it, yet I was reluctant to say anything, both because it would have been considered an unwarranted intrusion on my part and because Grete saw herself as a loving mother. She had enough burdens without the additional weight of my perceptions as an outsider. My observations of the interactional pattern between mother and son were climaxed painfully one afternoon when Harald burst out to his mother — "I wish you were dead!" This would not be an uncommon statement by a frustrated child in our culture, but Grete, hurt and shocked by it, retorted "I wish you were too!" Then, "That's a terrible thing to say to someone, Harald. If that's the way you feel, then I don't want to have anything to do with you." Harald by this point was visibly uneasy, trying to embrace his mother and erase the strong tension that surrounded them, but she ignored him and resumed her conversation with me.

Both of these types of situations, exemplified by the conversation with Inge and the afternoon with Grete and her family, entail revelations of self that the actor involved would be loath to present "publicly." As such, published description of them constitutes an invasion of the individuals' right to privacy. In the first case, as I have pointed out, the information was given to me as a trusted confidante and thereby is enmeshed in unspoken but mutually understood values about the responsibilities of friendship. In the second case, Grete was unaware of how much she was communicating, yet my understanding of its contextual significance and my being allowed to witness such a spontaneous outburst was in itself a reflection of growing friendship and trust between us.

The ethical implications of publication thus stem from the dual roles I played as (1) anthropological researcher with the goal of extending our understanding of human behavior and (2) participant in Danish daily life, who, as a human being, developed close personal relationships with many of the Danes I met. That I did not remain fully detached from the flow of Danish life might be seen as a failure in my role as objective analyst, yet to understand the subtle dynamics of Danish behavior *required* as detailed a knowledge of individual Danes as I had the capacity to acquire. Access to this information was made possible by friendship, and once established that relationship imposed standards of behavior at least as compelling (to me) as the rules of my discipline.

When I set forth on fieldwork one of my goals was to study the social networks of urban Danes, that is, the network of personal relationships in which people are involved and the types and characteristics of their relationships. Since Danish circles of kinsmen and friends tend to be closed to outsiders, we were very fortunate to be drawn into an established social network on our arrival. Members of this network thus became important sources of information. Another of my research goals was to discover the rules, values, and meanings that underlie interpersonal interaction in Denmark. This required, of course, that I observe as many instances of people interacting as I could. But it also entailed close attention to minute details of these events and to the subtleties of interpretation that participants made of them. In other words it required that I come to know the people involved very well — which inevitably went hand in hand with the growth of friendship between us. Thus the solicitous concern of our Danish hosts and their gracious acceptance of two foreigners in the midst of their daily lives was not just personally heartwarming but also very important for the success of the research. In fact it enabled me to penetrate to a depth of understanding of Danish culture that would otherwise have required several years of more superficial contact to acquire. A different choice of research problem might bypass the ethical conflicts this created.

If the researcher's focus is on abstract features of "social structure" or other types of analysis that are conceptually more or less divorced from the day-to-day reality of people's lives, such detail may be irrelevant to the scientific product as, for example, in a study of cultural ecology or an analysis of the social functions of ritual. It is when the researcher's central concern entails explanation of the microprocesses of human interaction (which ultimately generate the larger complex of behavior and understandings that we refer to as "social structure") that the ethical dilemma I have posed becomes critical. One reason for this is the rule governing any scientific enterprise, that is, that the scientist's analyses and conclusions must be adequately documented by reference to the concrete data on which they are based. Only in this way can conclusions presented be adequately assessed by other scholars and validated (or disconfirmed) by further research.

CONCLUSION

I have suggested that two ethical conflicts confronted me continually in my Danish research, the one inherent in my dual role as anthropologist and friend, the other a result of the disparity between what others willingly shared with me and what they revealed without realizing that they had done so. In the latter instance I played the role of professional "voyeur," a person who violates another's right to privacy by observing behavior that is not intended for public viewing. In the first case I have attempted to resolve the conflict by my choice of data for publication. As much as possible, I have drawn the data to document my analysis publicly from observations that did not violate my personal responsibilities to individual Danes. In the process much highly pertinent data has been omitted. In several instances, however, I felt compelled to include evidence that *did* violate the implicit expectations of privacy; so the ethical conflict remains. Certainly I have taken pains to change all names and edit out material that might pinpoint an individual's identity for those who know him, but even here I have not been entirely successful, for too radical a change would result in data that were not, in fact, representative of the reality I observed. My failures in this regard were brought home to me when I presented copies of my initial report to those with whom I had worked most closely — they had no difficulty seeing themselves behind the veneer of my editing nor in recognizing others whom they knew. That they were willing to set aside their feelings of unexpected exposure in the interest of continued friendship is a tribute to their tolerance and graciousness.

The second type of conflict has been more difficult to resolve. For the purposes of publication of data gathered in this way, I have made similar decisions, compromising between scientific requirements of adequate documentation and the rights of individuals to privacy. But is this enough? Is it ethical for someone highly trained in the art of penetrating "backstage" behavior to observe others who are not equipped, either by training or by expectation, to protect themselves from unwanted exposure? The importance of this question goes far beyond my own limited research, for social scientists in general are trained to be effective in just this way: as skillful snoopers. How then are we to protect the integrity of those we study in light of our research goals?

In discussing these aspects of anthropological ethics with others, I have encountered a range of reactions. Frequently the argument is made that, as long as the precise identity of individuals is disguised, the publication of confidential data is necessary for the "greater good" of scientific understanding and thereby of humanity. I would not dispute that the fuller our knowledge of human behavior, the more readily we may be able to solve the social problems that plague our world. However, I am skeptical of the significance of these efforts if, in the process, we reduce those with whom we interact (whether in the field or in our own society) to objects, by treating them merely as impersonal sources of data or as means to scientific ends. As an anthropologist committed to increasing cross-cultural and interpersonal understanding, I think it is vital that we realize the roles we play in the host communities we study, and respect the person-to-person relationships that develop between us and our informants as fully as we would those that characterize our private lives in our homeland. This does not preclude objective analysis of the data we gather, but it demands that we remember the *sources* of our insight, the human beings who gave of themselves in providing them. It demands that the requirements of our discipline for accurate and adequate documentation of results be balanced with responsible concern for the personal rights and well-being of those we study among. In concrete terms this means that we must not take our "rights of access" to the personal lives of our informants for granted. We must protect their rights to privacy as vigilantly as we protect our own. In telling others of the details of their lives, we must make every effort to do so in ways that do not violate their integrity as fellow human beings whose actual thoughts, acts, and feelings are far more complex than our descriptions can convey. The ethical standards of our profession can be met only if we examine very carefully the proposition that a "greater good" will be served by compromising the immediate bonds of trust and good faith. It is just such a consideration that prompts the present essay.

10
SECRET SOCIETIES AND THE ETHICS OF URBAN FIELDWORK

NOEL J. CHRISMAN

Noel J. Chrisman is an Assistant Professor in the Department of Comparative Nursing Care Systems, School of Nursing, University of Washington. He has carried out research in west coast cities examining the construction of social relationships and their implications for health behavior and urban adaptation. He has written "Middle Class Communitas: The Fraternal Order of Badgers," and "Situation and Social Network in Cities." He edited, with John Friedl, *City Ways: A Selective Reader in Urban Anthropology.* His current research focuses upon subcultural variation in health and illness behavior, particularly the relationship of social network composition to the process of lay consultation and referral.

My first foray into the Danish-American community in the San Francisco Bay Area took me to the home of Mr. and Mrs. Arne Ostergaard in November, 1964. Mrs. Ostergaard (this name, like those of all other participants in the study, has been changed to preserve some degree of anonymity), the primary spokesperson of the two, was obviously delighted to tell a visitor about *her* people. She showed me photographs taken in Denmark, her award from the D.A.R., and *Bien,* the Danish language newspaper. The paper, she said, was very important to Bay Area Danes because it reminded them of meetings and other future social events. She showed me the list of Danish clubs and associations with their meeting dates, touting her favorites.

After about an hour, Mrs. Ostergaard went to the kitchen to prepare *eftermiddagskaffe,* a snack of coffee and pastry that I later came to expect during any visit with a Danish immigrant. During her absence, I asked her husband if he belonged to any of the Danish voluntary associations. Mr. Ostergaard replied that he had belonged to the Danish Brotherhood in the past. When I asked him to tell me about it, he exhibited some embarrassment and said he could not because it was secret. Secrecy had been stressed during the initiation ritual when "they kind of scare ya." The subject was dropped when Mrs. Ostergaard returned with the refreshments and we returned to a discussion of her favorite Danish associations, none of which was secret. After another hour of conversation, I departed with fieldnotes, the address of the Danish newspaper, and two related ethical problems: the conflict of my multiple identities, and the problem of publicizing ritually secret behavior.

These two issues are not uncommon in anthropological research, but they were particularly salient in my investigation because the Danish-American community was residentially dispersed. If I were to study Danish-American social life, I was not going to find it on the streets of an urban district as William Foote Whyte had found his streetcorner Italian-Americans in Boston (1955). Ethnic life for these Danish immigrants was less public, more invisible to the outside world. Access to private lifeways would require a different, and more delicate, approach than that traditionally used by anthropologists in the field. Such an approach heightened the impact of the subtle interplay of my various personal identities. For example, my relative youth and Danish ancestry contributed in a positive way to the "participant" aspect of my participant-observer role. However, success as a native tended to overshadow the necessity to maintain the public researcher stance required to protect the private interests of informants.

Complicating the process of carrying out research among a dispersed population was the fact that two of the central ethnic institutions of the community were secret societies. I had determined that much of the behavior that could be labeled "ethnic" took place within the confines of these two fraternal organizations, protected from public scrutiny by walls of ritual secrecy. If Danish-American social life had been visible and had occurred in neighborhoods, as reported for other ethnic groups, I could have focused on this public behavior, hoping to gather data on the associations only as they had an impact on other spheres of life. In the absence of a localized community, however, this avenue was closed to me. In addition, I had discovered the futility of asking *about* the clubs from Mr. Ostergaard; even this former member refused to give me information. Thus, I decided to join the two secret societies, an action which would make me a member of this invisible community. Although I could foresee no immediate negative consequences of this decision, I realized that when the investigation was complete, it would be necessary to confront the issue of how to report ritually secret behavior.

On a conceptual level, the issues of multiple identity conflict and publicizing ritually secret behavior are temporally distant: the former is an immediate problem in defining the researcher's role; the latter is located at the conclusion of the study when results are to be published. Pragmatically, however, the two were closely intertwined during the conduct of the research project. For example, my membership in the secret societies identified me as a Danish-American community member, an identity that was immediately evident to all who met me in a lodge setting. It is not surprising, therefore, that the Danes tended to forget that I was doing research — a memory lapse that reduced their opportunities to conceal information from publication and increased the necessity for me to remind them. In addition, I had to carefully note data gathered during meetings, when I was bound by rules of ritual secrecy, so that I could refrain from publishing them if there were a question when the investigation was complete.

MULTIPLE IDENTITIES AND THE RESEARCHER ROLE

My choices of research role and investigative techniques for this project among Danish-American immigrants were conditioned most heavily by the traditional anthropological training I had received in graduate school. However, few ethnographic studies of urban American communities existed in 1964—1966 that could be used as models; and none of these had been written about "invisible" Northern European ethnic groups. I was committed to the technique of participant-observation as my primary field method and anticipated forming close personal relationships with informants. One advantage of such an approach is the degree of openness in social relationships with members of the studied group. This openness not only generates a better atmosphere for gathering data, but it also increases the researcher's empathy with the people among whom he or she works. This possible identification, through participation, suggests that the investigator may be in a position to assess native feelings about ethical issues. For example, I certainly felt more strongly about safeguarding fraternal secrets once I had been initiated into the lodges and was sworn to secrecy.

Being an observer as well as a participant requires that the researcher role be visible. In tribal situations such visibility is almost automatic — an anthropologist's national identity and nosy questions leave little doubt about his purposes in the village. However, I was working in my own country among people with a similar ethnic background. Nonetheless, having adopted participant-observation as a technique for gathering information, I used the model of the tribal researcher as an aid in making decisions about how to become integrated into the Danish-American community. Conceiving of the Danes as just one more human group to be studied eased any ethical problems involved in attempting to enter the secret societies for research purposes. I reasoned that if I clearly identified myself as a researcher wishing to document the patterns of urban social life among Danish immigrants, I could gain access to the associations — and, through them, to the community of Danish-Americans — and complete my research.

That this stance was overly simplistic and naive began to be apparent both from further reading in the anthropological literature and from further contacts with Danish community members. I recognized that non-Western villagers accepted intruding anthropologists partly because of their implied power as members of a complex industrial society; that is, as a representative of the United States, the anthropologist could be used to better the political or economic position of the village. In addition, the anthropologist frequently became a real economic resource through his ability to pay informants or to aid in accomplishing community projects. I realized that I had no such economic or political power to offer and that there was no reason for the Danes to accept me as a researcher; especially to the extent of allowing me to observe their secret behavior.

I also began to wonder about the possibility of gaining rapport with community members if I presented myself merely as a researcher: a person whose goal is to *take* data from people and give little in return. Where an ethnic community is localized, the field investigator can take a room in the area and begin establishing a few personal relationships and extend the set of social ties outward. For example, Whyte met "Doc," his major informant, through chance in a public place. This one contact was fruitful in that Whyte then met Doc's friends and engaged in their activities. Because the Danes were scattered throughout the Bay Area, there was no public area in which I could meet any informant, much less an informal leader such as Doc. Thus, for the purposes of gaining rapport with a dispersed population, I decided that it would be essential to present myself as an individual vitally and personally interested in the Danes and in what it was like to be Danish in the United States.

This decision generated the first of my multiple conflicting identities: "fellow Dane." I could express a credible research interest in learning about the Danish community if I phrased it partly as a personal interest. I was able to point out that my maternal grandparents were Danish and that I was amazed that Danish ethnic life continued to exist in this country. These same factors also influenced my choice of ethnic groups among whom to conduct the research in that I thought difficulties of gaining rapport might be eased. I could also be classed in a subcategory of "fellow Dane" by those members of the community who were aware of the phenomenon of third generation sons and daughters seeking their ethnic heritage. Thus, there was an existing native social position into which I could be placed by the immigrants.

Possessing a native identity is a clear advantage in using participant-observation as a research technique. That is, success in this mode of data gathering hinges to some extent on the fact that other participants will forget the researcher and his observational role and will display private behaviors. In addition, my shared native identity meant that I was included in feelings of ethnic solidarity and fraternal brotherhood that were present among members of the Danish-American community. The consequence of this integration from my point of view as an investigator was an automatic achievement of a high level of rapport with the studied group. This insured my access to the secret societies and to continuing relationships with Danish community members even though I had no political or economic benefits to offer "my villagers."

The ethical dilemma following on this seemingly ideal research situation was the difficulty of balancing my desire for rapport with my obligation to adequately protect the informants' rights to privacy. I reasoned, following the tribal model, that if I were clearly identified as a researcher, informants would be judicious in their self-presentations, recognizing the likelihood of their behavior becoming public. However, community members kept forgetting "who" I was. Near the end of the study, for example, a man *whose responses to interview questions I was tape recording,* asked: "what do you do?" I replied: "this." He said: "no, I mean what is your job to make money?" Again, I replied "this" and told him more about the study, reminding him that I was first introduced to him as the student doing research. My research role was evidently much more difficult to remember than my "fellow Dane" or "third generation ethnic" role, especially since the latter role implies a great deal of information seeking as normal behavior. Thus, for the Danes, my most salient identity (even if they watched my constant note taking, tape recording, and questioning) was my Danish one. This "confusion" on their part was, of course, useful for gathering data.

During the course of the fieldwork, I maintained the stance I had decided on in the initial stages. That is, I would be open about my research interests, attempting to inform everyone who was affected about the purposes of the project; and I would consider their continued acceptance of my presence as a researcher to be their consent to participate. This, of course, was balanced with the need for gaining rapport through stressing my identification with the Danes and my personal interest in their ways of life. I took this same position regarding the secret societies; that is, I would be completely open about my research purposes, *implying* their option to refuse my entry. I had also resolved that, if admitted, I would discuss the issue of secrecy and publication with lodge leaders.

As I began the intensive phase of the research — joining and participating in the voluntary associations and conducting interviews in people's homes — an unanticipated characteristic of the two secret societies and their members became apparent and generated the second identity conflicting with my position as a researcher: my age (25). I discovered that the lodges desired new members, particularly young ones. In addition, men gained prestige from sponsoring new recruits to the lodges. This second conflicting identity interacted with the first one, Danish ethnicity, to intensify my acceptance as a native, thus reducing my visibility as a researcher.

In contrast with the conflicting Danish identity which I had planned to stress in order to gain rapport, the implications of my "young man" identity became clear to me only after I had begun affiliating with the Danish-American community. This process was initiated when I made an appointment with the columnist who chronicled the activities of the two secret societies for the Danish language newspaper. When I met him, I introduced myself as a graduate student preparing for a research project on Danish immigrants and their descendants. I also remarked about my Danish ancestry and my personal interest in Danish life. Neither of these two facts about myself seemed to arouse much interest, but he was cordial and agreed to be interviewed. I collected a personal history and information about his contemporary friendships. We discussed the fact that many of his friends were Danish and that he spent a great deal of time with them at Danish Hall. At the conclusion of the interview, I asked about the possibility of joining the two secret ethnic associations of which he was a member. He responded by enumerating the membership requirements — a person must have some Danish ancestry or be the spouse of a member of the affiliated women's lodge — and by saying that he would pick up the appropriate forms from the lodge secretaries.

Once I had the forms, I visited the Brotherhood lodge and was interviewed for membership. The three committeemen who interviewed me seemed somewhat interested in the fact that I wanted to study them; but there was greater interest in attracting "new blood" into the association. They were especially pleased that such a young man as myself wanted to join. I later discovered that each lodge had experienced a decline in membership beginning about 1950. Few new members were initiated and only a small proportion of them were young. It is not surprising, then, that my interest in joining the two lodges stimulated a great deal of excitement and concern.

The committee from the Danish Brotherhood informed me that it would take two weeks to process my application and that I should return for initiation after that time. I doubt that the committee mentioned my study in their report to the lodge. At least, members gave no indication of foreknowledge when I announced that purpose following my initiation two weeks later. I had a similar experience when I was initiated into the Dania lodge the following week.

Generally, the members of both lodges were only politely interested in my research project. A small flurry of interest in the research was generated by my statement that one reason for my membership was to "find out about Danish-Americans in the San Francisco Bay Area." A few men approached me to volunteer to help, to lend history books, or to suggest particularly knowledgeable old men who could tell me about the "old lore." However, there was much more interest in me as a "young man/fellow Dane/new member," with little attention to "researcher." Members welcomed me warmly, hoping that I would enjoy myself and continue to participate in lodge life. One of the informal leaders, for example, expressed the sentiment that I "should get involved in lodge activities, be sure to get on a committee, so that you will really enjoy the lodge." Another man guided me to the bar and card room, pointing out the card games and explained that "these are a great bunch of guys; you can have a lot of fun here in the lodge." Another man said that "you might have to make an effort to get acquainted, but it is really worth it for you."

There were two consequences of this situation for my research. It was difficult for me to adequately insure that my role as researcher was *visible* — a primary requirement for maintaining informants' rights given the importance of participant-observation as a research technique. Second, I was unable to ascertain whether informants tolerated my constant probing because they recognized the research aims or because they did not want to alienate a new and younger member of their association. Although I was aware of the problems at the time and attempted to make my research role salient, I also recognized the value of "melting" into the research sample in order to collect data relatively unbiased by observer presence.

LODGE SECRECY

Despite my early planning, the issue of lodge secrecy did not have its full impact on me until I went through the rites of passage initiating me into the two Danish lodges. In each case, I agreed to observe lodge rules and took a ritual oath to that effect. Having made such a personal commitment to what had before been merely an object of anthropological curiosity, I realized the possibility that almost half the data I hoped to collect might remain the reminiscences of an "inside dopester."

To solve this problem, I quickly engaged lodge leaders, particularly Mort Jorgensen who was well respected in both lodges, in discussions of how to meet and reconcile the requirements of secrecy and dissemination of research results. These discussions continued sporadically during the entire year of intensive research in the lodges and were as valuable for making my research role salient as they were in reaching an agreement about lodge secrecy. In essence, leaders were not overly concerned about this issue in discussions of principle. (On the other hand, the events outlined below suggest that secrecy was a value for some members.) It became evident that secrecy had been more significant in the past during the heyday of lodge life in the 1930s. At that time, secrecy was a mark of prestige, as were other characteristics of secret fraternal organizations such as ritual regalia and official hierarchical positions. In addition, there were conflicts between the lodges and the Lutheran Church, resulting in the pragmatic value of maintaining secrecy regarding membership composition. In the 1960s, however, these factors were much less important and elicited little emotional response from members. Lodge members rarely discussed secrecy when they talked about lodge events or values. The issue arose once during a Dania meeting when a visitor from Denmark was to be invited to attend. Arguing that he spoke no English, and suggesting that the members not use secret signs while he was there, the president admitted the visitor.

The general lack of emphasis on lodge secrecy among members encouraged me to adopt a rather loose view of the issue. However, I wrote to the executive committees of each lodge (at the state and national levels of organization) informing them of the research and requesting guidance. In the one response, the secretary suggested that ritual secrets were really the most important aspect of the problem. This view was repeated at the local level where leaders pointed out that the ritual symbols and their meanings were secret. This perspective became the base for my own ethical judgments. A second suggestion (again at the local level) had less to do with the symbols and more with the specific content of meetings. Mort Jorgensen, for example, stated that "you shouldn't write about members' financial problems or troubles with their health." Other aspects could be discussed, he said, but "don't include embarrassing information."

With these guidelines in mind, I decided that it was not necessary to abandon gathering data during meetings. I made an exception to this in that I did not identify ritual symbols, meanings, and statements in my field notes. Where I judged these to be important to issues such as the ideology of fraternal brotherhood or the unity of ethnic heritage, I paraphrased the information.

Another strategy for reducing the proportion of data gathered during meetings was to rely more heavily on interviews with informants, either in their homes or at the lodge hall when meetings were not in session. In these instances, I attempted to discover personal responses to the immigrant experience and the relative importance of lodge membership in that experience. Clearly my common membership in the associations influenced the content of the interviews because I could refer to lodge events and personalities. However, I felt that the interview situation and the fact I used a tape recorder *implied* that these discussions were more a matter of public record than were lodge meetings. My view was occasionally reinforced when informants asked me to turn off the machine for some comments or would wait until I was leaving (with the tape recorder inoperative) before giving me answers to particular questions.

I did not cease my research during lodge meetings. And I generally took notes openly; although I imagine that only those sitting near me noticed my behavior. In addition, informants whom I knew best did not hesitate to explain the personal or factional implications of some discussions, both during and following meetings. Adhering to the ethical guidelines concerning ritual content or private personal characteristics involved little hardship since these data were not central to the theoretical issues on which I focused. At the same time, I felt that I had been accepted by lodge members and that my continued research presence was not causing them discomfort. (The reader should remember, however, that the issue of conflicting multiple identities was still present.) Thus, I embarked upon a plan midway in the research project to expand the number of men whom I could interview. The results of this seemingly minor action dramatically illuminated my position in the lodges and allowed members the opportunity to publically state their views of the research.

SECRECY AND THE MEMBERSHIP LISTS

In letters to the two lodges, I requested copies of membership lists, explaining that I wished to talk to more people in the Danish community. The first lodge to meet quickly acted on my request, agreeing to loan me their list, minutes, and other files. However, following the meeting, Mort Jorgensen took me aside and said he thought "the lodge might have set a bad precedent tonight. Those membership lists have always been secret. Members don't want some college kid coming by to ask a bunch of questions." He alluded to past difficulties with the church and to an earlier time when there was competition among the lodges for members. However, his position was balanced by the enthusiasm of other members in loading me up with records reaching back to the 1940s. They apologized for the lack of earlier information.

My letter was formally introduced to the other lodge branch two weeks later. Mort, who was the secretary, read the letter and noted that it would be discussed with other new business. After a few expressions of support and approval, Mort spoke against my plan, explicitly raising the issue of lodge secrecy about membership lists; not about lodge proceedings, an issue on which we had reached agreement. Predicated on lodge symbols and their meanings, Mort's argument centered on the importance of secrecy in lodge tradition. He related this to his belief that the members present should not vote to allow me to invade the privacy of others. More views were then expressed, the majority now in agreement with Mort. None doubted, indeed two praised, the research purposes; and everyone was careful not to attack me personally. Ultimately a compromise was reached in which I would be allowed to solicit the aid of volunteers through an appeal included with the next general mailing.

One member spoke to the issue of secrecy, pointing out that this was not as important now as it had been in the past. He added that perhaps my research would benefit the lodge by pointing out the causes of its membership decline. Those who disputed his support of my proposal did not strongly advocate strict adherence to secrecy rules. Instead, they stated that members should not be bothered if they had no desire to participate in the research. It should be noted that none of the opponents of the proposal refused to be interviewed when I asked.

The next event in this sequence began one month later with a phone call from Jorgensen a few hours before a scheduled lodge meeting. "Say," he said, "are you going to lodge tonight?" Receiving an affirmative, if puzzled answer, he continued: "Well, first nominations of officers for the new year is tonight and . . . well, I've been planning to step down as secretary and thought that you could really bring a lot to the job, you being in school and all. Would you accept the position if I nominated you? I don't think you would have any trouble with the job and it pays $25 a month." I responded that I would seriously consider his proposal and inform him of my decision at the meeting. Before the meeting began, I told Mort of my willingness to be nominated. This statement was overheard by the strongest proponent of my earlier request. He laughed and said: "Boy, you'll do *anything* to get those membership lists." I was nominated in a glowing speech in which Mort enumerated my capabilities for the position. He referred to our past disagreement, but stressed our continuing friendship. Significantly, he mentioned that I would learn much more about the lodge in this new position. Running without opposition, I won the election easily.

As secretary, I possessed all the papers and records of the lodge and, in addition, was responsible for adding to the records through writing the min-

utes for each meeting. I had been elected to the perfect research position —
I even had a copy of the ritual book. Although tempted by such easy access
to what I had previously been denied, I decided (after about a week) to continue observing the ethical guidelines which had been generated during the
first eight months of fieldwork. I felt that these understandings were shared
with the membership — hammered out in personal conversations, joint activities, and during the lodge discussions about the membership lists. Consequently, I did not select names from the list for interviewing purposes; instead, I interviewed the volunteers. Although I collected information on members' occupations from lodge records, I did so to develop a profile, disconnected from
names and personalities. I did not inform the members of this action, but
felt that I was sufficiently protecting their privacy.

CONCLUSION

Each anthropologist must contend with the problem of multiple identities that conflict with his or her research role, and all of us must adapt our
research aims to protect private information. The fact that the community
I studied was dispersed throughout an urban metropolitan area and composed of people like me heightened the impact of the ethical dilemmas I
faced. In order to gain entry to the Danish community, I had to stress my
Danish identity; an identification that frequently superseded my position as
researcher in people's minds. Adding to my invisibility as a researcher was my
relative youth, a personal characteristic that I had previously believed to be
unimportant. Although these "native" identities were useful in participant-observation, I attempted to remind people around me that I was doing research and intended to write about their behavior, thus making my researcher
role more salient.

The second dilemma, the problem of publicizing ritually secret behavior,
was also related to geographic dispersal of the community. Because there
were no easily accessible public arenas for community events, I could not engage in Danish-American activities without membership in the secret societies.
My response to this dilemma was to attempt to gather data about the lodges
without relying heavily on what I observed during meetings. In addition, I
discovered the areas of real concern — ritual secrets, embarrassing personal information, and membership lists — through public and private discussions and
avoided any specific references to these areas in my dissertation.

The underlying element in my response to the dilemmas was to be as
open as possible about what I was doing, frequently identifying the research
component of my behavior and discussing the ramifications of lodge secrecy.
Specific decisions, however, were made in concrete situations in which I at-

tempted to balance research aims and ethics, and my personal feelings and obligations arising from the process of engaging in research. In this process, the elements were continually changing, one modifying another at various points. Perhaps the most significant introduction of content regarding ethical concerns was the discussion in 1965 and 1966 of federal policy on the rights of human research subjects. The existence of this policy caused me to carefully consider the ways in which I treated informants. However, because I believed that I had been properly protecting informant rights, my behavior did not change substantially.

The most change occurred as I recognized the impact of personal obligations and relationships on the research. I had not been overly concerned with lodge secrecy as long as I viewed it from a distant theoretical perspective. However, accepting a ritual obligation forced me to carefully balance research aims with the rule of secrecy. Using mental gymnastics — collecting some lodge information from informants, for example — and the results of discussions with lodge leaders, I justified including some data gathered during lodge meetings in the final report. A factor that increased my confidence in the ethical position I had chosen was my continued acceptance by informants as I conducted the research. The men were eager to help as I interviewed them, and occasionally searched for books to lend from their libraries as an aid for expanding my knowledge. Frequently, however, I had to remind some of my research task.

As long as anthropological field methods and techniques include the traditional personal participation and commitment of the field-worker — and I see this as a basic condition of the discipline — one's ethical stance will be heavily influenced by events and feelings experienced in the field. However, the increasing number of formal and informal professional discussions of ethics and the existence of published accounts, such as those included in this volume, will allow a greater number of ethical decisions to be made before entering the field situation. This should reduce the number of alterations in research design and aims made in the field as a result of changes in ethical perspective.

REFERENCES

Chrisman, Noel J.

    1966   *Ethnic Influence on Urban Groups: The Danish-Americans.* Unpublished Ph.D. Dissertation. University of California, Berkeley.

Whyte, William Foote

    1955   *Street Corner Society: The Social Structure of an Italian Slum,* Enlarged Edition. Chicago: University of Chicago Press.

11
ETHNOLOGY IN A REVOLUTIONARY SETTING

JUNE NASH

June Nash is currently Professor of Anthropology at City College of New York and City University of New York. She recently returned from a field study of tin miners in Oruro, Bolivia. She has completed an autobiography of a tin miner entitled *He Agotado Mi Vida en la Mina* and is completing a book on the tin mining community. Her previous field work was with the Maya Indians of Chiapas, Mexico, on the basis of which she wrote a monograph entitled *In the Eyes of the Ancestors: Belief and Behavior in a Maya Community.*

There is a growing gulf between the anthropologist's two roles, that of field researcher and that of analyst.[1] In the first role, we share the lives of the people we study and identify with them in the conflicts they face (Gough, 1968:4; Henry, 1966) as we "try the intimate experience of another upon ourselves to test our hypotheses" (paraphrasing Levi-Strauss, 1969:51). In the second, we must objectify and distill our experiences. Ever since we discovered that secrecy was a defense against the dominant culture, we have been increasingly aware that our data may be used against those whose lives we have shared. In the period of decolonization, as Maquet (1964:48) has shown, the anthropologist has come to be classified with the enemy. Even where national independence is established, our material can be and is being used to counter popular uprisings. The people we study are often cut off from the data we publish by a language or literacy block. Without our knowledge, our material may be fed directly to the "man in the field with the civic action program; working with a military establishment . . . the person in psychological operations who has the basic fundamental studies that give him understanding of the masses" (in the words of Dante B. Fascell, chairman of the House of Representatives Subcommittee on Inter-American Affairs; see *Hearings,* 1969). Since we have no official audience with statesmen or policy makers, we do not know how or whether our publications influence policies that will affect the lives of the people we study. Lacking control over the product of our research, we have lost the basis for social responsibility.

The issues raised by Project Camelot and the publication of the Thailand counter-insurgency research reveal the need to set ethical standards within the profession (Jorgensen, 1961, Wolf and Jorgensen, 1970). Berreman (1968) has gone beyond the issue of professional standards to signal the danger of leaving the use of our data to others "politicians and journalist," "madmen and scoundrels," as well as "statesmen and benefactors." Stavenhagen (1971) has called for "decolonizing the profession."

In order to work out an understanding of the role we can begin to play, we need accounts of concrete field experiences such as those that Maquet (1964), Henry (1966), and Jones (1971) have given us. This report provides a comparative instance based on my recent field experience in the revolutionary setting of Bolivia. In my previous fieldwork with the Maya of Chiapas,

---

[1] Earlier versions of the paper were read by Gerald Berreman, Jorge Dandler, Brooke Schoepf, and Constance Sutton. I have benefited greatly from their comments, but recognize my own responsibility for statements and opinions expressed here.
My first trip to Bolivia in 1969 was supported by the Social Science Research Council Foreign Area Fellowship Program. My year's stay in 1970 was supported by the Fulbright-Hayes Title IV Act. I was able to write my findings during a year's leave supported by the Guggenheim Foundation. I am grateful to these granting agencies for making fieldwork and writing possible.
This chapter is a revised version of an earlier paper that appeared in the New York Academy of Sciences titled "Ethics and Politics in Social Science Research."

Mexico, the impact of modern change was only indirectly felt. The old power structure of curers and diviners who controlled the supernatural was breaking down, and men who had been protectors of the community were being killed as witches. Hostility was turned inward, as a rising incidence of homicide within the community indicated. The defensive insulation of the community against the outside world protected me from the kinds of issues that arise in studying groups in the mainstream of change. People did not involve me in the witchcraft conflict that was the central struggle in their lives.

In Bolivia it was not possible to choose the role of an impartial observer and still work in the tin mining community of Oruro, where I had gone to study ideology and social change. The miners, who spoke Quechua and or Aymara as well as Spanish, had entered the modern industrial sphere and were demanding power in it. The polarization of the class struggle made it necessary to take sides or to be cast by them on one side or the other. In a revolutionary situation, no neutrals are allowed.

In the 146 years since Bolivia's independence, there have been 186 uprisings, resulting in more than 150 changes of government. Only one of these movements resulted in the formation of a legitimized, democratically elected succession of leaders seeking structural changes that would warrant its being called a revolution: the uprising of the National Revolutionary Movement (MNR) on April 9, 1952, when the people fought for the right to seat president-elect Victor Paz Estenssoro after he had been refused power by the oligarchy of tin barons. Eventually Paz lost the confidence of the masses who had supported him as he turned to a false "development" based on loans and increasing external control. In the convulsive spring (our fall) of 1964, workers' strikes and student protest led to his withdrawal. Under the banner of the "revolution of reconstruction," Rene Barrientos Ortuno, a general who had become Paz's vice-president under pressure from the army, took advantage of the rebellion. Reneging on the promises he had made to labor, he instituted four years of the worst repression Bolivia had suffered since the days of the "Butcher" Mamerto Urriolagoitia, installed in the presidency by the tin oligarchy in 1948.

When I arrived in La Paz in July 1967, Che Guevara was still fighting in the tropics of Santa Cruz. Barrientos's troops had massacred 87 men, women, and children in Siglo XX Catavi on June 23. The massacre was precipitated by the Congress of Miners' Unions planned for the following day and was possibly an attempt to discourage workers from supporting Che Guevara's guerilla movement. I took a bus to the old mining center of Oruro, where I found the San Jose mine paralyzed by the reorganization of the mines according to plans proposed by the Inter-American Development Bank as a condition of its loan to the Nationalized Mining Corporation of Bolivia. The corporation had just fired over 200 women who had worked in the concentration of metals and replaced them with men and machines. I spoke to only a few people on my first visit, a teacher in the company school, who sympathized with the workers and told me some of their problems; a woman in *chola* dress (the sign of transition from an Indian culture to urban life) selling candy and fruit punch to miners as they came off their shift; and a gatekeeper who was no longer able to work inside the mines due to silicosis, the "professional illness" of miners but all of them spoke bitterly of the government and the nationalized administration. I read the writing on the walls of all the company buildings calling for the "fight against imperialism" and death to the military assassins and parasites," signed with the initials of the various political parties and union federations. In large red letters, dripping from the hastily executed inscription, the word LIBERACION dominated the walls of the company store. It was as though the cry of the French Revolution for "liberty, equality, and fraternity" had been reduced to its minimal demand-liberty to work out their own destiny. I was determined to return to this place that revealed, even in such a short visit, the turbulence of a society holding on to a precarious niche in an industrial empire at the same time as it was trying to come to grips with an imposed system of exploitation.

I returned to Bolivia for a summer field session in June 1969 to study the ideology of tin-miners. Barrientos had died in an air crash two months before, and his vice-president, Luis Adolfo Siles Salinas, had scheduled an election for May, 1970. Most of the mines were running, as they had for several years, at a loss, decapitalized by inefficient management and the transfer of capital into military equipment. Pensioned workers were not receiving subsistence checks that, even when they arrived, could not cover food costs. Government-employed teachers had not been paid for months. Union leaders were in hiding or exile, and "yellow" unions were serving as spies for the management. Mining police received more pay than miners. Their job was to catch *jucos,* usually employed miners, who entered deserted shafts at night and "stole" what they considered to be their national riches. Many of the older engineers felt that productivity would increase and costs decrease if the police were fired and the company bought the metal the *jucos* extracted.

I spent an afternoon in the local office of the mine management, waiting for permission from La Pax to go ahead with my study. I had already spoken to some of the officials in La Paz, but the administrator of the San Jose mines wanted direct communication from them. When the assistant to the manager of industrial relations finally received a telegram approving the project, he went far beyond what I had requested in the way of cooperation and arranged for me to conduct interviews in the anteroom of his office. Furthermore, he ordered the superintendent of mines to send miners to be interviewed when they finished work. I felt I couldn't refuse without arousing suspicion, so I started interviews on work conditions under these trying circumstances, where the assistant manager could hear everything that was said and where the men, tired after a day's work, were compelled to talk with a strange *gringa*.

One of the first miners I interviewed demanded that I explain what my study was about before he replied to my questions. I liked his forthright attitude and explained in detail. He seemed satisfied and spoke with interest and involvement. Another of the interviewees who impressed me in these early interviews was a watchman who, like all the others working in nonskilled jobs at the surface, could no longer work inside the mine because of silicosis. Since his duties were not pressing, he came by twice in the following week. He was more relaxed when I asked questions about ritual and folklore than when I questioned him about conditions in the mine. Once he brought up the massacres that had taken place in the mines, his tone turned from bitterness to compassion for the dead and he wept as he spoke of the massacre of December 21, 1942 in Siglo XX Catavi. Tears came to my eyes as he spoke of "our history" and of how Maria Barzola, a woman worker in the concentration of metal had seized the Bolivian flag during the march to the administrative offices to demand "more daily bread" and had been shot along with other men, women, and children by the soldiers called to the defense of the mine. Soon after that he and some of the other miners I had met in the course of my interviews invited me to their homes, and I could avoid the restrictive atmosphere of the administrative office. I think I had passed some kind of test that allowed me to go beyond a barrier to communication, a barrier that might never have been withdrawn, if I had remained a "stranger" (however desirable some ethnologists believe this to be [cf. Jarvie 1969]).

I was visiting in the mine one day when I heard that an agent of the Department of Criminal Investigation (DIC) had come to investigate what I was doing. When I returned to the house where I rented rooms, I found all my notes and tapes removed. I later learned that my student had taken them in a laundry sack to a friend's house in the mining community, but I had a few bad hours reflecting on the danger my notes could bring to my informants. The agent returned, and (remembering U Nu's "tension-releasing lunches" with his cabinet from my Burmese days of fieldwork), I invited him for breakfast the following day. That afternoon I received a call from one of my miner friends, who had begun an autobiography. He had heard the DIC was after me and was curious to know what had happened. I assured him that I would not let the DIC see any of his work, and said that I would burn it first if there was any danger. He protested against such drastic action; it made me feel good that he had confidence in me and was committed to the work we were doing. That evening we gave all the notes to a student who was traveling to La Paz retaining only a few myths and folk tales to show the DIC. The agent arrived promptly the following morning and waited for us to return from the anniversary mass of a friend's deceased mother. After we had chatted about folklore and rituals, he went on to tell us about his student days at the University of Wisconsin, where he said he had had a scholarship to study "counterinsurgency," and about his friendship with an American CIA agent working in Oruro. Then he left, after asking only to see our passports, although on the previous day he had demanded that we show him all our notes.

Political campaigns for a presidential election were underway when I left Bolivia in September. The Mayor of La Paz, Armando Escobar Uria, was gaining popularity as a candidate. I was not surprised to read shortly after that Alfredo Ovando, who had helped Barrientos attain power and who had little reason to believe that he could win a democratic election, had seized power on September 26. Desiring to outdo Siles, who had been promising to revise the oil code to increase the national share of the wealth of the American holdings in Santa Cruz, he nationalized the oil company. Economically, it would have been preferable to await the installation of a gas line to Argentina's markets, but the move was dictated by the political urgency of stabilizing a weak military coup. Yielding to pressure from intellectuals and workers, Ovando freed some of the jailed union directors, who returned to work in the mines. When I returned to Bolivia in January, 1970, I sensed the uncertainty that Ovando's moves had created among the miners. Some called for a position of *acerquismo*, getting closer to the center of power, by supporting Ovando and trying to influence policy. Others distrusted the attempts of what they felt was an opportunistic regime, still dominated by the military, to gain support among the masses. Wages and contracts cut in half by Barrientos in 1965 in a "temporary" austerity measure, remained at the same low level, a little under a dollar a day.

Labor had begun to rebuild its shattered organization. I visited the new secretary-general and presented my credentials and plan for a study of the mining community. (I had avoided the former representative because of the low esteem the miners had for him and their suspicion that he was a spy for management.) In April I attended a weeklong congress of the Federation of Mine Workers' Unions at Siglo XX Catavi, where old leaders and new gathered for the first time in five years to plan a program of action and elect a directorate. I was permitted to attend all of the sessions and to tape record the proceedings, except for those of the political commission. The regular attendance of myself and two assistants became something of a joke. It seemed too obvious a stunt for the CIA to pull — having a "blond" *gringa* sitting in front of a nearly all-male audience with a large paisley-covered taperecorder. For those with lingering doubts about my presence, it might even have been appealing that they had their own specially assigned agent bugging them. I felt that immediate feedback was essential to justify my presence to the miners, and so I wrote some of my impressions in an article published in *Temas Sociales* entitled "El XIVe Congreso y Después." In the months that followed, the union leadership concentrated on regaining the ground lost in the Barrientos period. The directors formulated a plan for reinstating wages at the pre-Barrientos level without producing inflation that had crippled the MNR government before currency stabilization in 1956. Their plan involved eliminating many of the bureaucratic and technical posts that had accumulated as the army invaded the administration and abolishing the mining police. Only one strike was called, and that was to demand replacements for machinery and tools in the mines. By the fall (our spring) of 1970, Ovando's government was beginning to swing farther to the right. The promised wage increase was not forthcoming and increased expenditures were made for armaments. One of the few left-of-center critics in the government, Marcelo Quiroga Santa Cruz, resigned from the Ministry of Mines and Petroleum in protest on May 18th. It wasn't just protest directly on mines wages but on a whole swing to right. He later revealed Ovando's intention of replacing all the civilian ministers with military men (*Presencia,* July 7, 1970). The only other civilian minister of the left, Kidrich Bailey, was forced to resign soon after. The union leaders alerted the workers to this swing to the right in the cabinet and called for an antiimperialist demonstration.

In the middle of July university students sent out a call to mobilize the National Army of Liberation, the guerrilla movement left over from the Che Guevara period, in Teoponte, and scores of students went there in the guise of literacy brigades. The 68 guerrillas were quickly defeated. As they were surrendering to the army, they were shot. Prisoners, some of them wounded, were killed with machine gun fire and hand grenades. Ovando refused to hand over the bodies of the victims to their families, perhaps, as rumor had it, because the thoroughly destroyed bodies revealed the brutality of the military operation. Not only relatives of the dead and political sympathizers, but many of the Bolivian people were outraged by this callous behavior. Other sectors of the middle class were alienated by Ovando's imprisonment and expulsion of priests in the middle of September.

A series of demonstrations in La Paz by university students protesting the government's bizarre handling of the dead guerrillas culminated in a march on September 21, the Day of Students. Usually a day for celebration of youth, when students crown their queens and dance, that year it was a day for rebellion against a regime that was falling into the old pattern of ineptness and repression of the resulting discontent. Union directors joined the students in a symbolic funeral of the dead guerrillas. Although the miners had rejected the movement when it was active, they proclaimed its martyrs when they were no longer a threat to their trade union aims. The streets for blocks around the university were still filled with the tear gas used to break up the demonstration when I passed by several hours later. My taxi driver said bitterly,

"Each one of those bombs costs us $U.S.10, and look what they do with them!" As I waited to meet a foundation representative in the lobby of one of the few luxury hotels in La Paz, I was appalled to overhear some of my compatriots, attending a medical convention, joking about this latest of Bolivia's revolutions. I wondered how anyone could laugh at people prepared to die rather than continue selling their lives everyday in a market over which they had no control.

The weeks following were a time of near anarchy. Ovando's government had lost its legitimacy. The big question was: When will it end?

The union in San Jose and other mining centers built up its antiimperialist campaign in these weeks of guerrilla action and student protest. The campaign came to focus more and more on *Yanqui* imperialism. Finally, I became the target. On October 3, Doris Widerkehr, who was beginning her dissertation research, went to tape a union meeting, as we had been doing for a special study of the rhetoric of worker organizations. She came back shaken and upset. One of the former leaders, who was himself accused by some of being a CIA agent had asked why we were allowed to tape the sessions and why we were doing the study. (Since I had had several conversations with him about the work we were doing, this seemed a tactic for diverting suspicion from himself.) The question had opened a general discussion of our role in the mining center. Three strangers from Argentina, one of whom claimed to be an anthropologist had said that they never used tape recorders in their work and that furthermore anthropologists need only 3 months for a field study and we had already been there 10 months. Doris had been asked to leave.

We discussed the events of the meeting with my compadre, a retired miner, during lunch. He advised me not to get angry when eating because the bile would burst and I might die. I tried to control my anger until the afternoon, when I went to see the secretary-general. Fortunately he was not there. Since I had not yet worked out a plan of action, I then went to see another of my compadres, who was a delegate with the union. He consulted with a compadre who had many years of experience in labor struggles, and they decided that I should draft a letter explaining my problem and methods of investigation in detail and distribute copies to all the delegates as well as to the secretary general, asking for an audience at the next meeting. I had, of course, discussed my work with the union before and had given the secretary-general copies of the articles I had published in Spanish, but changes in the union and in the political scene seemed to have made a reevaluation necessary. The strategy they outlined for me was to involve all of the men responsible for the operation of the union in the discourse, avoiding personal commitments to a single individual, who could then be suspected of being in complicity with me. I drafted the letter and revised it in accordance with comments from my compadre. The following day I passed out copies of the letter to the delegates as they were leaving a meeting concerned with an attempted coup in La Paz. The coup had begun on the morning of October 4, while Ovando was in Santa Cruz, with a radio-broadcast mandate signed by 64 officers calling for his renunciation of the presidency.

The following seven days have been called "The Week of the Generals" (Samuel Mendoza, *Presencia,* November 15, 1970). In the course of the week, six presidents entered and left the "Burned Palace." The contest became something like a football game between sectors of the armed forces, with the people listening to the radio with consternation, dismay, and a wild sense of the absurd as generals kicked the football of power from one to another.

Because I had not yet cleared up the question of whether I was an agent for the CIA, I did not go out except for brief trips to the plaza to see if any of the student demonstrations announced on the radio were taking place. A new group of DIC agents had taken possession of one of the benches in the plaza. I discovered their identity when I was about to take a photograph of soldiers massing near the Cathedral to block a scheduled student demonstration and one of the plainclothes agents rushed over to stop me, saying I had no right to photograph secret agents.

On Monday, October 5, as a result of the only "election" in two years, held in the Miraflores barracks, officers of the army called for Ovando (who had by now returned to the Palace) to renounce the presidency "for having defrauded the hopes of the people." General Rogelio Miranda, who had led the coup could not muster strong support even within the army, so he named a triumvirate to take control. Students and workers rallied behind General Juan Jose Torres, as the least imperialist, least Facist, and least reactionary of the lot, to oppose the trio. When a strike was threatened for the following day, the tide turned against the triumvirate. Torres was proclaimed president on the afternoon of October 6. He promised to form a government based on *campesinos* (agricultural workers), miners and factory workers, and university students, with the support of the army, the various ministries to be divided among these four sectors of the population. The representatives of the Bolivian Workers' Central (COB) at first rejected the plan of coparticipation, on the basis of their experience with the MNR government and criticism of the compromises resulting from that episode, but later agreed to accept the posts of Housing, Mines, and Labor. Torres's attempts to find a popular base for his new government threatened a rebellion if labor were to have as much participation in government as Torres had promised them. Fearing the seizure of power by the rightist wing, the Political Command of the COB agreed to leave the new president at liberty to choose his cabinet without including them.

Meanwhile, Doris and I had made preparations in case of an attack on the Anglo-American-owned apartment building in which we lived. I took my daughter to stay at the house of a friend. We took suitcases of notes to the house of another friend and copies to still another. Then we shuttered the windows and listened to the radio. That night it looked as though the crisis was over, and we celebrated the assignment of ministerial posts assigned to labor leaders, some of whom we knew.

The Workers' Central of the Department of Oruro had planned a strike and an anti-fascist demonstration in Oruro on October 7, with participation by miners from other centers as well as San José. From the window of a dentist's office that morning, I watched a crowd of young men converging on the offices of the DIC. The guards ran up to the roof with machine guns, but they did not fire on the crowd below, whether because of cowardice or good judgment I do not know. The youths came out carrying rifles. (We later discovered that the guns had no firing pins, but they looked menacing at the time.) Not far away, students were assaulting the U.S. Information Service building, where the doors of the library were bombed open and books and materials carried off or burned.

When I returned home, our cook told me that she had just bought a can of oil in the market when one of her neighbors pointed a rifle at her and tried to seize it. He did not recognize her until she screamed, "Don Roberto, what are you doing?" and then he let go of the can. Shortly after, one of the university students came with news of the assault on the USIS. He brought tear gas bombs and a vomit bomb, plainly marked U.S. Army, that he had liberated from the DIC office and gave them to us in case the Anglo-American school, as the only symbol of U.S. imperialism left, should be the next target. I was beginning to get irritated at some of the "revolutionary" tactics of the mob, and I didn't want to leave without at least some show of resistance. I felt that, while I had to demonstrate that not all Americans were imperialists, I also had to make them realize that not all actions in the name of revolution were revolutionary.

There was nothing to do but sit in the shuttered living room listening to the transistor radio, with the bombs close at hand. Radio Universidad announced the arrival of truckloads of miners from Machacamarca. Others from Catavi and Siglo XX were expected to join them for the afternoon demonstration. Suddenly a volley of shots was fired into the unarmed crowd in front of the central barracks. Whether it was triggered when civilians approached the door of the barracks, as some said or when a woman, hit by an orange peel thrown at the guards, screamed, is not verified. For the next eight hours there ensured a useless battle with random sniping, resulting in about 20 deaths and 100 injuries between desperate calls for a return to sanity radio announcers broadcast the lists of wounded and dead.

The teenage son of a miner came to visit us. He wanted to go out in the streets to see what was happening, but I made him help me bake a cake.

When it was done, I wanted to invite Doris, who lived across the street, to join us for tea, but the moment we opened the door a volley of bullets from a sniper sitting on a nearby hill discouraged us. I made the teenager stay overnight for fear that he would be shot going home to the mine. In the morning his parents arrived looking for him. As I had feared they had thought he was in the hospital or the morgue and had made the rounds early in the morning and seen the dead and suffering. However, they agreed that the precaution had been worth their night of anxiety. In the afternoon of the following day, we went to the wake of eight students and youths in the university auditorium and then to the mine office, where three workers who had died were on view. Thousands came to pay their last respects and then attended the mass funeral on the following day. The speakers tried to make of the deaths a noble sacrifice for the revolution, but the people knew that they were due to nothing more than the stupidity and ineptness of the command of the armed forces.

In the following days people waited and watched the new officials. The DIC office was still occupied by students, who had put a likeness of Che Guevara in guerrilla fatigues on the pillar in the entryway. They soon acquired a reputation of being as arbitrary in their handling of cases as their predecessors. One of the miners told us that a fight had broken out in his family and everyone was detained in the cold cells without cots or plumbing facilities, even his 15-year-old daughter (who, as a minor, should not have been imprisoned). In a country that lives with the constant expectation of revolution, there is little preparation for a successful outcome. During this period, there was relative freedom of expression in the press and on the radio. Union leadership was given full liberty to pursue the plans for the restitution of wages. There was no evidence of restraint or recrimination against any of the combatants.

A week after my accusation, I went to ask the secretary-general for time to explain my work to the delegates. He agreed to give me some time in the next meeting. In my presentation, I stressed that the tape recorder was a tool to get more accurate data and not an instrument of espionage. One of the delegates told me that the suspicion had arisen when I had lent the tape recorder to one of the delegates to a COB conference. Though the title of the tape on the machine had been erased, the tape itself had not and it contained accusations by one of the members against some of the directors. The delegate had played the tape for the other delegates to the conference and let it be known that it was mine. I was dismayed at what I had let happen after all my care, and assured them it was an error of stupidity and not evil intention. They seemed prepared to believe this. Despite their hatred of the CIA, they had a very high regard for the agency's performance, and this blunder did not fit the image. I felt that they had accepted my continued stay in the community when the directorate's intellectual advised me how I could improve and amplify the study by investigating work conditions of the women on the slag pile.

The episode, although disturbing and threatening the very possibility of continuing my work, yielded some ethnographic benefits. Enemies of the leadership became friendly to me when I was cast as an enemy of their enemy. They told me of the leaders' attempts to gain favor with the administration and described the circle of *llunkus,* men who curry favor with those in power, that surrounded each of them. They spoke more frankly of their own fear of being deceived by their leaders, the ever-present fear of the powerless. I learned of the corrupt union leader's technique of taking issues from the management, and introducing them as union demands, such as constructing additions to social service buildings (projects that meant a lot of graft), I discovered that I had been under almost constant surveillance by a neighbor whose husband worked in the mine, and that her report of my visitors' being only workers from the rank and file reassured the people that my interest in the mine stemmed from genuine sympathy. In the week of my own "suspension" I came to understand more fully the insecurity that robs working people of their revolutionary zeal.

Several days after my meeting with the union delegates, I saw the jeep station wagon put at the disposal of the union by the company raising a cloud of dust behind me as I walked down the road. Still not sure how they had taken my defense, I jumped into the ditch to avoid being run down; much to my surprise, the driver pulled up to me and the secretary-general asked me if I would like a ride. I was too overcome to think of an excuse, so I agreed, but I recovered my defense enough to decline a drink of chicha (the fermented drink of the workers). At that point I was afraid of being seen with him and his *llunkus.* The next time I showed up at a union meeting, two of my compadres came over and greeted me, using the formal address of *comadre,* thus establishing the relationship publicly. Later, when a newcomer who was trying to gain footing in the union tried to intercept my taking a photograph of two children listening in to the discussion at a meeting, two other friends came over and asked him what he thought he was doing. After the meeting a man invited me to be comadre of the soccer team. I could hardly refuse, although it meant buying socks for the 13 members.

Torres visited the San José mines in December, just after the announcement that the wage raises would go into effect in January. The crowd of 200 or so miners who came to the stadium to listen to him applauded his speech but saved most of their *vivas* for the working class and the martyrs of the union struggles. The president called for confidence in his government and the good will of the armed forces, and he pleaded for peace to work out a program for economic improvement. "You have fought enough," he told the miners," in the war of Nancahuasu and when Maria Barzola marched and sacrificed her life asking for more bread for the workers," the miners responded with a call for arms for the workers. Miners have learned that the words of presidents have little value unless they have confidence enough in the workers to give them weapons.

I left in December feeling somewhat optimistic about the future of the mines. When I returned in July, 1971, to make a film based on the miner's autobiography mentioned earlier, there was a new secretary-general, formerly a leader in Siglo XX who had been jailed during Barrientos's term of office. When he had been elected in December, one of the superintendents expressed relief that he had won over the more Marxist-revolutionary candidates, since he had a good reputation as a foreman concerned with production. He had already aroused some criticism from the rank and file for getting employment in the mines for members of his extended kin group. Furthermore, newspaper articles implicated him in the torture and slaying of a union leader during Ovando's period of office. The last thing he needed was a *gringa* working in the mines. He agreed to let me show the Super-8 film we had made the year before. I had looked forward to this as an opportunity of telling people in the mining community about the 16-mm film we proposed to do. When I arrived at the union hall, the order to permit the showing of the film had not been given. I sensed that I was going to have some opposition from official union sources in making the film and continuing my work, although my friends and compadres were cooperative throughout.

There had been a marked shift to the left in the Torres government. Two or more attempted coups in January (one by Hugo Banzer, who was to carry out the successful coup in August) had been put down with the help of miners. The right was on the defensive or in flight. The Popular Assembly, a kind of forum of union leaders, *campesinos,* and left politicians, opened in June. Ideologies and programs of the left were aired in what *Presencia* (August 6, 1971) referred to lyrically as a "symphony for the revolution." The main business of the Assembly became the working out of the details of coparticipation of workers in the administration of mines and factories. Workers in the mining center were doubtful about the program, since they felt that in the coparticipation phase of the MNR regime the union leadership had lost its revolutionary aims as it learned to participate in the spoils of the company. At an August meeting in San José mine, the director was unable to secure a quorum, and those present began to whistle and protest that the leaders had not come to advise them about the plan for coparticipation. The director turned to me and ordered me to go, thereby diverting the workers from their protest and eliminating a witness of the breakup of the meeting for lack of a quorum. After the meeting, rank-and-file members told me resentfully that they were again being used as "steps" in the rise of opportunistic labor leaders.

During July and August there were invasions of agricultural and business enterprises. Miners seized private holdings in Colquecharca, Postosi, and Catavi. Peasants seized the homes of the *hacendados* (estate owners) for whom they worked. Some of the presses and radio stations were taken over by the men who worked in them or by popular pressure groups and were turned into cooperatives. There was an air of apprehensiveness and expectation; people stood in their doorways, watching to see the next development, just as they did in the week of Carnival waiting for the dancers to come in. When I went to the University of Oruro's library on the morning of August 7, pensioned miners who had been on a hunger strike to gain their subsistence money surged into the building, which had once been the residence of a tin baron. As the men and women pressed into the main hall of the baroque mansion, shorter than I by a head, stunted by years of malnutrition and shaken with the racking cough of silicosis, I felt the full impact of the revolutionary pressures in an economy hedged in by foreign powers that did not have to yield to their demands.

In the early days of August, rumors of military plots originating in Santa Cruz led to the demand for arms for the people to "defend their revolution and take positive steps toward socialism" (*Presencia,* August 8, 1971). On August 14, union directors in Santa Cruz advised Torres of subversion in their capital. Torres failed to act, but the military began to prepare themselves; on August 16, students in the military college were assigned to the central barracks without any official explanation. The union leaders of Santa Cruz sent more urgent messages, and both union leaders and the Popular Assembly in Cochabamba asked for arms for the workers. On August 20, Hugo Banzer and 38 coconspirators were imprisoned. After a day of demonstrations in favor of his release, Banzer was set free and began to mobilize rebel forces.

In Oruro, miners were mobilizing from Siglo XX, Catavi, Huanuni, and Santa Fe to fight the rebels. On the morning of the 10th, union leaders of San Jose called for a work stoppage and a united demonstration of miners from the other centers. The call was broadcast on the union radio until 11 A.M. At 11:20 A.M. 14 truckloads of miners arrived in Oruro. The union leaders were no longer to be found. The mayor and government leaders had left their poses. At 12:45 P.M., the military guard of Oruro yielded to the insurgents. The demonstration was called off. On the following day, reinforcements arrived from Santa Cruz by air. Radio Pio XII, the Oblate mission station in Siglo XX, called for a withdrawal of miners still in the area to prevent bloodshed. At midnight the radio broadcast a speech, said to be by Victor Paz Estenssoro (whose MNR party, along with the Social Phalanx of Bolivia [FSB], was behind the rebellion), calling for their dispersal. (Those familiar with his voice say that it was difficult to recognize it because of the poor transcription.) Some of the miners left the city in response to his plea.

The miners were still under contradictory orders from their leaders on the following day. Over 1500 miners from Siglo XX and Huanuni, resolved to take the Oruro airport and hold it against the insurgents, were repelled by heavily armed forces, and 8 were killed. According to 2 miners taken prisoner, their leaders had told them that they would be joined by military forces under the command of President Torres (*Presencia,* August 23, 1971). The prisoners reported that the directors of the union escaped in some of the vehicles, leaving the dead and wounded without help (*Patria,* September 22, 1971).

The 280-day presidency of Juan José Torres ended after 3 days of fighting in the capital cities of Santa Cruz, Oruro, Cochabamba, and La Paz departments. Torres had given the country over nine months of freedom — freedom for workers to reorganize the unions, for students to march in protest against imperialism, and for politicians of the right as well as of the left to formulate positions and seek alliances. For some, this freedom meant only anarchy, but in a country that had lived in a state of dependency and subjugation to outside economic and political interests, it was a time to assess who Bolivians were as a people and where they were going.

Throughout his term, there had been persistent rumors of intervention by the United States. That the U.S. Embassy knew that a coup was about to take place is established by the warning to stock up on food supplies 48 hours before the coup in La Paz, reported by Cuban correspondent Ernesto Gonzales Bermejo. Reports indicate that Torres had himself reserved 60 places for exiles in the Chilean Embassy. The reported association of Major Robert J. Lundin with Banzer prior to and during the coup (*Washington Post* on August 29, 1971) has been denied as having had a serious impact on the movement of the rebels in Santa Cruz by General Remberto Iriarte (*Presencia,* August 31, 1971), but those who were in Bolivia during the coup attest to the importance of a network of radio communication linking the activities of rebels and demoralized government armed forces.

Despite the U.S. denial of military involvement, officials did not conceal their satisfaction at the success of the coup (*Presencia,* August 30, 1971). The financial support immediately offered the Banzer government indicated to Bolivians which side the United States was on. On August 28, *Presencia* reported a U.S. loan of $2,500,000 for cotton agriculture. On September 7, *Presencia* announced in large headlines U.S. offers of $100,000,000 credit with $3,000,000 earmarked for construction of three new markets. The Bank of America announced a $12,000,000 loan to the Nationalized Mining Corporation of Bolivia September 11, 1971. Victor Siracusa, U.S. Ambassador, promised special financing to Bolivia that would offset any problems with the proposed law restricting imports (*Presencia,* September 14, 1971). Brazil and Argentina added to U.S. promises loans totaling $10,000,000.

The new government is relying on military strength to hold on to what it has gained. The university and mines were occupied by troops until September. Recently armed tanks were delivered to Oruro, where the barracks are situated right next to the mining encampment. The two parties that backed the rebellion, the Social Phalanx of Bolivia and the National Revolutionary Movement, still maintain an uncertain alliance, but the old left-of-center supporters of the latter have urged Paz Estenssoro to denounce the government of Banzer for its treatment of students during the raid on the University of San Andres.

Reading the newspaper reports of the aftermath of the coup, I felt that I was back in 1954 in Guatemala, when Castillo Armas entered the country with 200 rebel troops equipped by the United Fruit Company and backed by promises of support from the U.S. government. I was living in an Indian town in the western highlands and saw trucks loading campesinos with nothing more than machetes to "defend their revolution" the night that Jack Purifoy, special representative of the U.S. government, maneuvered the ouster of President Arbenz. The coup also has a parallel in the U.S. invasion of the Dominican Republic, when President Johnson sent in Marines to take back control from a government considered too far left.

Recalling the consequences of our intervention in these countries, I began to reflect on the role we social scientists are called on to play. Do anthropologists go to these countries just to write epitaphs for the movements that are cut down when they go beyond the limits the U.S. government sets for them? Those of us who are concerned with the welfare of the people we study must reveal what we know about the U.S. involvement and what it means to them. In the months I worked in Oruro, I came to realize the CIA symbolized the American presence in Bolivia. Their agents act in secrecy and are protected by the State Department, while we, as American citizens, must bear the burden of guilt for their actions. It seems a corollary of this that we must dedicate ourselves to eradicating their influence on our government's policy.

The role of the participant-observer in a revolutionary setting has a special dynamic. Just by being there, threatening the existing role-structure and hovering in the conflict of identity, I became an instrument in the research. The attacks directed against me gave information of the inner conflicts of a people who had suffered "in their very flesh" the presence of the United States and the abhorred CIA agents. In evaluating my own role in the community, I realized that the CIA agent is not entirely different from the witch in the Maya community. The difference was that, while I despised the activities of the CIA of my own country, I felt neutral about witches in another country, and while I became one of the targets of accusation Bolivia my cultural distance protected me from becoming part of the witch hunt in the Maya community. This breakdown of my carefully cultivated "cultural relativist" position forced me to realize that it was premised on a colonialist attitude. I did not judge the witchcraft institutions because I felt removed from and impervious to them. In Bolivia I was no longer able to maintain this pose, because the CIA agents and I were part of the same historical continuum. I realized more fully the implications of Maquet's (1964) rejection of the scientific attitude of impersonal objectivity as inappropriate for the kind of research in which we by our very presences are instruments of that research. The world is no longer our laboratory, as Berreman has remarked (1970:100), but a community in which we are coparticipants with our informants.

Anthropologists are now at the crossroads in defining a participation-observer perspective more adequate to the load that revolutionary stress is putting on their role in the field. We must begin to specify the "degree of indeterminancy" (Heisenberg, quoted in Mannheim, 1936) arising from our own perspective. We can no longer retreat into the deceptive pose of neutrality (Henry, 1966). Science advances only by honest declaration of the convictions that influence our data gathering and analysis. It is a paradox that the physical sciences cast aside the pose of neutrality decades before the social sciences, with their presumably greater humanitarian orientation. In Bolivia I became convinced that part of our professional task as anthropologists is to attack the multifarious ways in which the U.S. State Department operates to destroy the independence movements of the countries that supply it with raw materials. Levi-Strauss (1969:52) announced prematurely that "our science arrived at maturity the day that Western man began to see that he would never understand himself as long as there was a single race or people on the surface of the earth that he treated as an object." We have yet to reach the goal he envisioned of becoming "an enterprise reviewing and atoning for the Renaissance, in order to spread humanism to all humanity".

REFERENCES

Berreman, Gerald D.

    1968   "Is Anthropology Alive?," *Current Anthropology,* **9**:391-396.

    1971   "The Greening of the American Anthropological Association: Address to the Council," American Anthropological Association, 69th Meeting, San Diego, November 19, 1970, *Critical Anthropology,* Spring.

Gough, Kathleen

    1968   "New Proposals for Anthropologists," *Current Anthropology,* **9**:403-407.

Henry, Frances

    1966   "The Role of a Fieldworker in an Explosive Political Situation," *Current Anthropology,* **7**:552-558.

Jarvie, I. C.

    1969   "The Problem of Ethical Integrity in Participant-Observeration," *Current Anthropology,* **10**:505-509.

Jones, Delmos J.

    1971   "Social Responsibility and the Belief in Basic Research: An Example from Thailand," *Current Anthropology,* **12**:347-350.

Jorgensen, Joseph G.

    1971   "On Ethics and Anthropology, *Current Anthropology,* **12**:321-335.

Levi-Strauss, Claude

    1969   *The Scope of Anthropology.* Bungay, Suffolk: Grossman.

Mannheim, Karl

    1966   *Ideology and Utopia.* New York: Harcourt, Brace.

Maquet, Jacques

    1964   "Objectivity in Anthropology," *Current Anthropology,* **5**:47-55.

Stavenhagen Rodolfo

    n. d.   "On Decolonizing Anthropology," *Human Organization.*

U.S. Government Printing Office, Washington, D.C.

    1969   Hearings before the Subcommittee on Inter-American Affairs of the Committee on Foreign Affairs, House of Representatives.

Wolf, Eric and Joseph G. Jorgensen

    1970   "Anthropology on the Warpath in Thailand," *New York Review of Books,* November 19, pp. 26-35.

12
PROFESSIONAL STANDARDS AND WHAT WE STUDY

LAURA NADER

Laura Nader is Professor of Anthropology at the University of California, Berkeley. She received her B.A. from Wells College in 1952 and her Ph.D. from Radcliffe College in 1961. She has done fieldwork among the Zapotec Indians in Oaxaca, Mexico, and among the Shia Moslems in South Lebanon. The producer of the film *To Make the Balance,* she is also author of *Talea and Juquila* and the editor of *The Ethnography of Law, Law in Culture and Society,* and (with T. Maretski) *Cultural Illness and Health.* She has been a Fellow at the Center for Advanced Study in the Behavioral Sciences at Stanford and a Visiting Professor at Yale Law School.

How does an anthropologist decide *what* to study? What is there about the profession that helps set priorities for study? If a doctor finds herself in an emergency room with two patients, one with a broken finger, and the other with a bullet in the chest, there are certain professional standards that rather quickly help sort out priorities on which patient to take care of first. However, if an anthropologist finds herself faced with numerous opportunities for conducting research, what professional standards help to set priorities and make choices. How does she answer the question, "What should I study?"

Choices reflect a system of values, and many times values underlying choice are comfortably hidden from review, and are not openly discussed. As I look back at my own research I can now separate a number of considerations that influenced my choice of problem and method. The values underlying these choices were latent and traditional early in my professional career, but gradually I became more self-conscious about the process of choice. This came as a result of a renewed awareness of the world from which our profession lives. I am conscious of a dialogue between myself — an anthropologist — and fellow citizens who are not anthropologists. This dialogue has delineated new directions in research. In this chapter I review the course of my own research pointing to the markers that have changed my course now and then.

TRADITIONAL PRIORITIES

Before I planned my first fieldwork I had spent about three-and-one-half years as a graduate student at the Peabody Museum at Harvard University. I recall having written three papers as a graduate student — none of which were based on field research in the Cambridge area. Although I do not remember anyone actually forbidding us to do term papers based on field research I can not remember anyone in my class doing so. The papers I wrote reflected the anthropological concerns of the time as well as my reaction to the academic world as I saw it. The first paper dealt rather abstractly with problems in the methodology of comparison and was written jointly with two other graduate students. The second paper was a cross-cultural library exploration of an American belief that "working women do not make 'good' mothers," a belief that implies that nonworking mothers do make good mothers. I searched the literature on non-Western cultures and concluded that no correlation existed between the variable good "mothering" and whether women worked or not. The third paper, "The Zapotec of Oaxaca," was an ethnographic description of the Zapotec peoples in Mexico. None of these papers were of publishable quality though they were important to my intellectual and personal development. The topics were chosen by me with little direction as to how one decides what to work on except to follow the widely accepted maxim: "Study what interests *you*."

There were no summer training grants prior to the major year of fieldwork. We were taught to be self-reliant and self-taught in using methods, in developing theoretical perspectives and in formulating problems. Instead of training or apprenticeship we received inspiration from people who were, after all, doing what we were training ourselves to do. All too often the model of researcher was in opposition to the model of teacher. Looking back now I feel that the exposure to teachers as devoted researchers rather than teachers as devoted teachers was a good model for the training of a researcher, though perhaps not for the training of a teacher of non-professionals.

I had to apply for funds to do fieldwork. I sent two applications into the only two places that seemed to be supporting social anthropological fieldwork in Mexico: the Doherty Foundation and the Mexican government through the Institute of International Education in New York. In order to apply for monies I had to know ahead what it was I was intending to do, and why. I had to have a problem, a theoretical perspective, and a methodological orientation. I had read most of what had been written about the Zapotec and in my readings had come across an article by Oscar Schmieder, a Univeristy of California geographer who had written about the settlement patterns and the geography of the Sierra Madre del Sur (1930), a mountain region of Oaxaca inhabited by Zapotec and Mixe Indians. He had a map of the area with which he was concerned, and on this area was a blank spot labeled the Rincon. Nobody knew much about this area encircled as it was by mountains; neither geographers, historians, archaeologists, linguists, or anthropologists had reported on the area. I would go there. I would fill in the blank. But what should I study? Settlement patterns struck me as a good umbrella, and one relevant to a variety of interests. It was also a topic that would have utility in an ever-crowding world.

During this first fieldwork and later I was influenced by certain values — tacitly accepted and unquestioned. At least the following could be identified as the "traditional ethics" underlying what it is that we were to study.

1. It was important to study non-Western cultures.

2. If you want to be an anthropologist, you must study such cultures.

3. Kinship is the most prestigious topic.

4. Description is of value as a means to generalization.

5. New data and new theory are stimulated by innovations in methods, and not vice versa.

6. Knowledge of previous work is imperative in the development of ideas.

These were values that influenced my choices and many continue to influence the choices of anthropologists today. Such values are tied into the system of ranking one anthropologist's work over that of another.

Upon arrival in Oaxaca in the spring of 1957 I located in the Rincon Zapotec area, the blank space on Schmeider's map, and proceeded, actually, to study the consequences of settlement pattern for social organization. I found two villages, one compact and one dispersed. Both were villages of approximately the same population size: some kind of controlled comparison seemed possible. I set about my work as planned. My methodology included participant observation, interview, and questionnaire, but I had the uncomfortable feeling that I could not validate what I was writing in my notes, except to say that I had seen it or heard it. During this time I was urged by my brother, who was in law school at the time, to collect law cases. I did and after my first field stay was to realize that the analysis of that case material could provide me with what I had been looking for, an independent validation of some of my observations about people in their roles and in their interactions with others.

When I returned to Cambridge I analyzed the cases to see how much about the society could be inferred and how much would check out with hypotheses that resulted from observation. In the process, however, I became interested in the subject matter for its own sake — what happened in courts was fascinating. It was highly patterned and apparently not completely open ended. It had boundaries that were at the time a relief to me, especially because the research on settlement was so all encompassing.

To this point my fieldwork had developed around topics somewhat by accident, a chain reaction of choices that followed from my first choice of research area and topic. The first choice grew directly out of the traditional value placed in anthropology on the importance of extending our knowledge of the range of diversity in human kind. What was not apparent to me at the time were the blanks that an anthropologist of another time might have given high priority. For example, an anthropologist with more of a historical sense that extended backward and forward might have been curious about the role of the lumber companies in planning the development of the area. Such a topic would have fallen squarely within the domain of change land use patterns, and the external relations of the Zapotec. Strangely enough my graduate training, which was so strong in the area of pre- and post-Conquest history, completely bypassed the concept of a more recent history that affected the people that anthropologists study.

During the second part of my fieldwork among the Zapotec (from December, 1959 to February, 1960) I concentrated on questions of law, starting with individuals and the trouble cases they were involved in. This made my investigations range in and out of court, depending on what individuals did with trouble. Choice and alternatives became problematic. What led some people to use courts and others not, and how was this related to patterns of kinship and authority? I completed my fieldwork on settlement patterns using the manner in which social control problems were handled as an indicator of larger patterned differences between the two villages. The thesis that resulted was a rather unwieldly controlled comparison, a study in inter- and intravillage regional variation on common themes, a study in micro- rather than macrochange, a study in village social structure as it was and as it appeared to be becoming.

In sum, the study was a contribution to the social organization of the Zapotecs in a region previously unexplored by scientists, by historians, or by reporters of any kind. It contained the seeds of much of the interesting questions which would come later (Nader, 1964; 1965; 1969). The work was published in English and has primarily been circulated among English speaking peoples (Nader, 1964). The work did not concern itself with wider relations with the state and federal governments. Internal imperialism was subtle and the impact of government and business I believed, naively, to be in great part controlled by the indigenes still, although signs of change in the region abounded — new roads were coming in, coffee as a cash crop was spreading as was cash cropping in general, and dependence on medical care was increasing.

POLITICAL POWER AND THE NATIONAL CONTEXT

My second fieldwork experience was short and problem oriented. I spent slightly over six weeks doing fieldwork in a south Lebanese village. My central question was straightforward. I had read in the Islamic literature about Islamic law. Since Islam was an urban religion I asked whether Islamic law really ever filtered into the villages of the Middle East. If so, how much, and in what way? Was it like Catholicism in Mexican Indian villages? Was there really a difference in the way villages of different religious sects settled conflicts? Or was there an indigenous "pre-Islamic" culture that overrode any impact that religious law could make in the villages.

I focused on case materials, on procedure, and essentially discovered what I had suspected — that Islamic law had only a small role to play in a

Shia Moslem village, that social structural variables, both in Lebanon and in Mexico, were greater deciding factors in forums of justice and in legal procedure than were the cultural factors.

My published report on this work was again comparative and oriented to hypothesis testing. My work was again published in English, although one of the essays resulting from this summer work (Nader, 1965), "Communication Between Village and City in the Modern Middle East," was translated in Syria and republished in Arabic. Initially, when I requested funding for this study I specifically argued that work on village law was necessary for developing nations. Such research would help those who were using the concept of unified law to strengthen their national base. However, with no sophisticated knowledge of national law I was not at the time able to make any connection between my findings and national development questions. Like my previous work on the Zapotec this work was written as a report for the major journal of anthropology in America, the *American Anthropologist*.

During this summer I looked at forms of conflict resolution and the relation between the rural and urban sectors of the country as reflected in a kind of political ward heeling whereby urban power brokers interact with villagers in trouble. I had in the space of four years since my first fieldwork turned my attention to the national scene as it affected and was affected by villages. Was this shift to the nation due to happenings in anthropology? For the most part it was due to the nature of Lebanese social structure within which, unlike Emerys Perers (1963), I found myself (while studying Shias) unable to ignore questions of power and nation. This was made all the more likely because I was staying in the home of an urban power broker.

This growing awareness of the importance of political power and the national context was to grow into a general call for studying "up" in anthropology (Nader, 1972). In the years that followed I was to become painfully aware that anthropologists, myself included, were caught in a mind set whereby we were trained to relate (and therefore to study) down rather than up. This was to make me aware of the presence of professional biases which determined the frame within which our choices are made.

After two years of teaching courses at Berkeley on kinship and law I was invited to spend 1963-1964 as a Fellow at the Center for Advanced Study in the Behavioral Sciences at Stanford. While there I developed two ideas for research proposals. This experience provoked the realization that the choice of what anthropologists study is not simply determined by professional values. I realized that as anthropologists *we* are subject to political power and the national context just as are the indigenes we study.

Of the two proposals submitted one was a project that I called the Berkeley Village Law Project, and the second was a proposal to do a comparative study of groomprice that would be both behavioral and historical.

The first project intended to train and send a team of graduate student researchers to various points on the globe on a descriptive and mapping mission in the hope that a group could accomplish more than a set of independent researchers. They were to use an agreed-on methodology and perspective to study the legal and extrajudicial systems of dispute settlement in villages.

Again I intended to fill the descriptive gap and more important to supplement what I thought was a perspective that was too narrow to help us develop any clear understanding of the role of law *in* society because of its overemphasis on understanding legal processes per se as to their systemic qualities. I felt that the paucity of theoretical development in the field was due either to too micro or too macro a picture, and that we needed to study choice on alternatives vis-à-vis justice forums. In this application there was only an apology for any practical need to study such phenomena: we need to know more about the disputing process in order to understand the etiology of conflict; new nations around the world were developing and integrating by means of the law and I argued they could develop their national legal systems more efficiently and more sensibly if they knew what was already the working law of their villages.

This proposal was sent to the National Institute of Mental Health and rejected for a variety of reasons one of which I was informed, was the youthful age of the principal investigator. We went ahead with the project anyway and supported the work piecemeal. Absence of general funding was not a deterrence as individual support was then available at such places as the NIMH, but again I became aware of the national political context that affected what anthropologists would be supported by government to study. I have watched throughout the 1960s and the 1970s in particular how government agencies influence the choice of questions for research by such strategies as contract research or targeted research. Anthropologists have, for the most part, been reactive rather than proactive in their relations with government agencies, and we will see later on some of the reasons for this defensive posture.

My second research proposal had a pure science intent with no apologies for applicability, and it was the most fun of the two proposals to write: "Groomprice: Its Place in a Cross-Cultural Investigation of Exchanges at Marriage." I was interested that the exchanges made at time of marriage seen on a global basis indicated that brideprice seemed to be associated with subsistence economies in which women participate, whereas dowry or groomprice were to be found in societies where the women have a lesser role in subsistence activities, in societies with a tendency toward patriliny, and with the concomitants of these patterns, urbanism and stratified society. Theories about marriage exchanges had raised more questions than they had answered about such topics as marriage stability and the distribution of property. In conjunction with the late Dr. Millicent Ayoub we planned to ferret out the concomitants of groomprice as a phenomena present through time and space. We had a modest proposal with clear-cut goals and some neat hypotheses. It was an exciting project, one selected on the basis of personal interest because the questions seemed ripe for theoretical breakthrough. We were funded by the National Science Foundation, a government organization that has traditionally supported scientific exploration rather than targeted research. Support for "pure" research places the burden of the ethical questions squarely on the shoulders of the research community that receives the support; for the most part, however, we have not felt that burden.

A NEW AWARENESS

I returned from the Center to my University duties. I had just had a baby and was to return to teaching in time to witness the beginnings of the Berkeley Free Speech movement. The 1960s had a great impact on the kinds of questions I was to ask in my research. So was the fact that I had three children during this decade. The impact was *not* one that made me decide to be more applied and less pure science in approach. It did, however, make me ask different kinds of questions. It led me to challenge the popular notion that all things are equally important to study *if* you the anthropologist are interested in the subject. It led me to question the idea that dealing with contemporary issues somehow made one has less objective, more biased than if studying more distant or bygone societies.

This awareness came about quite naturally. I had, by the early or middle 1960s, analyzed a great deal of my Zapotec data on law, and with the many legal questions being raised in the immediate context of that period I quite naturally began to ask questions bearing on the similarities and differences in the problem solving functions of American and Zapotec law. I found that the questions I asked were either greeted with puzzlement by my law colleagues or by simple statements of "I don't know." The first questions I asked pertained to use patterns in the law. Who uses the American legal system and to what purpose? I found an absence of knowledge at every turn. No one seemed to know what citizens did with their legal problems when they did not have access to law. The alternatives to the American judicial system had not been studied. The more I searched the more I realized that very little legal research had been dealing with understanding the legal system as it in fact operates. Uncharted — it must be studied. But what is it that must be studied first?

The American and Zapotec legal situations were in striking contrast along three important dimensions: the purpose or function of courts, their availability, and escalation patterns. The American system seemed to be one where access to courts was difficult for people with everyday living problems. There was apparently little use of mechanisms for deescalating disputes as in the face-to-face societies that anthropologists had studied. For example, most major student incidents during the 1960s escalated to the police and the courts without either going through student government or faculty government for hearing. Most often only University administrators heard the cases and since it was usual that the complaint was directed against University administration there was rarely a third-party hearing until the situation was out of hand.

I decided to focus research attention on extrajudicial mechanisms for dispute settlement because (1) no one knew much about it (e.g., uncharted), (2) I thought that legal change would be more likely to be brought about by extrajudicial means, and (3) such a strategy would best allow for the development of theory on legal change. The consumers of law were not allowed access to a court that had sometime ago changed its function from an institution whose prime function was to solve disputes to an institution primarily concerned with facilitating economic transactions in American society.

I interested a few undergraduate students to look into a number of extrajudicial complaint hearings institutions such as the California Insurance Commission, the Better Business Bureau, and the Bay Area Pollution Agency. This work developed into the Berkeley Complaint Management Project. Again we found ourselves mapping in an area that was relatively unknown. Our survey and ethnographic studies of complaint management in state and federal offices, in voluntary organizations, in the media (television, radio, and newspapers), in department stores, in ward politics, in unions, and in corporate practice were often firsts. For the first time in my research there were policy questions — should the United States develop better complaint management systems and, if so, at what level — in the law, extralegal, to meet individual needs, to make structural recommendations for change? There were also applied questions: How would we invent a system for complaint management that meets the various needs of people living in a democratic society? There were pure science questions: If we view the law as having systemic qualities, and the legal system as changing through time, what is it that explains the drift in a legal system?

Sir Henry Maine (1861) described the change in Western law as a movement from status to contract. This change accompanied the evolution in society from kin based to territorially based groups. Equally important shifts accompanied industrialization and the mass production and sale of goods whereby the majority of legal issues involve individuals with large-scale organizations such as industry or government, whereby access to the legal system became available only to people of wealth, whereby employment patterns changed most people's self-employed status to that of employee. Our research on

American law, a setting where access is extremely limited due principally to cost and crowdedness, led me to questions about the secondary consequences of no access to law such as objective and endemic powerlessness. What, we might ask, would Sir Henry Maine's conclusions have been if he had concentrated on all the users and potential users of the legal system rather than singling out legal specialists and the mechanisms available to them?

The 1960s were a time to rethink the academic disciplines and some of us did. Anthropology students at Berkeley were calling for courses on ethnography of elites. Law students were calling for courses on poverty and consumer law. I ventured to send two anthropology students to Washington to study a powerful law firm; one which was part of a small group of powerful law firms sometimes referred to as the fourth branch of government. The venture was unsuccessful; colleagues attributed the failure to the lack of experience and training of the students; I attributed the failure to a certain set of mind that is found in the social sciences generally, which results in training students to "relate down rather than up" (Nader, 1972).

Again the result was unsettling in terms of what it is that determines what anthropologists study. Anthropologists have covered the globe studying the range of variation in human society, yet we were ignoring perhaps the most extreme form of society ever conceived: a society where a few people are able to control the lives of many others by means of formal and "hidden" governments. It was not that anthropologists had not studied American society. Many had. It was that most of our studies had been of small groups, counterparts in small face-to-face societies — ethnicities, factories, and neighborhoods. There were some exceptions but, in the main, anthropologists had not studied vertical slices of American society (which would be the home version of cross-cultural), nor had we been concerned with power. Uncharted and powerful, the elites must be studied. Nobody had studied the insurance industry — its social organization, its power networks, and its impact on American culture. No one had studied the energy specialists and the organizations from which they operate. No one had studied the advertising industry as the single most efficient socializing agent in American society. No one had studied the multinational corporations — the nations within nations. No one had studied the food industry that has managed to put most people in this country on a completely untested diet — a first time in the history of people and a success story that should dazzle the dieticians. These areas of interest, it needs to be pointed out, raise no less serious scientific questions than traditional studies of neighborhood groups. Then, why, we ask, is not more ethnographic man and woman power distributed to such topics? Is it inertia? Is innovation impossible given certain types of professor-student relationships?

To date the only sense of urgency shared by the whole profession was that which related to the fact that there were peoples and cultures of the world that might become extinct before they were recorded, and we have committed ourself as a profession to study cultures before they become extinct. In the present case the argument for deployment of manpower needs to be made in terms of studying ourselves before we are extinct. We live in a time when institutionalized insanity is endemic; few of us are studying this phenomena. Why, when we have anthropologists that are studying health states of individuals and cultures?

PUBLIC SERVICE

Anthropologists engage in public service to greater or lesser degrees while they are teaching in the University. I have, during the past 10 years, engaged in much service work that has brought me in contact with a variety of professionals in many institutional contexts. Some of these professionals are academics and some, as with lawyers, are principally practitioners. As a result of the Complaints study, and the reading of hundreds of citizen complaint letters, I have also been in touch with "the thinking of the people" about their life problems. What I choose to study and what I will train students to work on is less and less determined by traditional subject matter which was high priority when I was being trained, but rather increasingly by the concerns of the world wider than academic anthropology. This is bound to happen to professionals who develop networks beyond their immediate professional ones: the stimuli are different.

For example, one of the realities in which academic anthropologists live is not only that of a shrinking academic marketplace, but also of shrinking research funds. Some years ago while I was serving on the Cultural Anthropology Committee of the NIMH I witnessed the virtual termination of support for predoctoral anthropology students and with it a blow to the predoctoral research that such training grants made possible. By virtue of the paucity of anthropologists at the National Institute of Mental Health (the maximum number at any one time was two, I believe) the CUAN committee found itself in an advocacy position. There were a variety of attempts to persuade the Institute to redistribute available funds that more anthropological work be funded. One such attempt was a conference on anthropological contributions to the understanding of mental health problems held at the Center for Advanced Study in October of 1971. I cochaired this conference with T. Maretzki and also coedited the volume that resulted, *Cultural Illness and Health* (1973). In the introduction to that volume I noted the costs of paying attention to anthropological studies such as those we presented. Ethnography is uncomfortably revealing at times when studying American society since the anthropologist is often studying the health system from the point of view of the client rather than from the point of view of the professional.

My experience in editing the *Cultural Illness* volume coupled with observations made in the process of attending professional meetings with lawyers, doctors, chemists, physicists, engineers, and the like, has stimulated new areas for ethnographic research relating to the belief patterns of professionals as they relate to specialized work performance. For example, a lawyer only "hears" that segment of a case that is law related, and it follows perhaps that process is missing from the handling of citizen problems by lawyers. Similarly, each type of child specialist looks at different needs of the child. Territoriality rather than cooperativeness is strong in American professionalism. What is interesting for the anthropologist is to develop an understanding of how professionals invent, feed on, and exacerbate many of America's so-called social problems, while others have a reverse impact: to study an engineer who says he is unable to discuss the question of safety "because it's built into the design," the physicist who says he can't ask questions about the breeder reactor "because it is not my specialty," or the judge who can't understand his insurance policy.

It's fascinating business finding out how in the development of professions we came to this. The science questions are there and the ethnographic data are desparately needed for living. The anthropologists who can teach civil servants "how to answer citizen requests in Americanese" will have many grateful citizens who will gladly pay for the research he or she is doing. The anthropologist who writes an ethnography of law for the Zapotecs that will give them some historical perspective on their relations with the Mexican state will be creating a new awareness in anthropology as well as among the Zapotec. These are questions that would not have occured to me in my pre- or postdoctoral periods, and maybe they should not have. But *the danger so often is that the questions that are top priority during one's graduate training become the questions we continue to work around as well developed professionals.*

A concluding example has influenced the way in which I would set priorities in my work and in the profession in general. Since 1972 I have served on the Carnegie Council on Children. The Council is a mixed group of individuals from diverse walks of life, mostly representative of various citizen's perspectives on children — not, for the most part, professional child specialists. Our charge has been to map out the present state of childhood in America, to envisage a better world for children, and to develop mechanisms for improving our children's chances for a livable future. Our assessment of the present situation has been "uncovered" by every White House Commission on Children since the early part of this century: the richest country in the world cannot boast about the way it is caring for its children, feeding its children, about the health care, the educational advancements, the realization of potential for many of our children. It became clear also that much of the research on children, since Freud, has focused on the intimate home environment in which children are brought up and within which they are said to develop. Most of our theories about how children are reared and the consequences of child rearing seek to explain the child as a product of family environment. As the Council meetings proceeded it became clear that in as technologically complex a society as ours, parents are less and less the determining factor in the development of their children.

New questions should revolve around the professionals and the industries that are rearing America's children. We need studies about the role of insurance, the social security administration, and the real estate industry as they affect the childhood development of every child. We need to understand how corporate rotation schemes affect the children of executives and engineers. We need the documents that explain the effects on children of the ways banks and the real estate industry are segregating America. And we could add similar questions about the linkages between the obstretricians, the pediatricians, the teachers, and the Atomic Energy Commission, and the rearing of America's children. The important subject matter is not our children and not the Atomic Energy Commission but the often uncomfortable connections and linkages between them that will make us realize exactly *how* all these people in large scale organizations are rearing our children along with us.

NEW PRIORITIES

The experiences of the past decade have resulted in three main reactions in our discipline. There are those of us who will continue to study areas that are esoteric and related to scientific problems that have long been with us in the discipline — subjects such as Mayan hieroglyphics or the kinship system of the Australian aborigines. There are those of us who will choose to take old scientific questions into new domains, such as studying the cognitive form of professional biases or mind sets, or variables that promote legal drift. There are those who will choose to emphasize the humanistic aspects of culture and who will interpret symbols and their meanings. We are doing all this in anthropology in a planless sort of way, however, with no understanding or knowledge of how we are distributing manpower in anthropology, and therefore, necessarily no understanding of how we should distribute our efforts except through rarely voiced but deep prejudices that the best schools should concern themselves with the most esoteric work in the most ivory tower manner (e.g., publishing articles written in specialized jargon in specialized scientific journals). The Midwestern or Southern schools, however, can concern themselves with the real world (presumably because anything that might have policy implications is of lesser importance and should be studied at lesser schools), and the lesser people should also be the ones to communicate anthropological findings to the public. It was not always so in anthropology. Boas (Columbia University) was concerned with public questions; Clyde Kluckhohn (Harvard University) wrote a prizewinning book and the last one on anthropology for the layman (1949).

I predict that if we do not become more self-conscious about how we should distribute our efforts the other professionals will more and more tell us what they need us to study, and this will include the granting agencies. They will do this because (except for minor efforts by organizations such as the Social Science Research Council or the National Science Foundation) nowhere do we have a set of priorities developed, either for the strictly scientific problems or for those questions that have scientific, policy, and applied components. If this trend continues then, in this world of increasing scarcity (funds, informants, etc.), it is just possible that anthropology will either atrophy, become attached, and finally absorbed in departments of history, or that we will become hand-maidens of others — such a state always has entailed a loss of integrity.

The first step in setting out the priorities in the discipline would be to encourage more explicit statements in meetings and in published works on why we have chosen to study something. Such a statement should include scientific and ethical reasons as well. Because something is interesting is a good reason — but it is not sufficient. A science that is simply satisfying the ego of individual scientists is doomed to repetitiveness and knowing more and more about less and less. A statement that says something about progress in the field that makes it possible to solve a new problem or a phase of an old problem suggests a science that is cumulative in effort. A statement that tells us that the area on the map is blank may be in the process of redistributing manpower in the profession. A statement that tells us that nobody has studied the insurance industry although virtually every American's life is touched by this industry is combining science with ethical considerations. Diversification is not only professionally adaptive behavior; it allows anthropologists to exploit the full potential of a discipline that is genuinely people based in orientation. If our discipline is too large to address itself to the central question of what we study and the distribution of anthropological talent, then individuals and perhaps even departments can take this step to ensure that our standards are indeed professional.

REFERENCES

Kluckhohn, Clyde

    1949   *Mirror for Man.* New York: Whittlesey House, McGraw-Hill.

Nader, Laura

    1964   "Talea and Juquila: A Comparison of Zapotec Social Organization," University of California Publications in *American Archaeology and Ethnology,* Vol. 48, No. 3, pp. 195-296.

    1965   "Communication between Village and City in the Modern Middle East," *Human Organization, Special Issue: Dimensions of Cultural Change in the Middle East,* John Gulick (ed.), pp. 18-24, Spring.

    1969   "Styles of Court Procedure: To Make the Balance" in *Law in Culture and Society.* Chicago: Aldine Press.

    1972   "Up the Anthropologist — Perspective Gained from Studying Up" in *Reinventing Anthropology,* Dell Hymes (ed.). New York: Pantheon Press.

    1973   (with T. Maretzki). "Cultural Illness and Health," Essays in Human Adaptation, *Anthropological Studies,* No. 9.

    1974   Review of "A Childhood for Every Child — The Politics of Parenthood" by Mark Gerzon, *Harvard Educational Review,* Fall.

Peters, Emrys L.

    1963   "Aspects of Rank and Status among Muslims in a Lebanese Village" in *Mediterranean Countrymen,* Julian Pitt-Rivers (ed.). La Haye, Mouton and Co., pp. 159-200.

Schmeider, Oscar

    1930   "The Settlements of the Tzapotec and Mije Indians," *University of California Publications in Geography,* **IV**, Berkeley.

APPENDIX

STATEMENTS ON ETHICS*

PRINCIPLES OF PROFESSIONAL RESPONSIBILITY
Adopted by the Council of the American Anthropological Association May 1971

>*Note:* This statement of principles is not intended to supersede previous statements and resolutions of the Association. Its intent is to clarify professional responsibilities in the chief areas of professional concern to anthropologists.

Preamble:

Anthropologists work in many parts of the world in close personal association with the peoples and situations they study. Their professional situation is, therefore, uniquely varied and complex. They are involved with their discipline, their colleagues, their students, their sponsors, their subjects, their own and host governments, the particular individuals and groups with whom they do their field work, other populations and interest groups in the nations within which they work, and the study of processes and issues affecting general human welfare. In a field of such complex involvements, misunderstandings, conflicts and the necessity to make choices among conflicting values are bound to arise and to generate ethical dilemmas. It is a prime responsibility of anthropologists to anticipate these and to plan to resolve them in such a way as to do damage neither to those whom they study nor, in so far as possible, to their scholarly community. Where these conditions cannot be met, the anthropologist would be well-advised not to pursue the particular piece of research.

The following principles are deemed fundamental to the anthropologist's responsible, ethical pursuit of his profession.

1. *Relations with those studied:*

    In research, an anthropologist's paramount responsibility is to those he studies. When there is a conflict of interest, these individuals must come first. The anthropologist must do everything within his power to protect their physical, social and psychological welfare and to honor their dignity and privacy.

    a. Where research involves the acquisition of material and information transferred on the assumption of trust between persons, it is axiomatic that the rights, interests, and sensitivities of those studied must be safeguarded.

*Reprinted with permission of the American Anthropological Association.

    b. The aims of the investigation should be communicated as well as possible to the informant.
    c. Informants have a right to remain anonymous. This right should be respected both where it has been promised explicitly and where no clear understanding to the contrary has been reached. These strictures apply to the collection of data by means of cameras, tape recorders, and other data-gathering devices, as well as to data collected in face-to-face interviews or in participant observation. Those being studied should understand the capacities of such devices; they should be free to reject them if they wish; and if they accept them, the results obtained should be consonant with the informant's right to welfare, dignity and privacy.

    Despite every effort being made to preserve anonymity it should be made clear to informants that such anonymity may be compromised unintentionally. (November 1975)
    d. There should be no exploitation of individual informants for personal gain. Fair return should be given them for all services.
    e. There is an obligation to reflect on the foreseeable repercussions of research and publication on the general population being studied.
    f. The anticipated consequences of research should be communicated as fully as possible to the individuals and groups likely to be affected.
    g. In accordance with the Association's general position on clandestine and secret research, no reports should be provided to sponsors that are not also available to the general public and, where practicable, to the population studied.
    h. Every effort should be exerted to cooperate with members of the host society in the planning and execution of research projects.
    i. All of the above points should be acted upon in full recognition of the social and cultural pluralism of host societies and the consequent plurality of values, interests and demands in those societies. This diversity complicates choice-making in research, but ignoring it leads to irresponsible decisions.

2. *Responsibility to the public:*

The anthropologist is also responsible to the public—all presumed consumers of his professional efforts. To them he owes a commitment to candor and to truth in the dissemination of his research results and in the statement of his opinions as a student of man.
    a. He should not communicate his findings secretly to some and withhold them from others.
    b. He should not knowingly falsify or color his findings.
    c. In providing professional opinions, he is responsible not only for their content but also for integrity in explaining both these opinions and their bases.
    d. As people who devote their professional lives to understanding man, anthropologists bear a positive responsibility to speak out publicly, both individually and collectively, on what they know and what they believe as a result of their professional expertise gained in the study of human beings. That is, they bear a professional responsibility to contribute to an "adequate definition of reality" upon which public opinion and public policy may be based.
    e. In public discourse, the anthropologist should be honest about his qualifications and cognizant of the limitations of anthropological expertise.

3. *Responsibility to the discipline:*

An anthropologist bears responsibility for the good reputation of his discipline and its practitioners.
    a. He should undertake no secret research or any research whose results cannot be freely derived and publicly reported.

b. He should avoid even the appearance of engaging in clandestine research, by fully and freely disclosing the aims and sponsorship of all his research.
c. He should attempt to maintain a level of integrity and rapport in the field such that by his behavior and example he will not jeopardize future research there. The responsibility is not to analyze and report so as to offend no one, but to conduct research in a way consistent with a commitment to honesty, open inquiry, clear communication of sponsorship and research aims, and concern for the welfare and privacy of informants.
d. He should not present as his own work, either in speaking or writing, materials directly taken from other sources. (October 1974)
e. When he participates in actions related to hiring, retention and advancement, he should ensure that no exclusionary practices be perpetuated against colleagues on the basis of sex, marital status, color, social class, religion, ethnic background, national origin, or other non-academic attributes. He should, furthermore, refrain from transmitting and resist the use of information irrelevant to professional performance in such personal actions. (November 1975)

4. *Responsibility to students:*

In relations with students an anthropologist should be candid, fair, nonexploitative and committed to their welfare and academic progress.

As Robert Lekachman has suggested, honesty is the essential quality of a good teacher, neutrality is not. Beyond honest teaching, the anthropologist as a teacher has ethical responsibilities in selection, instruction in ethics, career counseling, academic supervision, evaluation, compensation and placement.

a. He should select students in such a way as to preclude discrimination on the basis of sex, race, ethnic group, social class and other categories of people indistinguishable by their intellectual potential.
b. He should alert students to the ethical problems of research and discourage them from participating in projects employing questionable ethical standards. This should include providing them with information and discussions to protect them from unethical pressures and enticements emanating from possible sponsors, as well as helping them to find acceptable alternatives (see point i below).
c. He should be receptive and seriously responsive to students' interests, opinions and desires in all aspects of their academic work and relationships.
d. He should realistically counsel students regarding career opportunities.
e. He should conscientiously supervise, encourage and support students in their anthropological and other academic endeavors.
f. He should inform students of what is expected of them in their course of study. He should be fair in the evaluation of their performance. He should communicate evaluations to the students concerned.
g. He should acknowledge in print the student assistance he uses in his own publications, give appropriate credit (including co-authorship) when student research is used in publication, encourage and assist in publication of worthy student papers, and compensate students justly for the use of their time, energy and intelligence in research and teaching.
h. He should energetically assist students in securing legitimate research support and the necessary permissions to pursue research.
i. He should energetically assist students in securing professional employment upon completion of their studies.
j. He should strive to improve both our techniques of teaching and our techniques for evaluating the effectiveness of our methods of teaching.

5. *Responsibility to sponsors:*

In his relations with sponsors of research, an anthropologist should be honest about his qualifications, capabilities and aims. He thus faces the obligation, prior to entering any commitment for research, to reflect sincerely upon the purposes of his sponsors in terms of their past behavior. He should be especially careful not to promise or imply acceptance of conditions contrary to his professional ethics or competing commitments. This requires that he require of the sponsor full disclosure of the sources of funds, personnel, aims of the institution and the research project, disposition of research results. He must retain the right to make all ethical decisions in his research. He should enter into no secret agreement with the sponsor regarding the research, results or reports.

6. *Responsibilities to one's own government and to host governments:*

In his relation with his own government and with host governments, the research anthropologist should be honest and candid. He should demand assurance that he will not be required to compromise his professional responsibilities and ethics as a condition of his permission to pursue the research. Specifically, no secret research, no secret reports or debriefings of any kind should be agreed to or given. If these matters are clearly understood in advance, serious complications and misunderstandings can generally be avoided.

Epilogue:

In the final analysis, anthropological research is a human undertaking, dependent upon choices for which the individual bears ethical as well as scientific responsibility. That responsibility is a human, not superhuman responsibility. To err is human, to forgive humane. This statement of principles of professional responsibility is not designed to punish, but to provide guidelines which can minimize the occasions upon which there is a need to forgive. When an anthropologist, by his actions, jeopardizes peoples studied, professional colleagues, students or others, or if he otherwise betrays his professional commitments, his colleagues may legitimately inquire into the propriety of those actions, and take such measures as lie within the legitimate powers of their Association as the membership of the Association deems appropriate.

LIBRARY OF DAVIDSON COLLEGE